URBAN TOURISM AND URBAN CHANGE

This study of urban tourism provides both a sociological and cultural analysis of change that has taken place in many of the world's cities, and also the implications of these changes for urban management and planning, for success and failure in metropolitan change. Uniquely suited for teaching purposes, this text includes numerous case studies of cities worldwide to illuminate the significant impact and promise of tourism on urban image and economic development.

Costas Spirou is Professor in the Department of Social and Behavioral Sciences at National-Louis University in Chicago and a visiting fellow at the University of Notre Dame. His research interests include culture policy, urban redevelopment, tourism, and sports in society. He is co-author of *It's Hardly Sportin': Stadiums, Neighborhoods and the New Chicago*, a book about politics and community development, and author of *St. Charles: Culture and Leisure in an All-American Town*.

180°   150°W   120°W   90°W   60°W   30°W

Arctic Ocean

60°N

NORTH AMERICA

Detroit, Michigan, USA, p. 179
Cleveland, Ohio, USA, p. 119
Denver, Colorado, USA, p. 140
San Diego, California, USA, p. 167

Pittsburgh, Pennsylvania, USA, p. 2

30°N

Baltimore, Maryland, USA, p. 58
Greenville, South Carolina, USA, p. 188

Atlantic
Ocean

Pacific Ocean

Bogota, Colombia, p. 133

Equator (0°)

SOUTH
AMERICA

30°S

Dunedin, New Zealand, p. 50

60°S

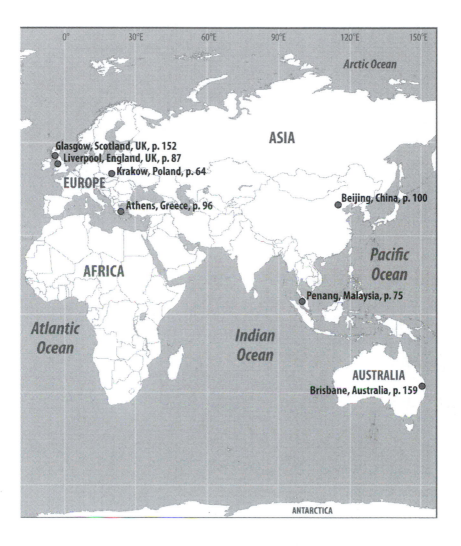

0°   30°E   60°E   90°E   120°E   150°E

Arctic Ocean

ASIA

Glasgow, Scotland, UK, p. 152
Liverpool, England, UK, p. 87
Krakow, Poland, p. 64

EUROPE

Athens, Greece, p. 96

Beijing, China, p. 100

AFRICA

Pacific
Ocean

Penang, Malaysia, p. 75

Atlantic
Ocean

Indian
Ocean

AUSTRALIA
Brisbane, Australia, p. 159

ANTARCTICA

METROPOLIS AND MODERN LIFE

A Routledge Series
Edited by Anthony Orum, University of Illinois, Chicago
and Zachary Neal, Michigan State Universitiy, East Lansing

This Series brings original perspectives on key topics in urban research to today's students in a series of short accessible texts, guided readers, and practical handbooks. Each volume examines how long-standing urban phenomena continue to be relevant in an increasingly urban and global world, and in doing so, connects the best new scholarship with the wider concerns of students seeking to understand life in the 21st century metropolis.

Books in the Series:

Common Ground: Readings, Reflections, and New Frontiers edited by Anthony Orum and Zachary Neal

The Gentrification Debates edited by Japonica Brown-Saracino

The Power of Urban Ethnic Places by Jan Lin

Forthcoming:

The Urban Instinct by Nan Ellin

The Connected City by Zachary Neal

URBAN TOURISM AND URBAN CHANGE

Cities in a Global Economy

Costas Spirou

National-Louis University

Routledge
Taylor & Francis Group

NEW YORK AND LONDON

First published 2011
by Routledge
711 Third Avenue, New York, NY 10017

Simultaneously published in the UK
by Routledge
2 Park Square, Milton Park, Abingdon, Oxon OX14 4RN

Routledge is an imprint of the Taylor & Francis Group, an informa business

© 2011 Taylor & Francis

Typeset in Caslon, Copperplate, and Trade Gothic by EvS Communication Networx, Inc.

Library of Congress Cataloging-in-Publication Data
Spirou, Costas.
Urban tourism and urban change : cities in a global economy / Costas Spirou.
p. cm. (Metropolis and modern life)
1. Tourism. 2. Cities and towns. 3. Sociology, Urban. 4. City planning. 5. Economic development. I. Title.
G155.A1S6244 2011
307.1'416dc22
2010023418

ISBN 13: 978-0-415-80162-1 (hbk)
ISBN 13: 978-0-415-80163-8 (pbk)
ISBN 13: 978-0-203-83580-7 (ebk)

To Patrice,
Jack, Tara, Mary Eve, and Stelios

Contents

SERIES FOREWORD

This series brings original perspectives on key topics in urban research to today's students in a series of short, accessible texts, guided readers, and practical handbooks. Each volume examines how long-standing urban phenomena continue to be relevant in an increasingly urban and global world, and in doing so, connects the best new scholarship with the wider concerns of students to understand life in the twenty-first century metropolis.

In this addition to the series, Costas Spirou addresses how tourism has economically and socially transformed cities as they enter a global era. Do vacations to the beach, or trips downtown for dinner and a movie really impact large, modern cities? Combining over a century of historical material with up-to-date examples from cities around the world, in this book Spirou tells a compelling and engaging story that answers this question. Yes, urban tourism does matter. Although tourism is frequently viewed as less important to cities than other more traditional activities like manufacturing or finance, it has played a major role in the development and redevelopment of cities around the world. He begins by tracing the history of tourism for cities and the commodification of leisure in the early twentieth century, then turns his attention to the complex forces that shape cities today: globalization, war, economic booms and busts, politics, and the "creative class." In each chapter, Spirou introduces the reader to a key dimension of the world of cities in a global era, illustrating with examples and photographs how urban tourism fits in. Throughout, the discussion is supplemented with minicase studies of tourism projects in cities on nearly every continent, including Dunedin (New Zealand), Krakow (Poland), Penang (Malaysia), Beijing (China), Bogota (Columbia), as well as many American cities, including Baltimore, Cleveland, and Denver. Both timely and accessible, this book illuminates the pivotal role of tourism for the modern metropolis, answering some questions, while also prompting new ones for both students and scholars.

Anthony Orum
Zachary Neal
Series Editors

Preface

Why I Wrote This Book

Over the years I have had the opportunity to teach undergraduate courses to students in urban sociology and political sociology. I have also taught more focused classes in urban and community development, culture and urban change, and sport and society. My experience has been that students have always found these subjects interesting. However, when classroom discussions centered on the recent reorganization of cities, especially in downtowns, students were markedly curious and particularly engaged. Many would share personal observations and reflections about the rapid physical remaking of these spaces. Furthermore, lively conversations often included commentaries on the qualitative aspects of these transformations. For example, students were able to quickly identify the considerable resource allocations made in terms of culture, leisure, and tourism. Questions such as: What is the historical context of this urban restructuring? Why do cities invest so extensively in entertainment oriented facilities? Are these investments worth it and how about access issues? Do all residents frequent these new attractions and are they affordable? Or are these mostly geared for visitors? Should the money be spent instead to address social issues such as education, housing, transportation? What about the significant residential development that has sprung up in recent years, in and around downtown areas? Is there a relationship between this and the rise of urban tourism and amenities development? How about gentrification and displacement? These discussions would often end by recognizing the changing nature of cities and by concluding that urban centers are now aggressively focused on capturing tourist dollars within a consumption driven economy.

It is the need for a comprehensive response to these classroom conversations which motivated me to embark on writing this book. Existing instructional material on the study of tourism tends to either utilize a management or a marketing standpoint, making the need for a social science treatment of the subject imperative. In fact there are few publications that employ a social science approach. Those are typically edited from a cultural studies or geographic perspective. Furthermore they possess limited emphasis on sociological forces and lack the inclusion of economic development rationales and the role of political actors and public/private partnerships. This work integrates these elements and explains how tourism, culture, and entertainment helped transform urban centers during the recent decades.

Intellectual Motivations

This book is about the evolving nature of contemporary cities and the dynamic change which characterized urban centers during the latter part of the twentieth century. Historically, cities served multiple functions, showcasing not only the strength of economic, political, and religious institutions, but also serving as centers of intellectual power and artistic and technological advancements. With the birth of the industrial revolution cities were positioned center stage and often came to be viewed as a barometer of human civilization.

For much of history, tourism was on the periphery of human experience. Though people desired to see other places, travel limitations and cost kept the number of travelers low. Travel was for the wealthy. Therefore the masses alternatively sought recreation through trips to the beach and parks, mostly away from the cities. Escaping the density, pollution, and difficult living conditions evident in the manufacturing surroundings and reconnecting with nature was appealing.

However, during the first half of the twentieth century, the nature of leisure started to slowly shift, from being passive to becoming active. Labor laws reduced the time people spent at work, the standard of living increased, the rise of air transport and the construction of the highway system eased travel, television and other forms of mass media exposed Americans to the world, and the rise of corporations and business trips all proved significant in the way Americans engaged tourism. Travel was not only possible; it was within reach and also desirable. Cities, especially during the postwar era, came to be viewed as attractive places where one can experience the cultural institutions, visit sites, and become connected to the settings in the forefront of human progress.

It is within this framework that urban tourism emerges as a powerful force. At a time when many cities were struggling to address the devastating effects of deindustrialization and urban decline this sector becomes a significant economic development strategy. Industrial cities looked to convert to tourism centers and invested millions in that transformation. However, the rise of urban tourism in recent decades is also influenced by other forces. Chapter 2 discusses the role of globalization and of urban competition. Both of these factors helped position tourism as a viable industry, one that came to quickly be viewed as capable of generating positive economic impacts. Chapter 3 presents a variety of tourism policies embraced by local policymakers aiming to bring about growth. Tourism districts are one example that played a key role in this process.

The dynamics of building the infrastructure needed to sustain urban tourism and finance massive development projects is discussed in chapter 4. Convention centers and stadiums for professional sports franchises represent that type of investment. Support for waterfront development, parks, festivals, and art spaces, as well as urban beautification programs, prove equally important in refacing and altering the look and function of many spaces. These significant expenditures subsequently give rise to new amenities which help attract a distinct human capital, drawn in by improved quality of life conditions. This process, as well as the effect of urban tourism in remaking the culture of the city is covered in chapter 5.

However, a reconstituted urban environment, with amenities and considerable investments in leisure oriented infrastructure, proved to have additional effects. Newcomers, attracted by the new urban culture, reshaped the physical landscape by placing considerable pressure on local housing markets. Extensive residential development followed in the form of new construction and conversions. These trends are discussed in chapter 6 and point to the restructuring of downtowns.

All of these changes generate numerous questions about the future of the city. For example, as urban tourism fueled the restructuring of cities along lines of leisure and entertainment, and high income residents came to occupy revitalized neighborhoods, a set of new issues emerge. Gentrification and displacement, uneven development, concerns regarding cultural authenticity, and questions about the role of the public sector in assisting the development of private enterprise abound. Chapter 7 discusses these complex, social inequality related debates. On the one hand, we can point to the unanticipated social implications of these urban tourism investments, while on the other, these same practices helped breathe new life to once distressed and dilapidated cities.

Urban tourism is a powerful force and has significantly influenced the ways cities think about their role and future direction. Projections indicate that in the next decade, capital investments in tourism across all continents will near the $2 trillion mark. Governments will continue to search for ways to attract visitors and their spending and seek out partnerships with corporations and business leaders to provide memorable tourist experiences. Because of this, the physical landscape of urban centers will be altered. However, when one considers the seasonal nature and low paying jobs generated by this sector, this dynamic change is going to produce new forms of social inequalities. The necessity for tourism sustainability extends to the urban environment and points to the need for us to address and remedy these conditions.

Teaching Motivations

The recent urban restructuring caused by investments in tourism, culture, and entertainment services requires the adoption of a text for teaching that is timely and comprehensive. *Urban Tourism and Urban*

Change: Cities in a Global Economy fills that void and in the process, serves the needs of both students and instructors. My goal is to provide a unique blend of readability and scholarship that presents sociological concepts with a wealth of cross-cultural and global examples.

The book includes numerous teaching elements not present in other publications on this subject. Specifically, it offers a historical framework of the development of urban tourism within the context of postwar urban change. This helps students gain a better understanding of its genesis and evolution including the value placed on this industry by local governments, civic coalitions and private interests. Numerous case studies of U.S. and international cities amplify various aspects of the book, inviting students to engage in the pursuit of understanding this economic sector. The integration of sociological factors on leisure and commodification expand knowledge of the social world, allowing for an opportunity to see how the advancement of urban tourism can have direct implications for other areas of human experience. Treatment of how smaller cities embraced similar trends shows the distinct relationship between urban tourism and urban change.

The descriptive and analytical nature of the material, augmented by photographs and relevant tables, draws students into the subject matter and helps them gain a better understanding. The integrated case studies offer a unique perspective since they provide instructors and students with an opportunity to understand the global nature of these developments. Finally, the questions for writing, reflection, and debate, found at the end of every chapter, provide ample opportunities for classroom discussion and further engage the student in the subject matter. Because of these features, this book is appropriate for use in numerous courses and various disciplines. I would like to acknowledge all the instructors who are going to adopt the book in their courses and invite them to contact me with feedback.

Costas Spirou

Acknowledgments

The idea for this book began more than a decade ago when I came to see firsthand the physical transformation of Chicago along the lakefront. Multibillion dollar investments in parks, museums, a stadium, convention center upgrades, beautification, festivals, and new entertainment venues were all made along the lines of leisure and tourism. The city's Loop or downtown area also evolved. During the 1980s, at the end of the work day, office workers rushed to the suburban train stations for a quick exit from the city. Today, vibrant street life and residential redevelopment has altered the image of this environment. Is there a connection between these two developments? This project attempts to address this question and puts urban tourism at the forefront of this makeover. My travels in the United States and abroad further solidified this reality of urban change and I also came to realize that even smaller cities and suburban communities refocused on their downtowns and employed tourism as a means of achieving their revitalization.

There are numerous individuals who supported this work and made it possible. I owe much gratitude to editors Anthony Orum, University of Illinois at Chicago and Zachary Neal, Michigan State University who not only expressed interest in this project but also provided needed feedback and encouragement. I want to thank Steve Rutter, Publisher at Routledge for giving me this opportunity and Leah Babb-Rosenfeld, Senior Editorial Assistant who assisted with many and varied details. Because of them, the process of bringing this manuscript to life became a reality.

I would like to thank the reviewers, who were instrumental in the development of the manuscript: Richard Benfield of Central Connecticut State University, Robyne Turner of Rutgers University, Mark Rosentraub of The University of Michigan, Gabe Cherem of Eastern Michigan University, and Boaz Kahana of Cleveland State University.

Larry Bennett, DePaul University deserves special recognition. A friend, colleague, mentor, he has over the years helped me appreciate how social forces affect urban change. I have learned much from him as his insights and scholarship continues to illuminate the evolving dynamics of cities. Larry offered a valuable critique of earlier drafts of this manuscript and has been a great source of support. My numerous conversations with Dennis Judd, University of Illinois at Chicago about cities and tourism over the years helped me think about its role in urban development. His extensive scholarship on the subject provided guidance on formulating some of the themes in the book. I also want to thank a group of Chicago colleagues who offered constructive feedback. Dick Simpson, Michael Pagano, David Perry, Karen Mossberger, and Yue Zhang, all at the University of Illinois at Chicago, Terry Clark, University of Chicago, Annette Steinacker, Loyola University Chicago, and Jim Lewis at the Chicago Community Trust.

I also want to recognize a number of individuals that helped me with various aspects of my research. Chuck Suchar, DePaul University provided unique photos, William Owen and Rich Majka assisted with technical aspects of the images, and Jill Talabay and Robin Hunter, Marketing Department at National-Louis University aided me with the acquisition of many photographs. I received additional research assistance from Olivia Pantoja, Public Policy graduate assistant at National-Louis University and Carole Kabel at the National-Louis University Library. A special thank you goes to Mary Eve Spirou who helped me with data management. My appreciation is also extended to my parents, Ploutarchos and Yvonni Spirou for their value of education, to the late Anthony Dades, and to Mary Dades and Stacy Popovich who have been instrumental in my journey.

The greatest aid and support for all this derives from my wife Patrice who has patiently and graciously endured the challenges of completing this project and who offered feedback on earlier versions. Patrice heard me talk about these issues for a very long time. Over the many years she has been a true inspiration, a source of continuous aid and comfort and the one who has kept me focused on the purpose of it all. This book is dedicated to her and our children Jack, Tara, Mary Eve, and Stelios.

1

CHANGING CITIES AND THE COMMODIFICATION OF LEISURE

During the second half of the twentieth century, the rise of the suburbs and ensuing problems in the inner cities, especially during the 1960s and 1970s, caused significant geographic restructuring along with major changes in social relations. This book focuses on one aspect of that restructuring; namely, the role of urban tourism in the revitalization of downtown areas and the surrounding neighborhoods. Specifically, how the intersection of "a second iteration of leisure," a condition that emerged during the post-World War II era, coupled with urban economic development initiatives contributed to major investment in urban infrastructure and the marketing of cities as places of entertainment and play for both those who are on vacation and those who are visiting for business reasons.

These culture-driven strategies in urban development were fueled by the fact that citizens now have more leisure-expendable income than ever before. This prompted city governments to increase expenditures on culture and specialized bureaucracies. In order to cater to a growing, more sophisticated, and differentiated public demand, policy-making bodies ventured to enhance their provision of cultural services. The outcome of these trends resulted in the development of an economy of urban tourism. Thus, we can observe cities and their governments turning their attention to showcasing their heritage and exporting their cultural identity, with hope of translating these policies into revenue streams capable of bringing about social and economic transformation.

This investigation of the rise and importance of urban tourism is structured around four key interlocking themes so that the topic can be understood via a developmental perspective within a broad historical and socioeconomic framework. First, postwar urban restructuring forced cities to search for alternative means of economic development. Rapidly evolving elements of globalization furthered this quest by injecting competition between cities (for business and recreational visitors), and leading them to embrace a variety of entrepreneurial strategies. Second, the emergence of urban tourism as a fiscal growth strategy reorganized the physical landscape of cities. The massive development of infrastructure that followed changed the built environment in ways not visible since the early period of city building, evident during the latter part of the nineteenth and early years of the twentieth centuries. Third, the remaking of the urban core through tourism also altered the culture of cities, attracting younger workers. Increased cultural amenities, for example, drew greater numbers of people who worked in the arts at all levels to urban areas. Fourth, some of the implications associated with the rise of urban tourism included questionable social and economic benefits, diversion of valuable resources, and the difficulties of sustaining a dual city that catered both to visitors and residents, a system which tended to aid the interests of the corporate elite.

The issues outlined above are demonstrated by the city of Pittsburgh. At the turn of the twentieth century Pittsburgh was on top of the world. The city was synonymous with steel production, providing more than a third of the total national output, exemplifying the prowess of the American economy in the midst of major industrial growth. By 1950, Pittsburgh had the highest population in its history. The professional football team, the Steelers, and the locally produced Iron City Beer, reflected the cultural integration of the city's manufacturing identity. However, Pittsburgh's fortunes were soon reversed. Once it had been the steel capital of the world, but massive declines in manufacturing jobs, which caused significant depopulation, led to the disintegration of the local economy following extensive plant closings. Many neighborhoods were ravaged, especially in the north side of the city. There were empty factories with rows of smokestacks and a vast array of vacant buildings, commercial and residential. During the 1970s the city's population declined by almost 14 percent and in the 1980s by more than 18 percent. Equally significant was the weakening of the corporate leadership which had played a critical role in the city's earlier industrial development.[1]

But in May of 2009 the White House, to the surprise of many, announced that the city would serve as the site for the September 2009 G-20 Economic Summit. It was Pittsburgh, rather than New York or Chicago that was to be presented as a shining case of a previously depressed manufacturing center that had managed to successfully revitalize itself into a postindustrial city. One indicator of Pittsburgh's reversal of fortune was the national and international attention it received as the recipient of numerous accolades for livability. In 2005, *The Economist* ranked it as the most livable city in the United States and 26th worldwide. In 2007, *Places Rated Almanac* recognized it as "America's Most Livable City"[2] and in 2009, *The Economist* placed Pittsburgh once again in the number one position nationally and 29th worldwide.[3] In 2009, *Forbes Magazine* ranked it as America's 10th most livable city among 379 contenders. Of the five indicators used (income growth, cost of living index, culture index, crime rate per 1 million residents, and unemployment), Pittsburgh received the highest mark in the culture index (37 of 379 competitor cities). In 2010, the same publication identified Pittsburgh as the most livable city in the country, giving it a ranking of 26th in arts and leisure among the country's 200 largest metropolitan areas.[4]

This renaissance can be attributed to many factors. Since the mid- to late 1990s, Pittsburgh had pursued a diversified economy. Focus had been placed on upgrading local business conditions by attracting companies in the healthcare and medical sectors, technology, robotics, and financial services. In addition, institutions of higher education like Carnegie Mellon University and the University of Pittsburgh improved their status, helping advance the city's new image.

But Pittsburgh also saw itself as a regional recreational and convention destination. City officials endeavored to build an infrastructure that would support the advancement of this industry and significantly upgrade its current standing. For example, the David L. Lawrence Convention Center, opened in 2003, is owned by the Sports and Exposition Authority of Pittsburgh and Allegheny County. The $375 million facility was developed as a result of a public–private partnership that included philanthropic contributions and corporate sponsorships with the state providing more than $150 million. Viewed as the keystone of the hospitality industry in western Pennsylvania, the riverfront project, which offers more than 1.5 million square feet of space, replaced the previous convention center, which had been built in 1981 and had just 130,000 square feet.

The construction of the convention center is the result of a new strategic direction and an ambitious financial framework that was introduced in 1997. Revenues were drawn from various local sources, but all were for the benefit of restructuring the city. They included adding a 1 percent county sales tax on top of the existing 6 percent base sales tax, as well as parking, hotel/motel taxes, federal and state contributions, and even a payroll tax on nonresident athletes. The result of this initiative was the unveiling of the Regional Destination Financing Plan. Introduced in 1998, the plan included over $1 billion in development projects.

In addition to the convention center and related infrastructural costs, a large portion of these funds went to the construction of new sporting facilities on the North Shore, an area where Three Rivers Stadium once hosted the city's professional baseball and professional football teams. Demolition of the old stadium made room for two separate structures, PNC Park (home of the Pirates) and Heinz Field (home of the Steelers). City officials then looked beyond sports. According to then Mayor Tom Murphy there was a need for a park that would "be visually attractive, but also have the feel of an adventure playground, so that families would bring their kids there." The $31 million North Shore Riverfront Park introduced greenery and connected the North Shore with the downtown, bringing more people to the once barren area. In fact, such development prompted one observer to exclaim that "the new amenities have bolstered the city's mood...I think people

Figure 1.1   Aerial view of Pittsburgh, Pennsylvania. The North Shore (foreground) includes concentrated investments in the development of the Carnegie Science Center and the UPMC Sports Works, Heinz Field, PNC Park, the Children's Museum, the Andy Warhol Museum and the National Aviary. The addition of parkland and bridges connects these attractions to the downtown, including the Cultural District and Point State Park (Courtesy lo Foto, Shutterstock Images).

have begun to see that life after steel is possible. All the old industrial detritus around here is gone."[5]

Pittsburgh's array of projects was intended to recast the downtown as a premier location for tourists, businesses, residents, and for those seeking entertainment opportunities. A number of organizations led the charge. The Pittsburgh Downtown Partnership, formed in 1994, marketed the area as a vibrant location for visitors and locals. The Urban Redevelopment Authority directed the revitalization of downtown by introducing Three PNC Plaza ($133 million) and Piatt Place ($70 million), two mixed use projects that provide office and retail space, a hotel, and condominiums. In addition to these facilities, the $40 million, state of the art August Wilson Center for African American Culture, parks, and high rise residential structures, also helped change the image of the core.

These investments proved to have a powerful impact. The once dominant view of the city was being altered right in the midst of an ongoing population exodus. The number of young people had drastically diminished with a high ratio of elderly residents staying behind.

However, one 2006 analysis identified a reversing trend, concluding that among "Pittsburghers 25–34 years old, 41.9% have graduated from university, placing the city among America's top ten. More than 17% of those young people have also earned an additional graduate or professional degree: the fourth-highest share in the country, behind only Washington, DC (think lawyers), Boston and San Francisco."[6] The 2007 to 2008 estimated annual population loss was by far the smallest in this decade.[7]

The city sought to retain this younger and highly educated group. For example, The Propel Pittsburgh Commission is a mayoral committee whose mission is to give "young professionals of Pittsburgh a major role in moving the City of Pittsburgh forward."[8] Its interest for the creative class, or knowledge-intensive workers, was combined with industrial brownfield site redevelopment.[9] A good example of that is the SouthSide Works complex which opened in 2005 and is a 34-acre project, once the site of an old Jones and Laughlin steel plant along the Monongahela River. The neighborhood built at the site includes upscale ethnic restaurants, high end apartments, art galleries, shopping outlets, along with an extensive array of entertainment opportunities. The development also complements the East Carson Street business district, aimed at serving young professionals who can combine living, working, and playing within its boundaries. Future plans include a riverfront pavilion and a fitness center.[10]

It is clear from the case of Pittsburgh that cities are reorganizing themselves by utilizing cultural strategies to craft new urban identities, employing numerous initiatives aimed at reviving and growing their local economies. In response to fiscal pressures and other, larger socioeconomic structural changes, cities have aggressively embarked on plans to reinterpret or romanticize their past. In turn, they are endeavoring to replace former identities by constructing and promoting new, culturally based images that rely on entertainment, leisure activities, urban tourism, along with convention business. Museums, festivals, revamped public spaces, tourism bubbles, sports stadiums, theater districts, ethnic precincts, convention centers, and urban beautification programs are some of the tools utilized to advance this new direction.

To better understand these significant developments, it is important to first focus on the conditions that helped propel the reorganization of American cities into places of culture, leisure, and entertainment. I provide a treatment of two distinct, yet interconnected forces. First, after World War II the restructuring of urban spaces was signaled by extensive transformations that came to reshape the built environment. The second point centers on the commodification of leisure and its role in assisting the formulation and growth of urban tourism. I examine these issues, offering a historical framework that serves as a basis for considering the remaking of cities.

Manufacturing and the Rise of Urban Centers

As the United States entered the second half of the nineteenth century the mechanization of manual labor, begun a century earlier, brought about changes in agriculture and textile manufacture. Many of these changes impacted the eastern area of the nation, which was then the industrial center of the country. Steam boiler technology brought about new transportation opportunities and expanded commercial activity. Its introduction was fortuitous, because at that time the country was looking west, searching for new economic growth opportunities.

This westward expansion was fueled by a second industrialization movement that would prove more robust than the first one. The change fundamentally reorganized social relations and eventually restructured society. At its core was the rapidly evolving railroad system, the high point of which was the opening of the First Transcontinental Railroad in 1869. Via an expansive network, the rail grid allowed for an efficient transportation of goods.

Workers laid railroad tracks at a dizzying pace. In 1830 there were only 39.8 miles of track, all in the eastern part of the country. By 1860, 28,919 miles were spread across all parts of the nation; by 1890 that number was an impressive 163,562 miles.[11] The new rail system encouraged the development of a new type of American city. Population centers were transformed by the rapid expansion of the steel, textile, and iron industries; the rise of manufacturing; the growth of meatpacking; and the application of technological advancements such as electricity, the telegraph, and the telephone; combined with the available natural resources in the interior of the country.

For example, the citizens of Philadelphia saw their core of economic activity move away from the docks along the Delaware River to new inland manufacturing districts. This changed the character and physical function of the area. It was during this time that Philadelphia's downtown or central business district, the Center City, was developed.[12]

The result of these broad-spectrum changes was a series of newly created downtowns in cities across the country. These areas housed a variety of businesses, including hotels, banks, and other financial services. Increasingly, these new downtowns offered more differentiated shopping and entertainment opportunities through department stores and theater productions. All of these areas shared a typical pattern of development: emerging manufacturing districts included proximity to rail access and work and living environments were separate.

Like Philadelphia, by the latter part of the nineteenth century Chicago saw its robust economy along the mouth of the Chicago River give way to successful machinery and textile manufacturing areas on the west side and printing on the near south side. Further south, the Union Stockyards employed thousands. During the 1920s, Chicago processed more meat than any other location in the world.[13] Much of this processing was accomplished by the use of railroad lines, which allowed for rapid shipping in of cattle and other animals to the slaughterhouses and the subsequent distribution of the meat products both within Chicago and to other cities.

As noted above, work and family life also become spatially differentiated. Efficient transportation enabled the separation of factories from workers' housing. Neighborhoods, such as Back of the Yards that were crowded by laborers from the nearby Union Stockyards, were initially positioned within walking distance of factories. In some cases, like the Pullman Palace Car Company in far south Chicago, wealthy industrialist and founder George Pullman envisioned a workers' paradise—a uniquely designed setting that incorporated family life and work (the production of railroad cars)—within the same isolated grounds. That experiment failed as the workers revolted with strikes against Pullman, quickly ending this innovative form of labor relations and social engineering.

As residential neighborhoods were subsequently located farther away from manufacturing districts, mass transportation became critical. The electric trolley, elevated train, and subway all served the needs of the economy within this newly developing industrial city. In addition, social relations shaped new residential patterns. Chestnut Hill in Philadelphia and Prairie Avenue in Chicago housed middle-class and upper middle-class families, and could be found far away from factory workers' homes.

Cities served as the entry points for newcomers from both U.S. rural areas and from Europe, who sought to improve their lot in life. Urban centers were expanded by the influx of immigrants from the second half of the 1800s to the early part of the 1900s. Internally, the Great Migration of African Americans from the South to the northern industrial cities also provided the needed labor to meet the needs of the expanding manufacturing capacity and business development. By 1960 robust expansion characterized American cities, many of them seeing their population nearing or exceeding 1 million residents (see Table 1.1).

Leisure and the Urban Environment: 1880–1950

As urban centers in the United States grew, leisure began to rapidly evolve: what had traditionally been left to individual choice now became part of a planned effort. Urbanization and immigration made it critically imperative to consider the consequences of dense urban living conditions. This section describes the rise of a "first iteration of leisure" occurring during this period and identifies two emerging themes: (1) its institutionalization, and (2) its use as a means of social control.

By focusing on the availability and use of open spaces, leisure penetrated the social fabric of American life. During the latter part of the nineteenth century, the Progressive Movement helped found the "playground movement" by questioning the consequences of a new

Table 1.1 The Ten Most Populated Urban Centers in the United Center, 1880–1960

1880		1900		1920		1940		1960	
New York, NY	1,206,299	New York, NY	3,437,202	New York, NY	5,620,048	New York, NY	7,454,995	New York, NY	7,781,984
Philadelphia, PA	847,170	Chicago, IL	1,698,575	Chicago, IL	2,701,705	Chicago, IL	3,396,808	Chicago, IL	3,550,404
Brooklyn, NY	566,663	Philadelphia, PA	1,293,697	Philadelphia, PA	1,823,779	Philadelphia, PA	1,931,334	Los Angeles, Calif.	2,479,015
Chicago, IL	503,185	St. Louis, MO	575,238	Detroit, Mich.	993,078	Detroit, Mich.	1,623,452	Philadelphia, PA	2,002,512
Boston, MA	362,839	Boston, MA	560,892	Cleveland, Ohio	796,841	Los Angeles, Calif.	1,504,277	Detroit, Mich.	1,670,144
St. Louis, MO	350,518	Baltimore, MD	508,957	St. Louis, Mo.	772,897	Cleveland, Ohio	878,336	Baltimore, Md.	939,024
Baltimore, MD	332,313	Cleveland, OH	381,768	Boston, Mass.	748,060	Baltimore, Md.	859,100	Houston, TX	938,219
Cincinnati, OH	255,139	Buffalo, NY	352,387	Baltimore, Md.	733,826	St. Louis, Mo.	816,048	Cleveland, Ohio	876,050
San Francisco, CA	233,959	San Francisco, CA	342,782	Pittsburgh, Pa.	588,343	Boston, Mass.	770,816	Washington, DC	763,956
New Orleans, LA	216,090	Cincinnati, OH	325,902	Los Angeles, Calif.	576,673	Pittsburgh, Pa.	671,659	St. Louis, Mo.	750,026

Source: U.S. Census Bureau.

urban lifestyle. Jane Addams's support for reforms and call for action started the commitment to providing a safe haven for children and began addressing the problems of crime-ridden streets.[14]

As an offshoot of the women's suffrage movement, which was developing in the late 1800s, the Mother's and Children's Movement focused on supporting schools and protecting children from abusive labor practices. By 1902, nearly 800 cities had organized municipal park systems. In 1905, Chicago invested $5 million in building 10 neighborhood parks. Settlement houses were also part of the playground movement since their mission was to serve impoverished and struggling communities—recreational activities flourished in many of these institutions. In Cleveland some of the oldest settlement houses, such as the Alta House (1895), Hiram House (1896), and Rainey Institute (1904), provided gymnasiums and swimming pools in newly built facilities.[15]

As the playground movement became connected to the national agenda, local governments began providing many of these services, which were often part of social reform efforts to Americanize the newly arrived masses. Civic leaders viewed organized recreational activities as being central to assisting new residents adjust to life in the United States. Programs designed to help participants become productive contributors to the city's economic and social well-being proved popular. Even the acquisition of proper citizenship would be attributed to the movement and, in the process, help expand support for the initiative. In 1906, the Playground Association of America was founded. A year later, President Theodore Roosevelt referred to the Chicago parks as "one of the most notable civic achievements of any American city."[16]

In addition to the civic value of leisure and play this era brought another shift in society's attitude along religious and moral lines. A Victorian outlook had dominated civic leaders' view of theaters, sports, and dance halls during much of the nineteenth century. Immoral behavior, which was defined as drinking, gambling, and sexual conduct, became closely associated with these entertainment settings. However, in the first part of the twentieth century, this restrictive approach changed.

First, civic leaders viewed structured recreational opportunities as an antidote to the social ills that seemed to attract the youngsters who wandered the streets. They urged a national involvement of municipalities offering organized recreational activities. In 1906, 41 cities sponsored public programs and by 1920 465 cities were involved. The enactment of laws authorized local governments to become involved in the organization and delivery of recreation. As a result, the number of buildings for recreational use quadrupled between 1925 and 1935.[17]

Second, there was more leisure time available to the average worker. The labor unrest that dominated many American urban centers during the latter part of the nineteenth century led activists to focus, in the early years of the twentieth century, on reducing the average number of hours worked per week. The amount of time spent at work steadily declined after the Civil War; however, between 1900 and 1920, there was a more rapid decline in the time spent on the job. Between 1913 and 1919, weekly hours decreased by 8 percent. During the 1920s, Americans saw their hours per work week drop by about 10 hours from the upper 50s to the upper 40s. During the 1930s, Americans saw that number further diminish below the 40-hour mark.[18]

As Americans enjoyed more available time away from the factory and turned to leisure, recreation began to have an economic effect. During the 1920s, savvy business leaders engaged in promoting "the new economic gospel of consumption." Some feared that the increased periods of leisure time and focus away from work would directly slow economic growth. They countered this fear by advancing marketing activities; it was hoped that workers would want to acquire more consumer goods and that advertising would lead to an increase in productivity to meet this need.

With more people having more free time, the period also saw an increased presence of establishments related to leisure and entertainment. A variety of recreational outlets were provided, given the rise of commercial amusements, such as dance halls, social clubs, regular theaters, movie theaters, public parks, beaches, and professional sports grounds. This also led to concerns about the moral values conveyed by some of these activities, especially dance halls and similar clubs, which were viewed to promote sexually promiscuous behavior and gambling. However, this was increasingly becoming part of a new lifestyle that was adopted by the masses and in the process helped construct a new culture that was more open, progressive, and a departure from the traditional Victorian values and practices of the past that focused on the importance of religion, morality, and industrialism.[19]

So, as we see, by the 1920s leisure time and entertainment had become essential elements of society. For most people leisure activity meant not being at work. By the 1930s, when the country experienced the harsh effects of the Great Depression, leisure activities alone seemed to offer a panacea. The government aggressively engaged in facility and program development aimed at boosting entertainment options. Campgrounds, outdoor common areas, and field houses sprang up across the country. From 1932 to 1937, more than $1.5 billion was allocated to realizing these pursuits. The Works Progress Administration (WPA) distributed $11 billion for the construction of 12,700 playgrounds, 8,500 gymnasiums, 750 swimming pools, 1,000 ice skating rinks, and 64 ski jumps, which accounted for 30 percent of the WPA's total budget.[20]

In the early 1940s, during World War II, the military provided recreational activities for servicemen and women, as well as in communities across the country, and to those who worked in war-related manufacturing plants. As a way to reduce labor tension, a condition that always threatened the maximizing of profits, employers extended support for sport activities. Indirectly, this focus also led to increased assimilation of workers separated by ethnic and racial ties, so that they became better integrated into the capitalist system.[21] According to the 1944 conference proceedings of the Industrial Recreation Association, "well-paid workers today and the minority groups that are continually coming to the fore have had tastes of power that can be redirected into a fighting game of basketball and close competition in bowling or some of our other dynamic athletic and sport events."[22]

By the late 1940s, the institutionalization of leisure time meant that playgrounds, settlement houses, parks, gymnasiums, and commercial establishments now housed organized activities. Furthermore, leisure emerges as an instrument of social control and becomes connected to the Americanization of immigrants. It also kept the labor force distracted from organizing against factory conditions and unequal treatment. But leisure would undergo an additional shift, a "second iteration" during the postwar era, a period of considerable economic growth and urban change.

Postwar Restructuring and the Changing Nature of Leisure

The end of WWII signaled the start of a fundamental economic reorganization. Cities were in the midst of that process. Before the 1940s, urban centers maintained a differentiated and highly functional role as business and financial services. Office headquarters and legal services could be found in downtown areas. Furthermore, in adjacent areas light manufacturing industries, specialized factory districts, warehousing, and wholesalers helped create robust commerce locales offering continuous employment opportunities.

The leadership of urban centers in the 1950s and 1960s viewed fiscal growth opportunities in the same manner as their predecessors had approached city building decades earlier. The prominent modes for assessing current and future economic development opportunities were investment in manufacturing and reliance on the export-base theory. In fact, quite a bit of emphasis was placed on these two factors; the building up of a downtown as the main core for financial activity, and the upgrading of a city's physical infrastructure. These developments helped cities respond to the rising use of automobiles and airplanes through the construction of highways and airports.[23]

But at the same time, the manufacturing economy showed signs of weakness. The decline of heavy industry accelerated in the postwar period and forced economic reorganization and restructuring. For the cities of the Northeast and upper Midwest, which had relied for decades on industrialization to provide a tax base, the rapid deindustrialization proved devastating. In many cases, plant and business relocation further accelerated the decline and caused high rates of unemployment. During the 1970s, a total of 30 to 50 million jobs were lost and almost three-fourths of all private-sector jobs that were in place in 1970 had disappeared from many Northern and Midwestern cities by the end of the decade.[24]

The postwar decline in manufacturing employment persisted into the latter part of the twentieth century and was exacerbated by recessionary periods (see Figure 1.2). While many factors were influenced by this shift, the rise of the service economy advanced this dislocation and proved one of the major contributors to urban restructuring. In 1947, 11.3 percent of the work force was connected to the agricultural sector. By 1966, that figure decreased to just 2.7 percent. During that same period, manufacturing, which also included mining and construction, decreased from 33.8 percent to 21.1 percent of the work force. On the other hand, the service sector grew from 54.7 percent in 1947 to 76.6 percent in 1966 and included transportation, communication, wholesale, retail, finance, insurance, real estate, government, education, law, and accounting. Such profound economic shifts were bound to bring about changes in leisure activities.[25]

In 1934, sociologist George Lundberg and his colleagues had defined leisure as "the time we are free from the more obvious and formal duties which a paid job or other obligatory occupation imposes upon us."[26] Sociologist Josef Pieper had argued in the 1950s

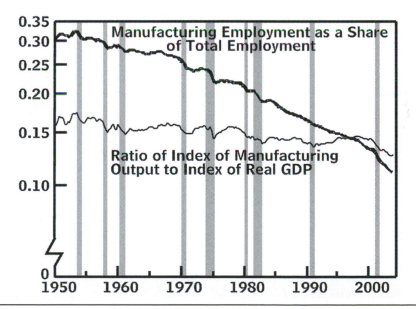

Figure 1.2   Output and employment in the manufacturing sector, 1950–2000. *Note:* The vertical bars indicate periods of recession as defined by the National Bureau of Economic Research. *Source:* David Bauer. What Accounts for the Decline in Manufacturing Employment? *Economic and Budget Issues Briefs,* Congressional Budget Office, February 18, 2004, pp. 1–4.

that "leisure implies an attitude of non-activity, of inward calm, of silence."[27] However, during the 1950s, a decade of prosperity, America was in the midst of profound social and cultural changes. The growth of mass culture that evolved from a rapidly developing consumerism significantly altered the impressions and practice of leisure.

In February 1949, art historian Russell Lynes wrote an article for *Harper's* magazine, titled "Highbrow, Lowbrow, Middlebrow" drawing national attention to the social effect of leisure-oriented practices. Lynes created a chart, classifying the tastes of Americans by integrating objects, interests, and activities. The reaction to Lynes's article was so extensive that it appeared in *Life* magazine a couple of months later, furthering the debate.

Lynes's assessment documented Americans' changing behaviors, but it also clearly showed that a new system of social classification was beginning to emerge. In postwar America, class was not solely defined by the traditional signifiers of wealth, education, and background. Within the parameters of a new leisure framework, social classification was also drawn from the amount and way in which Americans spent their free time. In a 1983 interview, Lynes explained that,

> Corporate support of art exhibitions makes possible these blockbuster museum shows, to which hundreds of thousands of people go and stand in line for hours to see King Tut's mask or whatever. This moves a whole lot of people into museums, for better or worse. Partly it's a matter of corporate or government support, and also there's been an enormous increase in the amount of leisure people have. Work hours are shorter, leaving more time for people to do things they want to or think they want to.[28]

The new standing of leisure complemented other major cultural shifts that were underway following World War II. Sociologist David Riesman examined the dynamics of this new society, within which leisure was rapidly being transformed. In his 1950 book *The Lonely Crowd*, Riesman tried to explain the historical shift by offering a three-stage typology.

Riesman termed the first stage as the "tradition directed" style in which values already established by society are embraced. The second stage was termed the "inner directed" style, which drew from actions that focused on parental understanding and was characterized by a sense of commitment to immediate guidelines directed by an inner conscience. The third stage, identified as "other directed," was where a mass culture allowed for a fundamentally changing nature of the social character that is not fixed and rigid. At this stage, people were more likely to respond and embrace an outward outlook, influenced by the peer group, and therefore capable of developing changing desires and evolving tastes. Leisure could now be viewed and examined within a very different framework.

It is important to note here that this reformatted nature of leisure in the postwar era was taking place in the midst of rapidly evolving urban conditions. Urban decline and renewal, population movement to the Sunbelt and suburbanization, along with the rise of edge cities provide us with the context within which urban tourism emerges as a tool of economic growth and a preferred option for policymakers seeking to turn around urban decay. The rise of leisure and the significance of tourism cannot be viewed independent of the conditions which brought about stress to the once dominating urban cores. An understanding of urban tourism thus necessitates placing that process within a broader historical context of American urban experience.

Postwar changes impacted the cities in fundamental ways, especially as the economic functions that once characterized urban centers were undergoing restructuring. Production, warehousing, wholesale and retail trading, finance, and related business services had became synonymous with urban life. These industries had roots in smaller medium-sized communities of the upper Midwest and Northeast. There was an infusion of a large labor pool of immigrants; African Americans traveled from the South to the North where employment possibilities were excellent. Cities' economies benefited and markets slowly became differentiated, which fueled continued production and unprecedented growth.

But manufacturing jobs rapidly declined after the 1950s because technological advances transformed the production process and required a smaller number of workers. On the other hand, the service sector grew dramatically in both professional positions and support staff. The United States also experienced an increased level of educational attainment (see Figure 1.3), causing considerable demand for

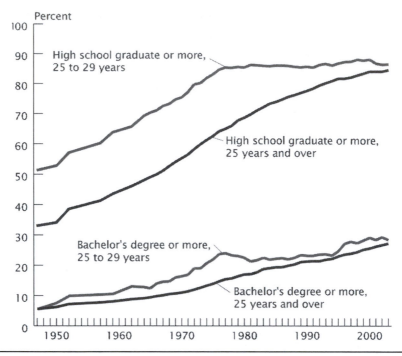

Figure 1.3   Postwar education levels in the United States, 1948–2003. *Source:* Current Population Reports, Series P20-550, Educational Attainment in the United States: June 2004.

white-collar workers, such as lawyers, financial advisors, accountants, and others. At the same time, the economy's move away from production toward a closer alignment with consumption resulted in the rise of large retail businesses and services that included sales, administrative support, and restaurant personnel.

An analysis of seven Northeastern and Midwestern metropolitan areas between 1970 and 1997 shows that the percentage of those employed in the manufacturing sector decreased from 30.1 percent (1970) to 12.5 percent (1997) while the finance, insurance, and real estate sector increased from 6.4 percent (1970) to 9.9 percent (1997). The services sector nearly doubled from 18.4 percent (1970) to 35.6 percent (1997).[29]

Loss of manufacturing was not the only reason for the decline of the urban core. Suburbanization and the concurrent white flight, greatly contributed to the altering fortunes of cities. Federal policies exacerbated the decline. The Federal Highway Act of 1956 under President Dwight D. Eisenhower unknowingly led to this downward trend.

The fund was meant to create an impressive transportation system and to encourage the mass production of automobiles coming out of Detroit. This drove down prices, which made it easier for consumers to purchase cars. The government issued $25 billion in bonds for the construction of more than 41,000 miles of highway for the interstate highway system, the largest in the world.

But the highways also fueled metropolitan expansion, especially following the development of auxiliary interstate expressways. These adjoining networks were put together with the aim of circumventing the main highway routes through cities. Many of the bypasses and spur thoroughfares provided the needed access for the massive post-war suburbanization.

Manufacturers also searched for opportunities to move away from the restrictions of space and cost that were found in traditional city centers. As the new transportation system started to take shape, location became more important in the decision-making process of business operations. In the past, the labor concentration and the presence of railroad hubs in urban cores were the rationale behind the positioning of commercial activities. Vast pools of workers and highly developed railroad networks meant that production and distribution demands could be supplied effectively and efficiently. Because workers could now live outside the city core, retailing and manufacturing activities were relocated to the suburbs. Some companies went beyond the immediate regions to other parts of the country, relying on the flourishing trucking business to easily move goods across the country. Other enterprises looked abroad, taking advantage of weaker environmental restrictions and cheap labor conditions.

The federal government responded by assisting cities that were now experiencing economic decline, as residents fled to the suburbs. The Housing Act of 1949 provided considerable funding for urban redevelopment programs. During a three-decade period, these renewal programs focused on numerous outcomes. Slum clearance, housing construction, and economic development proved central tenets of these efforts. In 1960, $706 million was expended on slum clearance; in 1970, $3.8 billion was spent.[30] The result was the removal of huge portions of downtown neighborhoods, often replaced with office buildings, open spaces, and parks.

But urban renewal programs could not effectively revive dying urban cores and economic development opportunities would prove limited. Furthermore, the federal government slowly withdrew its attention from cities, leaving local leaders to search for other revenue sources. The decline of urban centers also had social consequences. Populations of American cities became predominately African American, characterized by joblessness and concentrated poverty. Housing decay and widespread social problems were overwhelming. The manufacturing jobs that had brought African Americans north to Detroit, Milwaukee, Buffalo, and other cities were now gone. By the late 1960s, riots engulfed urban neighborhoods and reached their height in 1968. In 1968 and 1969, 289 riots extended over many days with 66 dead, 5,302 injured, and 31,680 arrested. From 1965 to 1970, 221 people died in these urban uprisings.[31] The onset of these riots contributed to the image of cities as crime-ridden, deteriorated, and violent places with increasing black ghettos where drug addiction and welfare dependency were considered the norm.

An additional outcome of the urban decline was the rise of social inequality and community division. The postwar crisis, fueled by capitalism, resulted in furthering the racial divide and disproportionately affected African Americans who found themselves concentrated and trapped in the urban core. In 1960, the economic distress in Detroit meant widely varying unemployment rates for African Americans (15.9 percent) and European Americans (5.8 percent). According to one analysis, while the city of Detroit lost population, qualitatively it also changed as it "grew poorer and blacker."[32] In Youngstown, Ohio, the closing of industrial facilities during the 1970s and 1980s impacted the local culture and the individual identity of its residents, which for generations had been structured around steel making. This loss caused division among residents, some of whom favored holding onto the past, while others advocated for a new approach to the city's employment problems.[33]

By the 1960s and 1970s, mass production and distribution of goods can be observed, with leisure itself becoming a commodity and part of a commercial industry. Middle-class and working-class Americans could now possess the goods and also engage in conspicuous consumption practices, something that a generation earlier was reserved for the upper middle class and wealthy.

The Commodification of Leisure

Industrial city centers struggled, given that they were ill-equipped and without a strategy in place to address the significant population and manufacturing shifts during the 1960s and 1970s. Leaders proved incapable of providing an effective response to extensive economic restructuring. Increased population and business flight to the suburbs were more than a statistical outcome. Its implications meant massive job losses, significant increases in social problems, a diminishing tax base, reduced city services, and rapid urban decay. The mismatched, progrowth, postwar policies unfortunately also reached into the response cycle. The introduction of urban renewal programs failed to resurrect the once economically dominant cities; thus the edge cities were slowly gaining financial prominence in outlying suburbia.

During the twentieth century, municipal reformers' planning efforts, which included large-scale public projects, proved to have adverse social effects. Robert Moses modernized New York City's parks and recreation facilities. Known as the Parks Czar, the influential planner promoted the idea of intergenerational recreation. During his long reign, Moses transformed New York's aquatic landscape not only by modernizing existing spaces, but also by adding 17 swimming pools, 11 bathhouses, 73 wading pools, and 225 new playgrounds, revamping two zoos; and building a new beach pavilion. In just two years, Moses expended more than $113 million on parks and recreation.[34]

These administrative successes and extraordinary building plans appealed to an emerging middle class which embraced the automobile industry. Moses's favoring of a city transportation system that focused on highways versus mass transit had additional ramifications. The vast recreation facilities would become segregated, strengthening the patterns of urban social inequality that were slowly becoming visible across the nation's cities.

Existing ethnic and racial prejudices contributed to the nature of public policy decisions that made various groups experience recreational opportunities differently. The lower classes had limited access to parks and beaches. In many cases, public projects helped maintain the division and isolation that typified the urban environment. The powerful, no-nonsense centralized style that characterized Moses's leadership approach also meant inattention to the interests of neighborhoods composed largely of immigrants, racial minorities, and working-class residents.[35]

While urban restructuring was in full force, another set of changes was also in effect, and Moses was cognizant of the new direction and emerging ideals related to recreation. The affluence that characterized post-World War II America significantly altered the perception of leisure. Leisure for most Americans evolved from being a passive occurrence to becoming a sought after activity. For many years, vacations were reserved for the wealthy; however, by the 1960s and 1970s, more families were able to enjoy trips to the beach or to the countryside. Between 1940 and 1970, disposable income more than doubled and the monthly income of families more than tripled. Specifically, from 1950 to 1959, the average family wages increased 41 percent and from 1960 to 1969, the average family wage increased 43 percent. From 1980 to 1996, the average family wage increased 9 percent.[36]

Technological advancements, higher levels of education, and the integration and influence of media in households had marked consequences. Leisure activities consumed more goods and services, a fact further fueled by the commodification of "community" as social mobility characterized postwar suburbanization. The barbeque on the backyard patio and the basketball hoop on the garage meant expanded recreational pursuits associated with the middle-class lifestyle.

Arthur Baum, a reporter for the *Saturday Evening Post* reported in a 1953 newspaper article on the emerging postwar trend by noting that American families became increasingly involved in backyard sports. Paddle tennis, miniature golf, badminton, tetherball, archery, croquet, and other games captured the country's imagination and became part of everyday life. Economically packaged sporting equipment was used to take advantage of 50-foot home plots.

Leisure growth was good for business as manufacturers reported expanding sales. In the early part of the 1950s, sales for backyard archery equipment increased at an unprecedented rate; one manufacturing executive noted that the popularity of archery sets was "practically out of control."[37] In addition, Americans rushed to purchase and install plastic pools in their backyards at a fraction of the cost of a standard swimming pool.

But the acceptance of these sporting experiences was more than a pastime activity. Suburbanization, coupled with spare time and money influenced Americans to adopt a new mantra: "Any American can be a household athlete."[38] Following World War II, personal service and consumption expenditures increased (see Table 1.2).

Within a new economic environment, leisure was also connected to consumerism and commodification. Success at work meant

Table 1.2 Personal Service Expenditures as Percentages of Gross National Product and Total Personal Consumption Expenditures (1940 through 1960)

YEAR	IN BILLIONS OF 1960 DOLLARS			% SERVICES OF GROSS NATIONAL PRODUCT	% SERVICES OF PERSONAL CONSUMPTION EXPENDITURES
	GROSS NATIONAL PRODUCT	PERSONAL CONSUMPTION EXPENDITURES	SERVICES		
1940	100.6	71.9	26.9	26.7	37.4
1941	125.8	81.9	29.0	23.1	35.4
1945	213.6	121.7	40.4	18.9	33.2
1946	210.7	147.1	46.4	22.0	31.5
1947	234.3	165.4	51.4	21.9	31.1
1948	259.4	178.3	56.9	21.9	31.9
1950	284.6	195.0	64.9	22.8	33.3
1952	347.0	219.8	75.6	21.8	34.4
1954	363.1	238.0	86.3	23.8	36.3
1955	397.5	256.9	92.5	23.3	36.0
1956	419.2	269.9	100.0	23.9	37.1
1957	442.8	285.2	107.1	24.2	37.6
1958	444.2	293.5	114.2	25.7	38.9
1959	482.1	313.8	122.8	25.5	39.1
1960	504.4	328.9	132.2	26.2	40.2

Source: Regan, William J. 1963. "The Service Revolution." *Journal of Marketing 27*(3):57–62.

distribution of economic rewards, and these resources provided consumers with the ability to purchase leisure activities, which became connected to a materialistic lifestyle, evident within modernization and a postindustrial society. Jürgen Habermas differentiates between free time (culture consuming) and leisure (culture creating), each one containing different social roles. Free time contains an element of communication, sociability, and engagement, while leisure has shifted into the consumption arena.[39] From this perspective, leisure does not produce emancipatory environments since it does not necessarily increase individual freedom.[40]

Inseparable from capitalism, leisure is structured by the economic system and the related markets it creates. Commodified consumption is directly connected to the production process. An analysis of the model airplane hobby industry illustrates how technical advancements transformed this fun activity. The postwar introduction of plastics reorganized the traditional core of this hobby: the construction and flying of model airplanes. For many years, enthusiasts focused on the flying aspects, and the model display was secondary. Being able to construct and fly a model plane required extensive skills and aeronautic knowledge; thus, the market was small. But the introduction of molding to modeling created a shift in focus. The use of plastics altered the hobby by creating two distinct groups of fans. On the one hand, there were fans who were interested in model display. On the other hand, there were fans for whom model building meant being able to fly the plane.

In addition, the introduction of the plastic molding made it easier to meet the skill sets of eager younger enthusiasts. In fact, plastic kits helped fuel the popularity of making model airplanes, since mass production of prefabricated parts eased the assembly process. As the leisure industry's capital flowed more vigorously, the market expanded into modeling of other objects, such as ships and cars. Advertisements included the distribution of these kits through general department stores, making them part of the children's toy market. The "deskilling" of the hobby shows how within capitalism "the mode of production shapes cultural activities in [a] form consistent with its own needs."[41]

The Sunbelt, Suburbanization, and Edge Cities

The declining condition of industrial cities after World War II was advanced by decentralization, the population shift from the city center to the suburbs, and the parallel development of cities in the South and Southwest, giving rise to the Sunbelt. These demographic movements placed considerable fiscal pressure on an already fragile urban core; however, in the process, they contributed to one of the most powerful economic booms. Recently dubbed by urban planning scholar Robert Beauregard as the "short American century," these movements helped maintain America's exceptionalism.[42]

Not bound by the constraints of the traditional industrialized city center design, cities in the Sunbelt experienced rapid growth. From 1950 to 1970, Phoenix experienced an increase from 106,000 to 581,000 residents. San Jose experienced an increase from 95,000 to 445,000 residents, and Jacksonville experienced an increase from 204,000 to 528,000 residents. Growth was everywhere; Dallas, Los Angeles, Austin, Charlotte, San Diego, San Antonio, Las Vegas, and many other cities continued to see population growth into the 2000 census. From 1990 to 2000, California's population increased 13.6 percent, Arizona's population increased 40 percent, New Mexico's population increased 20.1 percent, Texas's population increased 22.8 percent, and Georgia's population increased 26.4 percent.

These patterns can be attributed to many factors. The integration of technology in the production process required new types of plants and assembly formats. The older manufacturing cities lacked the requisite infrastructure, and the newer cities were ready to provide needed transportation and communication networks. Local governments aggressively engaged in attracting businesses, which viewed this as an opportunity to escape the increasingly powerful labor unions. In addition, the federal government expended billions in military development in locations throughout the South and the West.

Like the movement to the Sunbelt, postwar suburbanization proved one of the most powerful internal migration movements, significantly restructuring the spatial dynamics of American cities. Philadelphia's population decreased from 2.07 million in 1950 to 1.51 million in 2000, Chicago declined from 3.62 million in 1950 to 2.89 million in 2000, and Detroit from 1.84 million in 1950 to 0.95 million in 2000. During that same period (1950 to 2000), St. Louis's population declined from 0.85 million to 0.33 million and Pittsburgh's population decreased from 0.68 million to 0.32 million.

An analysis of data from the U.S. Census Bureau that presented central city and suburban population change clearly shows the dramatic transformation. From 1950 to 1959, the 26 largest cities in the country lost 2.43 million residents while during that period the suburban areas of these same cities gained 8.24 million residents. A similar trend is observed in the decades that followed: from 1960 to 1990, the 26 largest cities lost 9.428 million residents and the suburban population increased by 22.047 million.[43]

This population deconcentration is the outcome of multiple factors, including white flight, home mortgage subsidies, highway construction, educational and mortgage assistance to veterans returning from World War II, economic globalization, and business relocation. In addition, the idealized image of suburbanization, popularized during the early part of the twentieth century, could now become realized by the masses.

Another postwar trend, the rise of edge cities, furthered this population movement to the outskirts. New employment centers formed in suburbs, increasingly surpassing the geographic size and number of jobs available in nearby downtown areas. By the 1980s, the typical commute was from a suburban home to a suburban job, reversing the previous trends of traveling downtown. Extensive business relocations during the 1960s and 1970s followed the new labor force and customer base.[44]

Metropolitan dispersal persisted in the 1990s as edge cities evolved to contain the majority of office space. According to one analysis, there was less office space in downtown Boston (37.4 percent of total metro area) compared to the office space in the outskirts (58 percent of total metro area). There was less office space in downtown Denver (30.4 percent of total in metro area) compared to the office space outside the core (65.3 percent of total metro area), and downtown Dallas held one-fifth of the space (20.5 percent of total metro area) compared to office space outside the core (74.9 percent of total metro area). Similar trends occurred in Philadelphia, Miami, Atlanta, Houston, Los Angeles, and San Francisco. Edge cities helped redefine the metropolitan areas, assisting suburbs to become self-sustaining.[45]

The issues addressed in the sections above clearly convey the social and economic difficulties that the once powerful and dominant American cities of the Frostbelt faced following World War II. Population and business decline, unrest, poor services, along with housing decay, now characterized city neighborhoods. Suburban communities on the other hand, experienced robust affluence and rapid growth. In addition, the concurrent restructuring of leisure practices and the associated fiscal potential would emerge as an opportunity to revive these struggling urban cores.

Positioning tourism as a viable economic development option for cities was furthered by two additional postwar trends. The following sections explore these developments in greater detail. First, the preservation movement and the rise of historic districts meant that visitors could be drawn to new attractions. Second, the professionalization of travel and its development into a major industry ensured that the increased demand could be met. This is also related to the rise of corporations and of the associated convention meetings and conferences which necessitated tourism service providers. Finally the availability of leisure persisted, even at a time when Americans complained that they spent too much time at work.

The Preservation Movement and the Rise of Historic Districts

The rise of the preservation movement contributed to urban tourism and business travel by helping create additional destinations across the country. A number of legislative acts and organizational initiatives following World War II set the stage for an increase in the number of historic districts. For years, local citizen outreach drives through private sources operated separately from government, successfully identifying, protecting, and preserving the nation's historical places. These public and private efforts came together, initially through the formation of the National Council for Historic Sites and Buildings, and later by the induction of the National Trust for Historic Preservation in 1949.

The National Historic Preservation Act of 1966 would prove the most important legislation. Enacted after a National Trust for Historic Preservation report released in 1965, the law called for a new direction. The document, titled *With Heritage So Rich*, urged for a renewed commitment across all levels of government to preserve important structures and settings. The document pushed for the completion of a national survey that would identify historically significant buildings, sites, and districts.

The Act's impact was extensive and included many other elements. It established the National Register of Historic Places and the Advisory Council on Historic Preservation, and introduced the idea that historic districts should be certified. This allowed fund preservation activities to receive support from legislative acts. The result of this Act cannot be underestimated. By the mid-1980s, between 2,000 and 3,000 organizations were observed, engaged in preservation, education, advocacy, and restoration work. The National Trust for Historic Preservation saw its membership increase from 10,700 in 1966 to 185,000 in 1986. In addition, more than 35 university courses in various aspects of historic preservation appeared in the curriculums of colleges and universities across the country, professionalizing this field and employing more than 54,000 people in its administration.[46]

The 1966 Act also redefined historic districts. In previous years, only individual structures could receive that designation. However, the National Trust for Historic Preservation legislation recognized that historic objects often exist within a broader physical context, making the surrounding environment equally important. The notion that building groups could be identified in the designation proved unique, not only from a preservation perspective, but also from a tourist perspective, since visitors would be able to gain a more comprehensive understanding and appreciation for the location.

Subsequent legislative acts, the Tax Reform Act (1976) and the Revenue Act (1978), helped further solidify the preservation movement. The removal of existing incentives to destroy deteriorated buildings was also significant. Instead, tax benefits would be offered for rehabbing historic structures.

These developments had a direct impact on the number of historic areas and districts that were introduced. In 1973, Santa Fe, New Mexico, was formally added to the National Register of Historic Places. The city square, considered for years to be the center of community life, benefited from the landmark status. Performing arts stages and multiple markets attracted thousands of tourists who traveled to experience the display and the fusion of Mexican, Spanish, and Indian cultures. Similar designations spread across the country.

These changes increased the number of national parks, monuments, and historical and military areas from 157 in 1940 to 277 in 1970. The number of tourists who visited parks after World War II also grew significantly, but these parks were lacking accommodations and visitor services. To meet the increased demand in this area, Congress provided more than $1 billion in the 1950s and 1960s.[47] By 2004, more than 387 national park units were administered by the National Park Service. An upward trend has been observed in recent years. In 2009, the government designated nine new historic landmarks, bringing the total number of historical places close to 2,500. Then Interior Secretary Dirk Kempthorne noted "the historical and cultural developments reflected by these new National Historic Landmarks is tremendous. Each of the nine sites provides all Americans with [an] opportunity to learn."[48]

Interestingly, while these designations increased tourism, they also proved to positively impact economic development. Many cities looked to historic preservation as a way to revitalize their neighborhoods. In recent years, historic district properties have gone from 17,000 in 2000 to 34,400 in 2005. In Memphis, Tennessee, the number of neighborhood historic districts included from 2003 to 2005 doubled in comparison to those added in previous periods.[49]

The Travel Industry, the Rise of Corporations, and the Convention Business

According to a 1953 newspaper account, one of the key challenges facing travel agents related to the increased demand for travel to foreign countries. This caused customers to develop peculiar demands for transportation and accommodations. The story noted:

> Twenty years ago the typical tourists in Europe were a retired executive and his wife, who spent $6,200 on a six week trip. Today, the two largest groups going to Europe are students and housewives with tight budgets of $1,100, or less, for six weeks. There still is a good deal of plush travel, but all-expense tours geared to middle-class incomes now produce the most revenues.... A woman wants to go to Bermuda—by train. A man specifies a baritone gondolier in Venice. Girls on cruises all want men, men, men! And if the trip flops, the travel agent gets it in the neck.[50]

In an interesting way, this report outlines the postwar popularity of travel. But it would be the expansion of the computer reservations system (CRS) that fundamentally converted the industry. Originally, only the airlines could use the system to make reservations and complete transactions. The increased demand for travel required that the system be made available to agents as well.

Travel service providers slowly became professionalized. As agents, convention and visitor bureau personnel, and hotel and tour operators achieved an "expert" status, they transformed the sector into a burgeoning industry. The National Tour Association formed in 1951; the U.S. Travel Data Center formed in 1973, and the National Council of Area and Regional Travel Agencies formed in 1976. By becoming professionalized, tour operators became global in their outreach. Founded in 1972, the membership of the United States Tour Operators Association (USTOA) is currently responsible for serving more than 11 million passengers annually with a sales volume nearing $10 billion every year.

Travel agencies would continue to thrive even during the deregulation of the airline industry in the late 1970s and early 1980s. With high travel demand in the midst of a competitive environment, air travel experienced reduced airfares and complicated formulas that included various departure and arrival dates and times. Travel offices could now shift through these complex formulas and provide customers with the lowest possible prices.

The popularity of Disneyland and other resort areas, extraordinary hotel growth, rise of the fast food industry, falling cost, and spread of air travel, along with increased automobile usage furthered the standing and value of the tourism industry. With suburbanization also came a sense of nostalgia for the "old neighborhoods," giving rise to a unique group of travelers, the day-trippers. All of these developments injected strong elements of Fordism; a model driven by technological progress, standardization, and economic growth based on mass production.[51]

In 1972, the tourism industry ranked as the second largest retail business in the country and was first among the top three industries in 46 of 50 states. Authorities recorded tourism-related expenditures at $61 billion that year. In 2000, the domestic travel market in the United States surpassed the $500 billion mark. Domestic travelers accounted for 86 percent of all travel spending in the country.[52]

Cities could play a very important role in this growing industry because they provided many of the attractions sought by visitors. In addition, the increase in the U.S. population living in urban centers would help the growth of tourism. In 1950, according to census data, 64 percent of the population lived in urban areas. In 1980, it was 73.74 percent and in 2000 it was 75.21 percent. The actual number of urban residents increased from 96.84 million in 1960 to 222.36 million in 2000. Many of the trends that gave rise to urban centers in the postwar era also contributed to the growth of urban tourism.

The substantial postwar rise of educational attainment in the United States also solidified the role of cities in the forefront of culture. The proportion of 25- to 29-year-old high school graduates rose from 38.1 percent in 1940 to 86.7 percent in 1993. This placed cultural institutions in the forefront of mass culture consumption as museum visits and related tours and activities gained favor with visitors.

But beyond the demand side (the tourist in search of the experience), we must also consider the supply side (the making of the experience). Urban centers aggressively pursued promotional campaigns to remake themselves as ideal environments for work, leisure, and residential living. Local boosters supported the transformation of cities into tourist sites, not only by marketing the various attractions, but also by supporting aggressive construction of needed infrastructure.

These initiatives are part of regeneration and local economic development rationales. The outcome of these efforts, visible across many cities, has been the construction of convention centers, new hotels, sport stadiums, casinos, and expansive entertainment complexes—all of which extensively reorganized the urban landscape. Cities competed with one another to attract visitors to their locales. In 2006, while Los Angeles (58.6 million), Orlando (47.8 million), New York City (44 million), and Chicago (41.3 million) reported a greater number of visitors, Las Vegas showcased the highest weighted score and emerged in the number one position when factoring the sale of rooms. In the "sale of rooms" category, Las Vegas surpassed all other cities by selling 40 million rooms, followed by Orlando (27.2 million), Los Angeles (25.5 million), and Chicago (24.8 million). According to this formula, Baltimore, Fort Lauderdale, Kansas City, and Nashville were the least visited cities in the country.[53]

Las Vegas recently engaged in aggressive marketing practices to promote itself beyond its attractions. The city departed from past efforts that focused on informing prospective visitors about various destinations to initiatives that endorse the individual experience. The highly successful "What Happens Here, Stays Here" is now complemented with "Your Vegas is Showing" (YVIS). According to a vice president for marketing, "This campaign is about how Vegas, its energy and excitement, can help transform a person."[54]

The postwar era brought extraordinary periods of economic growth and affluence, capturing the world's attention. Non-Americans singled out the nation's popular culture and goods that Americans consumed. In addition, they looked to the United States as the pacesetter of the future. The country had the capacity to transfer various technological advancements and discoveries into everyday life, making the economic expansion remarkable.

U.S. financial growth was so extensive that even the ideological opponents of capitalism recognized the success. A 1968 analysis by one socialist publication conceded "the economic superiority of the United States following the Second World War needs little recapitulation...[in 1953] the U.S. gross national product was still more than twice as high as the combined GNP's of France, Germany, Italy,

Belgium, Luxemburg, Britain and Japan."[55] Even policies to reduce poverty would be revisited. Many viewed technological changes capable of generating enough wealth to retire existing redistributive plans.[56]

The geographic restructuring of metropolitan areas impacted corporations given that these enterprises were at the center of the country's economic boom. Suburbanization fueled office construction. By taking advantage of the new telecommunications technologies, executives could coordinate business expansion that included exporting goods at unprecedented rates.

The number of corporations in the United States increased from 365,000 in 1947 to 923,200 in 1963 and to 1,280,800 in 1971. The total receipts of these corporations increased considerably from $466.4 billion in 1947 to $1,208 trillion in 1971 (1958 dollars).[57] The development of expansive networks helped many of these sectors become international. The rapid growth of services significantly increased business travel. Information gained widespread value as a form of communication and business exchange, and the growth of large corporations in multiple cities required face-to-face interaction. Trade shows, conferences, and conventions rapidly turned out to be a necessary part of commerce.

From 1957 to 1968, the number of conventions for various associations increased annually from 22,000 to 35,000. During that same timeframe, attendance rose from 10 million to 12 million attendees, contributing $1.2 billion in 1957 and $2.2 billion in 1968 to various urban economies. Overall, it was estimated in 1968 that Americans expended a total of $6.1 billion on conventions.[58]

In the years that followed, cities aggressively engaged in building convention centers to attract and retain conferences, meetings, and exhibits. The rise of corporations obviously helped make convention business a major part of the urban tourism strategy and injected competition as cities sought to secure these economically significant events. Construction of hotels, restaurants, and additional support services followed. By the late 1990s the development craze placed extensive pressure on cities. Many of them came to expect immediate success following the introduction of these facilities. The next chapter goes into greater detail, examining this urban competition and the tourism industry.

It is clear that the continued availability of leisure time is central to the development of urban tourism. Even though the United States is often referred to as the "no vacation-nation," recent research shows that time away from prescribed tasks saw a considerable increase. This contradicts Current Population Survey data that tends to overstate Americans' reported "hours worked."[59]

Specifically, a 2007 study between 1965 and 2005 reveals that women experienced a decrease in their domestic duties by around 10 hours per week, and that men labor fewer hours for paid work today compared to decades ago. The same analysis shows that leisure for men during that period increased by 6 to 9 hours per week and for women by 4 to 8 hours per week. This is quite significant since the extra free time would amount to about seven additional weeks of vacation per year, which is equivalent to a 13 percent increase in annual pay.[60] These findings are consistent with other studies that reached the same conclusion: Americans are working less and as a result they are able to spend more time engaged in leisure activities.[61]

Personal consumption expenditures on recreation increased from 6.6 percent in 1970 to 7.6 percent in 1990 to 8.7 percent in 2005, and the inflation-adjusted spending on recreation per capita (2005 dollars) increased from $854 in 1970 to $1,612 in 1990 to $2,551 in 2005. The annual number of spectators at professional baseball games rose from 29,191,000 in 1970 to 55,512,000 in 1990 to 76,285,917 in 2005. Average attendance at games also rose sharply.[62]

Ticket prices at professional sporting events also increased in recent years and an analysis of average salaries in major sports leagues revealed dramatic changes. In the postwar period, players' salaries rose slowly; however, in the 1980s, professional athletes experienced significant income increases. In 1950, the ratio of average National Basketball Association (NBA) salaries relative to median family income was 1.3/1; in 1980, it was 9/1; and in 2007, it was 54/1. While free agency helped boost these ratios, the willingness of Americans to expend considerable resources and to consume the entertainment product offered by the basketball league also helped boost these ratios.[63]

Overseas travel also changed following World War II. During the last three decades, a greater number of adults engaged in overseas travel (see Table 1.3 below). From 1970 to 2005, that number more than tripled. In addition to the availability of time and disposable income, the ease of travel, as well as the educational value placed on travel, contributed to these increases.

Conclusion

If we are to understand the rise of the leisure class in the United States its emergence must be positioned within a broader historical context. When leisure and recreation are placed in the urban political economy framework it not only provides insights on the changing nature of social class, but also offers a perspective on how leisure and recreation have influenced the transformation of cities. Settlement patterns are informed by structural factors, a relationship that helps reveal the dynamic nature of urban change.

Numerous forces that can be traced to the postwar era shaped the current condition of cities. Decentralization, deindustrialization, and economic restructuring caused the fortunes of many urban centers to decline with accompanying population loss and social problems. At the same time, the second half of the twentieth century gave rise to new residential and commercial settlement patterns farther away from the center. The economic prosperity that ensued resulted in

Table 1.3 Overseas Trips per 1,000 Adults (16 years of age or older)

2005	124.4
2000	123.3
1995	93.4
1990	83.2
1985	67.4
1980	47.5
1975	40.5
1970	37.0

Source: US Census Bureau, Statistical Abstract of the United States: 2007, Table 1250, and US Census Bureau, Statistical Abstract of the United States: 1987, Table 390.

the restructuring and commodification of leisure. Travel and tourism emerged as a multibillion-dollar industry and held the promise of aiding the ailing urban cores.

At the same time, the perceived positive outcomes of the rapidly developing tourism industry injected urban competition, forcing cities to invest considerable resources as they sought to attract visitors and their expenditures. Urban recreational and business travel, like other trends and conditions, was influenced by globalization. These issues are further examined next, including the entrepreneurism exemplified by local policymakers in developing and marketing their tourism product.

Writing, Reflection, and Debate

Discussion Questions

How old are the cities you have lived in? Do you see any traces of earlier eras of city building?

Think about the things you do for fun. Would Habermas consider these things "free time" or "leisure." Do these activities depend more heavily on buying things or on creating things?

2

GLOBALIZATION, URBAN COMPETITION, AND TOURISM

The previous chapter traced how major events in America's urban past—the birth of the railroads, the rise of manufacturing, World War II, and the decline of manufacturing—carved a path for the development of urban leisure and travel for recreational purposes (tourism), and for business. Over the course of nearly 200 years, the way Americans spent their free time changed dramatically, rising and falling with economic conditions, shifting toward activities driven by spending, consumption, and the careful planning of cities' leisure landscapes. However, urban leisure and tourism have not been influenced by domestic factors alone. This chapter explores how globalization would also prove to have a significant impact on the development of tourism. For example, international trade and commerce require the creation of entertainment outlets. Convention centers and exhibitions are often regarded as a prerequisite of travel, whether recreational or for business, to urban areas. Business travel not only necessitates appropriate visitor sites, as those attending conventions seek a recreational environment, perhaps to entertain potential customers, but also helps establish related markets and networks. In the last few decades, the explosion of this international industry gave countries and cities across the globe the opportunity to promote themselves with the hope of attracting the accompanying expenditures of large volumes of visitors.[1]

The globalization of tourism and business travel has meant that cities must intensify their planning efforts. This injects competition as urban centers embrace entrepreneurial practices. And while both the private and public sectors are extensively involved on an individual basis, it is private–public partnerships that dominate these emerging practices. This is not surprising; it is consistent with past modes of city building.

One of the key outcomes of this strategy is the reimaging of former industrial cities and the development of new urban identities. Investments in marketing the new image of these cities are significant, and the benefits are inherently advantageous. The redevelopment of urban spaces around culture is evident in cities across the world. For example, Bilbao in Spain received international attention as new cultural facilities, in particular the Frank Gehry designed Guggenheim Museum, reshaped its environment. The progressive design forever changed the way the world thinks about museums and gave the city global media attention, elevating its reputation to attract tourists and multinational businesses.[2] Other highly acclaimed architects were hired to refashion key attractions and introduce new ones.

Singapore advanced cultural consumption by building the Esplanade, a major arts facility capable of supporting international performers. A key goal of this initiative was to rebrand the southern part of the city as an artistic hub. In Dakshinachitra, Chennai, India, the development of a cultural complex focusing on traditional crafts was aimed at not only showcasing artifacts and educating visitors about the distinctive styles, but also at serving as a global exporter of artisans' high-quality creations. These efforts gave the city a unique identity as a cultural center.[3]

Cases like these are plentiful. Cities across the world have turned to culture and globalization has helped drive the rapid expansion of travel whether for business or pleasure. But there have been negative effects too in the form of environmental degradation, and labor issues have also surfaced, two elements that threaten the reputation of the travel industry. Furthermore, while Bilbao has been a success story, the overdevelopment of Cancun, Mexico raises questions about economic growth at the expense of ecological disintegration.

Globalization and Travel

Post-World War II global economic expansion fueled the development of air travel in the 1950s, and there has been an average increase of 9 percent annually since that time. The introduction of the first frequent flyer program by American Airlines in 1981 set the stage for other carriers to reward distant travel. Current estimates indicate that the world aircraft fleet will reach 23,000 airplanes by 2016, double the 1996 number.[4]

In addition to air travel, a number of other factors contributed to growth. Hotels evolved and became international in focus, developing global networks to serve travelers. The Hyatt Corporation, for example, was founded in 1957 in Los Angeles and by 1969 there were 13 Hyatt hotels in the United States. That same year, they unveiled their first international hotel, the Hyatt Regency Hong Kong. With the 1980 opening of Hyatt Regency Maui, the organization moved aggressively into the global resorts business. In 2009, the corporation operated more than 391 hotels and resorts (more than 136,000 rooms) in 44 countries.[5]

The globalization of tourism is the outcome of the same political and economic factors that can be identified in other industries. The rise of a worldwide economic system is supported by cultural and social changes in information technology and mass media. As business entrepreneurs engaged in activities across all continents, differentiating between travel, tourism, leisure, and accommodations grew more difficult, blurring their relationship.[6] These activities would become increasingly interconnected, slowly morphing into one general area that today not only encompasses multiple industries and markets, but also operates across boundaries.

The most recent 2008–2009 report by the World Travel and Tourism Council provides a comprehensive assessment of the tourism sector by noting that the current economic crisis is part of a broader

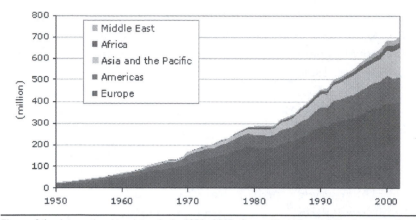

Figure 2.1   International tourist arrivals, 1950–2005. *Source:* World Travel & Tourism Council.

cyclical downturn and is not expected to have a long-term impact on the status of the industry. The report also notes that Africa (+5.9 percent), Asia Pacific (+5.7 percent), and the Middle East (+5.2 percent) are experiencing higher growth rates than the world average. On the other hand, the Americas (-2.1 percent) and Europe (-2.3 percent) are falling below the threshold.[7]

According to the World Tourism Organization, 2007 was a banner year for tourism with new arrivals reaching a record figure worldwide—close to 900 million. There were 52 million more arrivals that year compared to 2006. This number is impressive, especially when one considers longitudinal data that show international tourist arrivals at about 25 million travelers in 1950, and 550 million travelers in 1996 (see Table 2.1). They attribute this growth trend to the popularity of travel at a time of a strong world economy. In fact, the past two decades are the industry's longest period of sustained expansion.[8]

This surge reflects the successful introduction of new destinations, especially in Asia and the Pacific. Since the 1950s, Europe and the Americas lacked the average growth found in the developing nations; however, both of these continents remained the world's main tourist-receiving regions from 1950 to 2000. The two regions comprised 95 percent of the total market share in 1950, 82 percent in 1990, and 76 percent in 2000. In 2004, tourism represented $132 billion in the Americas and $328.5 billion in Europe. Asia and the Pacific accounted for $129.5 billion of the total receipts that year. In 2004, the total worldwide revenues were $634.7 billion.[9]

Global travel and tourism are expected to continue on an upward trajectory (see Table 2.1). The Council outlined a mature but steady phase of growth between 2009 and 2018. Averaging 4.4 percent per year through 2018, travel and tourism can support 297 million jobs worldwide and possess 10.5 percent of the global GDP. Both the public and private sectors will make considerable investments in the industry. Capital expenditures are expected to more than double from 2008 to 2018 ($1,354 billion to $3,146 billion). Revenues from business travel and personal tourism will also help boost employment. It is projected that in 2018, 1 out 10.8 jobs will be tied to this sector.

The potential of travel and tourism is extraordinary. The economic development prospects are so significant that the United Nations identified this as a key contributor to help reduce poverty and protect the

Table 2.1   Various Aspects of Global Tourism, 2008 and 2018

WORLDWIDE	2008			2018		
	US$ BN	% TOTAL	GROWTH[1]	US$ BN	% TOTAL	GROWTH[2]
Personal Travel & Tourism	3,212	9.2	3.0	5,460	9.4	3.5
Business Travel	843	1.4	3.0	1,443	1.4	3.5
Government Expenditures	381	3.8	2.2	616	4.0	3.0
Capital Investment	1,354	9.4	3.7	3,146	9.8	5.6
Visitor Exports	1,118	5.8	3.1	2,189	5.4	5.3
Other Exports	985	5.1	5.1	1,984	4.9	6.0
T&T Demand	7,892	10.1	3.3	14,838	10.3	4.4
Direct Industry GDP	2,008	3.4	2.7	3,362	3.2	3.3
T&T Economy GDP	5,890	9.9	3.0	10,855	10.5	4.0
Direct Industry Employment[3]	80,749	2.8	2.0	97,983	3.1	2.0
T&T Economy Employment[3]	238,277	8.4	2.4	296,252	9.2	2.2

1. 2008 real growth adjusted for inflation (%)
2. 2009–18 annualized real growth adjusted for inflation (%)
3. '000 jobs
Source: World Travel & Tourism Council.

environment from impending global threats such as climate change. While considerable community capacity building opportunities exist, tourism also carries some of the social inequalities typically associated with globalization. For example, the economic advancement also can have environmental ramifications. Ecological consequences are visible in Cancun, Mexico, which rapidly evolved since the mid-1970s to become the most popular destination in that country. The Mexican government identified the area and promoted its standing as a Caribbean resort area during the 1960s. However, this highly planned environment eventually matured into a model of mass tourism. Market forces viewed the explosive growth in Cancun as an opportunity to maximize their profits. The government slowly withdrew its involvement in the city, allowing for a model of disorganized capitalism to dominate. In addition to corruption, drug investment, money laundering, and rapid construction, Cancun's mass tourist development had a detrimental effect on the natural environment.[10]

Left uncontrolled, tourism can pose major threats to indigenous populations and can reduce cultural diversity. There are even issues of access. According to the World Trade Organization, 7 percent of the world population will be able to travel abroad by 2020, which is double the 1996 figure of 3.5 percent.[11]

Expansion in accommodations to support visitors is a visible outgrowth of urban tourism, but here too we can observe the negative effects of this globalized industry such as environmental impacts. At the end of 2003, 1,903 hotels and 246,895 rooms were scheduled for construction in the United States. By the end of the third quarter of 2005, that number increased to 2,792 hotels with 377,077 rooms.[12] In 2006, there were 3,067 projects with 415,977 rooms, the highest rate since 2000.[13] Expenditures in this area refashioned the physical makeup of many urban centers.

City governments typically welcome hotel projects, viewing them as a form of private investment that can help revive depressed cores. In May 2005, development of the $30 million Hilton Garden Inn began in Portsmouth, New Hampshire's downtown district. This was the city's largest construction project in recent history and with 131 rooms it promised to attract tourists to the area. Plans also included condominiums and street level retail space. Even though public funds did not support the hotel, more than $13 million in public bond financing assisted development of the adjacent conference center, a nearby park, and a marina. The need for additional hotel rooms in downtown Portsmouth encouraged developers to propose more projects, including a 1,240 room hotel with a Venetian theme, an Atlantic style casino, an expansion of the Sheraton Harborside, and the Parade Mall Westin Hotel.[14]

Globalization fueled the growth of the hotel industry. Large corporations increasingly position themselves internationally to take advantage of the increased opportunities in this sector. In 2008, InterContinental Hotels Group (IHG) operated in 100 countries, Starwood Hotels & Resorts Worldwide in 95 countries, and Accor in 90 countries. By franchising their assets, these entities can improve the management of their operations, which allows them to operate in more countries and generate higher profits. In 2008, the Wyndham Hotel Group franchised the most hotels, over 6,544 globally, followed by Choice Hotels International (5,570 hotels) and InterContinental Hotels Group (3,392 hotels).[15] In spite of the recent economic downturn, Starwood Hotels & Resorts Worldwide continued its aggressive expansion in the Asia Pacific by 70 percent in 2008. Hilton added 32,000 rooms globally in 2007 and plans for further growth beyond its U.S. business activities. During the next decade, Marriott has scheduled the addition of 130,000 more rooms worldwide.[16] The healthy occupancy rates worldwide (see Table 2.2) further that commitment.

Changes in the composition of the U.S. labor force also contributed to hotel growth. According to the U.S. Department of Labor, Hispanics are consistently more likely than any other group to be employed in the leisure and hospitality sector. In 2007, 21.7 percent (20.2 percent in 2003) of all accommodation and food services employees were Hispanic or Latino compared to 6.5 percent who were Asian and 11.2 percent who were African American. The number of Hispanic or Latino workers in the accommodation industry was 23.7 percent (24 percent in 2003) and even higher in the area of traveler accommodation at 24.8 percent (25.2 percent in 2003). When one considers the occupational category of maids and housekeeping cleaners, the

Table 2.2   Hotel Occupancy Rates in Cities, 2005–2009

	2009	2008	2007	2006	2005
North America					
Atlanta, GA	52.6	58.5	62.8	64.3	64.6
Boston, MA	62.2	66.3	68.3	66.9	65.2
Chicago, IL	56.4	63.1	67.5	67.4	64.0
Los Angeles-Long Beach, CA	64.1	70.9	74.8	75.1	74.5
New York, NY	77.1	81.7	83.2	82.3	82.7
San Francisco-San Mateo, CA	71.4	75.1	75.0	72.8	71.4
Europe					
Amsterdam	66.5	73.0	78.4	79.1	75.2
Berlin	67.5	68.8	69.9	66.8	63.1
Brussels	63.8	69.3	71.0	69.2	65.5
London	80.3	79.3	80.6	80.0	73.9
Madrid	57.4	64.1	68.9	67.8	68.4
Paris	73.5	77.2	78.2	74.3	70.6
Rome	61.8	64.2	77.5	74.9	72.2
Vienna	65.9	71.0	75.4	75.9	73.5
Asia Pacific					
Auckland	67.1	70.7	69.9	70.1	71.0
Beijing	51.9	55.6	68.8	71.1	73.9
Hong Kong	73.8	81.3	84.1	83.1	81.9
Singapore	73.3	77.2	83.2	81.2	89.6
Sydney	78.1	77.9	80.1	77.6	76.0
Tokyo	70.3	75.1	78.7	81.0	78.9
Latin America					
Buenos Aires	55.0	67.5	69.5	70.4	71.2
Mexico City	50.0	61.1	60.0	60.9	63.5
Santiago	61.1	73.6	72.4	70.5	64.2
Sao Paulo	59.0	63.8	61.6	57.5	52.6
Middle East					
Cairo	65.3	74.3	76.2	73.5	72.0
Dubai	68.8	76.6	82.1	82.3	84.0
Riyadh	58.7	70.8	71.0	68.0	64.6

Source: STR Global.

proportion of Hispanics is overwhelming, reaching 40.4 percent of all workers. In addition, 36.6 percent of dishwashers in 2007 were Hispanics.[17]

Mexican migrant workers are equally critical to the continued success of the hotel industry. A major study by the Pew Hispanic Center in 2005 concluded that most of these newcomers (54 percent of the survey respondents) spoke little or no English. Approximately half of women (47 percent) and nearly two-thirds (61 percent) of the males were employed in three industries—hospitality, construction, and manufacturing. Mexican migrants in New York (26 percent) and Chicago (17 percent) reported working in the hospitality industry.[18]

Over the years, the relationship between the hotel industry and the Hispanic labor organizations has been contentious, since the latter groups view corporations as unresponsive to their needs. The National Council of La Raza, the largest national Latino civil rights and advocacy organization in the United States, withdrew its 2006 annual conference from Los Angeles because of a labor disagreement between the Los Angeles Hotel Employers' Council and UNITE HERE, the labor union representing the hotel workers.

Disputes over labor wages are common across the country in the hotel industry, resulting in strikes and sit-ins. Wages for nearly 1.5 million workers in the hotel industry vary extensively across the country, and are usually kept low, forcing unions to aggressively pursue and succeed in expanding unionization. For example, San Francisco hotel workers make approximately $15 per hour, but in Boston and Chicago workers average between $12 and $13 per hour. In Atlanta and Phoenix, workers average between $8 and $9 per hour. While these workers have not benefited from the extraordinary expansion of tourism and other travel during the 1990s, capital–labor relations must be improved.[19]

Nevertheless, within an increasingly globalized environment, travel growth and its extended economic benefits are the basis for which cities would revise their direction and search for revival opportunities. The ensuing competition will intensify their efforts for needed revenues. By the latter part of the 20th century, these conditions will trigger massive public and private urban investments—not seen since the late 1800s and early 1900s.

Urban Competition and the Search for Alternative Development Strategies

Urban tourism and related cultural forms did not fit the planning mix of economic development practices in the 1950s and 1960s. At best, they were viewed as an inconsequential element of financial activity. The post–World War II urban restructuring caused chronic fiscal stress, which was most visible during the 1970s. Municipal governments were thus forced to search for new sources of economic growth.

Many cities sought to diversify their various trade and industry sectors. Investments in mega-projects such as airports came to be viewed as a major economic indicator and a sign of future expansion. Between 1955 and 1960, commercial air passenger trips increased by nearly 800 percent. After 1955, they surpassed the number of inter-city railroad passenger trips. As a result, capital spending on airport improvements doubled between 1956 and 1960. Airport development was a local endeavor, since the federal government contributions in this area were nominal.[20]

It is within this framework of economic uncertainty that urban tourism emerges as an appealing alternative, one that slowly gains favor with civic boosters and local officials who perceive it as a viable development tool.[21] As a result, we begin to see the emergence of public investments and private sector development in the form of infrastructure and programming geared toward the advancement of the tourism industry. However, a number of issues must be considered. For example, who invests and why? How is the public interest defined? What are the community benefits of this process?

Urban centers searched to enhance their spaces and take advantage of this new growth potential. They faced numerous challenges, though mainly in the areas of urban identity and urban competition. To be more specific, how can a city with a formerly strong and nationally/internationally identifiable manufacturing economy convert itself into a tourist destination? Most importantly, how does it convince potential visitors of the viability of its new services and sense of attractiveness? It is through the interplay between structure and agency that we are able to gain insights into the transformation of urban centers into tourist cities. Local leaders must respond to structural conditions, and urban processes beyond their control and their vision must become realigned with their quest to achieve this new status.

With this approach, the rise of urban tourism requires cities to be entrepreneurial and businesslike. Thus, the city is no different from the corporation that must engage in image-building activities, promote its products, and be prepared to deal with change if it wants to maintain its competitive edge and grow its market share. Given this new economic outlook, it is apparent that the financial stakes are very high.[22] As a result, we observe the remaking of local policymakers from service providers to active participants in local economic affairs.

The Role of the Public Sector in Urban Tourism and Business Travel

There are two broad areas within which we can find the public sector playing a significant role in the advancement of urban tourism and business travel. The first area concerns expenditures for state offices of tourism and business travel (e.g., for conventions) and municipal units that primarily focus on promotional and marketing strategies. These entities also coordinate and manage various attractions and events. They are typically structured as dedicated governmental units, or are found within divisions of economic development, community affairs, or commerce. At the local level, departments of tourism report to the office of the mayor as do departments seeking to encourage business travel to a city. The second area regards the public financing of infrastructure necessary to provide the services for promoting the tourism strategy. These services include sports facilities, beautification, parks, and convention centers among others.

In 2005, the Michigan Department of Labor and Economic Growth reported that during the first four months of the year, leisure and hospitality jobs rose across the state by 1.2 percent compared to the same period in 2004. The sector includes a range of businesses such as museums, casinos, and hotels/motels. As one of few industries to showcase growth, Michael O'Callaghan, executive vice president and COO of the Detroit Metro Convention and Visitors Bureau, noted: "We have a jewel here. Our concern is that there is a big industry out there that just isn't being marketed as well as it should be."[23]

This cry is common in the travel industry, especially from leaders of convention and tourism agencies. Thirty years ago, cities promoted a few attractions; now a broader strategy includes multiple venues for business and recreational travelers that must be continuously updated and kept fresh. In addition, at a time when tourism and business travelers are viewed as part of the city's economic development strategy, there is considerable pressure to grow the size of this sector (Figure 2.2). Municipal governments are constantly on the outlook for ways to increase their share of the market in this area by increasing promotional expenditures.

Just like cities, states approach promotional spending through the utilization of cost/benefit rationales. In 2007, the average annual state tourism budget across the country was $13.6 million. The State of Oregon increased its annual investment in tourism marketing from

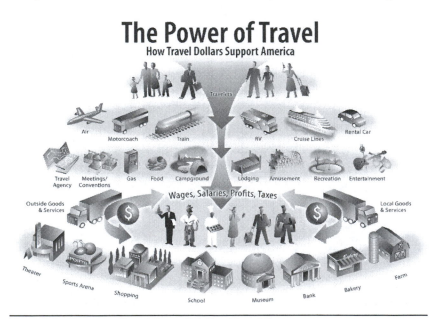

Figure 2.2   The power of travel. *Source:* U.S. Travel Association.

Table 2.3   State of Oregon Earnings from Tourism in 2003 and 2007

	2003	2007	DIFFERENCE
Taxes (State/Local)	$246 million	$320 million	+28%
Earnings	$1.7 Billion	$2.0 Billion	+ 6%
Direct Employment	85,700 Jobs	91,100 Jobs	+18%
Visitor Spending	$6.5 Billion	$8.3 Billion	+30%

Source: Oregon Tourism Commission.

$3.2 million in 2003 (46th in the country) to more than $9 million in 2007 (29th in the country).[24] These additional resources are expected to maximize the return of the public investment. Thus, according to Oregon state officials, for every $1 spent on marketing, the return was $159 in visitor spending; for every $1 spent on state marketing, the return was $6 in state and local tax revenues (see Table 2.3).

Cities are recipients of state contributions, but there is also direct municipal spending on local tourism activities. Dedicated funds typically assist convention offices and visitor bureaus. In 2007, the city of San Diego dedicated $8.8 million to the San Diego Convention and Visitors Bureau.[25] In 2008, the city of San Francisco funded their Convention Visitors Bureau with $8.3 million.[26] However, the majority of resources from local governments are derived from taxes on hotel stays, car rentals, and destinations. This strategy requires a balancing act given that extensive taxation can also reduce the attractiveness of a location.

The second area of public sector involvement can be found in the development of the infrastructure, which in recent years experienced considerable growth. Cities pursued aggressive construction plans in downtown areas which were focused on meeting visitors' needs. These programs produced some of the most extensive city building of the post-World War II era. Sports stadiums and arenas, as well as convention centers and hotels, have been popular projects that were embraced by municipal governments across the country.

In 2001, the city of Miami, Florida engaged in a major upgrading of the city's infrastructure by issuing $255 million in bonds. After receiving approval by the voters, an additional $241 million helped jump-start an ambitious 10-year capital program. According to the plan, more than 50 percent of the expenditures are allocated for parks and recreation, 15 percent for quality of life, and 2 percent for historic preservation. Bicentennial Park, Little Haiti Park, Margaret Pace Park, Miami Marine Stadium, the Orange Bowl, the Miami Art Museum, and the Museum of Science are some of the key outcomes of this massive infrastructure investment.[27]

After the 2008 Olympics, Beijing was slated to spend approximately $150 million to finish new tourist attractions—part of an aggressive plan to grow the city's reputation for overseas and domestic visitors. The upgrades will complement existing tourist zones in traditional culture, modern entertainment, and nature. China aims to become recognized as the world's top destination. By 2015, the goal is to draw 200 million visitors annually—in 2006 there were 124 million visitors to China.[28]

At the same time, the extensive nature of public sector involvement during the late 1980s and through the 1990s, caused citizens to question the justification for these expenditures, citing misdirected priorities and spending inefficiencies. One of the main debates in city councils regarding these outlays centers on the revenues from tourism and business visitors weighed against taxpayer costs. The case of the city of Dunedin in New Zealand, discussed below, reveals the debates between local government officials and residents over the construction of a new stadium, which is intended to raise the international profile of a struggling community.

Stadium Development in Dunedin, New Zealand

The city of Dunedin, New Zealand has a population of 122,000 residents (2008) and is the second largest city in the South Island (Christchurch has 320,000 residents). Dunedin grew during the second half of the nineteenth century following the discovery of gold in the 1860s. European immigrants poured into the city to work the gold mines in the surrounding Otago region. In the early part of the twentieth century, the city constructed the impressive Dunedin Railway Station, which opened in 1906 and quickly became the busiest station in the country, handling as many as 100 trains daily.

Figure 2.3 Dunedin's historic railway station in New Zealand is one of the city's main tourist attractions and one of the country's architectural gems (Courtesy Bs Wei, Shutterstock Images).

Following World War II, Dunedin experienced additional growth but had lost its national influence, slipping as the country's fourth largest urban area. By the late 1970s and early 1980s, the city was in the midst of a population decline. However, the growth of the University of Otago helped maintain its vibrancy through the development of a music and arts scene. City officials focused on transforming Dunedin into a heritage city by showcasing its unique history and culture and encouraging tourism.[29]

Within this framework, the Dunedin City Council embraced sports and proposed, in partnership with the University of Otago, the construction of a new stadium. The new facility would replace the famed Carisbrook, which opened in 1883 and lacked the amenities found in other sports venues. Rugby and soccer have been played at Carisbrook, which is affectionately referred to as the "House of Pain"—a reputation derived from the passionate crowds who cheer there for their home team. The All Blacks, New Zealand's national rugby union team, also played at Carisbrook, losing only three contests in 100 years.

By employing the argument that Dunedin will be the recipient of increased tourism and that a new strategy is needed to recapture the city's past national standing, advocates of the stadium posited

Dunedin needs to move in a new direction. We cannot afford to stay behind. We must act decisively and realize that this is not a stadium; it is a world-class civic, academic, cultural, sports, and entertainment facility. This is capable of transforming the city, since now we can compete for national and international events. We must figure out a way to make this happen and make Dunedin a desirable place to live. The stadium is a key to the future of our city.[30]

But at a cost nearing NZ$190 million, the 30,000-person capacity, glass-covered, multifunctional stadium proposal included considerable public funding, estimated at nearly NZ$70 million. Private funding was set at NZ$27 million in order for the project to qualify for final council approval. In early 2009, the Forsyth Barr Company, an investment banking firm, signed a 10-year naming lease agreement, shaping the structure's final name as the Forsyth Barr Stadium at University Plaza. The involvement of the firm substantially helped finance the project's expected private sector contribution.

Opposition to these plans by many residents who viewed this as an unnecessary public investment at a time of hard economic times grew intense. With groups such as "Stop the Stadium" and the "Dunedin Rate and Householder Association" pitted against the Carisbrook Stadium Trust, the Dunedin City Council, and the University of Otago, the small, stable community was now divided. Another group, "What if? Stadium of Dunedin," advocated the idea for a different construction site and design.

Regardless, residents overall rejected the Dunedin stadium plan. A study found that 71.7 percent did not approve of the project and 78.2 percent opposed public funding for the structure.[31] In January of 2009, more than 1,000 people took to the streets to protest against the city's proposed stadium.

The turn of events in Dunedin is common and indicative of the issues that typically arise from these planning initiatives in cities across the world. Stadium development projects are viewed as capable of redefining the urban image and assisting economically struggling communities. However, the benefits of this strategy remain unclear, rarely justifying the public financial investments. This small city embraced this approach, placing faith in a stadium that it expects will bring about needed national and international visibility and propel it onto the international map.

The Role of the Private Sector in Urban Tourism

Given the multitrillion-dollar size of the world travel and entertainment industry, it is obvious that, in addition to public support, the private sector plays an increasingly critical role. Driven by profit, business entrepreneurs look for opportunities to maximize their investment. Travel and entertainment rapidly emerged as an excellent growth market with considerable potential returns. Thus, professional team owners, hotel chain corporations, restaurants, and other food service and tour providers, embraced the growth of urban tourism and business travel by becoming active participants in its economy.

There are two categories of private sector involvement. The first type regards direct investment in the tourism sector and the second type relates to indirect urban investment derived from the revitalization of the urban core. The outcome of the second type is partly attributed to the development of culture, leisure, and entertainment in cities across the country.

The city of Detroit, for example, looks to casinos and gambling to increase tourism and business travel in the form of conventions. Recent private investment comes from three major casinos, Greektown, MotorCity, and the MGM Grand Detroit, which invested $1.5 billion to develop new hotels and to upgrade the facilities. Totaling 1,200 luxury rooms, these corporations are also interested in retaining the day-trippers for longer stays. MGM Grand's investment produced a $765 million complex that includes a 17-story hotel with electronic concierges in each room. The restaurants offer celebrity chefs Wolfgang Puck and Michael Mina who operate their own facilities. Greektown Casino spent $475 million with a 20-story hotel, and MotorCity Casino introduced a 17-story hotel and other amenities for $275 million.[32]

The private sector in countries abroad also took advantage of the major growth in both recreational and business travel. Between 2001 and 2006 in Mexico, more than $11.6 billion in private investments were recorded, and that amount surpassed government projections by 29 percent. Nayarit State received $92.5 million from private sources and more than 60 percent of that money went to the city of Nuevo Vallarta. Between that same timeframe, Quintana Roo received $2.47 billion, an amount that contributed to the urbanization of the state's Caribbean coastline.[33] In Australia, the city of Perth experienced aggressive private sector investment. In 1999, $A635 million for private tourism development included $A62 million for three new sizable hotels and additional expenditures to upgrade the city's infrastructure.[34]

Even corporations that are not directly involved in the tourism industry look to the urban core more favorably as they come to appreciate the more vibrant, safe, and inviting city centers. In 2005, the city of Chattanooga, Tennessee completed a very ambitious $200 million transformation of its 12-mile waterfront property along the Tennessee River. The 21st Century Waterfront Plan includes new museum attractions and a stadium for minor league baseball; and this is just the beginning of further development. Blue Cross and Blue Shield of Tennessee seriously considered leaving the city. However, because of the renewed commitment to the waterfront, the company not only decided to stay, but also invested more than $300 million in the development of the Cameron Hill Campus. The new complex employs 4,500 workers. In addition, more than $350 million in revenue brought new condominiums to downtown Chattanooga. Many other cities such as Phoenix, Arizona, which is pursuing an ambitious CityScape project, expect similar private sector investment following initiatives to recreate the urban core along lines of leisure and recreation.

While separate observations can be made on the involvement of the public and private sectors, their differentiation does not offer a comprehensive understanding of recent urban development and change. It has been both sectors working together that propelled the growth of urban tourism, and consequently the refashioning of cities. In the form of partnerships, local government and business interests look for ways to leverage each other in their quest to meet different goals. On the one hand, businesses are concerned with maximizing profit, while on the other, city authorities desire to grow their communities, provide public services, and meet budgetary needs.

Urban Tourism and the Rise of Private–Public Partnerships

A conventional analysis would place public and private sectors as separate entities, but they work closely together on tourism development. In fact, the building and operating of an economy of culture and leisure allow us to observe what political scientist David Perry refers to as the "privatizing discourse of public infrastructure." Increasingly, private sector participation entails investment, ownership, or management in city building. Urban tourism development reveals the pressure of an expanded and deeper connection between state and capital, which has emerged as the prevailing force in the creation of the entertainment infrastructure.[35]

This intersection gives rise to discretionary purpose authorities and special districts. These units are popular as local governments are called upon to meet various goals. Community development, transportation, economic development, parks and recreation, medical and health, environment, and criminal justice are some of the areas within which we see the presence of these governmental units. In 2009, the State of Colorado reported 3,099 such local governments actively engaged in various practices. Both the Denver Metropolitan Major League Baseball Stadium District and the Denver Metropolitan Scientific and Cultural Facilities District aggressively pursued the advancement of tourism.

In Chicago, expansion of McCormick Place, currently the largest convention complex in the world, included the construction of an 800-room hotel to accommodate the large volume of visitors. The Metropolitan Pier and Exposition Authority financed the project by floating $130 million in revenue bonds. The Authority owns the hotel and partnered with the Hyatt Corporation, which manages its operation. The Authority is currently considering adding 600 rooms to the Hyatt McCormick Place Hotel at a projected cost of $145 million.[36]

The use of private–public partnerships in building the city of leisure is increasingly a common, sought after strategy. The logic centers on

Figure 2.4   Cloud Gate sculpture in Millennium Park, Chicago, Illinois. One of the park's focal attractions, the display is affectionately referenced by the public as "the bean." The park opened in 2004 at a cost of half a billion dollars and was the outcome of a public-private partnership (Courtesy Author).

the notion that growth is central to urban well-being, and urban tourism is simply another means to achieving that goal. The purpose of public subsidies is to induce private investment and entice commerce ventures. Businesses are expected to create jobs and a healthy tax base, which is then utilized by the municipality to improve basic services as well as maintain and expand infrastructure. Prosperity and a good business climate will in turn encourage additional private investment. The outcome of this strategy is the rise of local growth coalitions and regimes that aggressively pursue tactics that focus on attracting and retaining corporate investment. It is within this scheme that the promotion of tourism, culture, leisure, and entertainment is rapidly replacing the once dominant manufacturing economy. The city of Toronto, Canada is a good example of this approach (see "Writing, Reflection, and Debate" section at end of the chapter). However, this strategy is also visible in smaller cities.

The South African coastal cities of Buffalo City and Virginia Beach share a common goal and strategize how best to take advantage of their status along the Indian Ocean. The cities identified a number of niche markets, including ecotourism, events and festivals, sports tourism, and a new convention center. The private sector is central to these efforts. For example, the city of Virginia Beach allocates about R3.5 million to tourism development annually, of which 37 percent is expected to derive from the private sector.[37]

These initiatives are controversial and many question the public value of these practices. Opponents argue that local governments often go too far in their efforts to attract investment, charging that these policies are advanced at the expense of taxpayers. Consequently, in some instances, referendums stalled the construction of stadiums that involved the use of public funding. Local newspaper editorials and community groups led antiapproval efforts, referring to these practices as examples of corporate welfare. In 2007, the Cincinnati Reds saw the voters of Sarasota, Florida reject a taxpayer-supported stadium project. The team sought $16 million to help pay for a $45 million renovation of their spring training facility.[38] In 2006, Seattle, Washington voters approved a ballot initiative that restricted taxpayer subsidies for professional sports teams. This hampered plans for the construction of a $500 million arena complex which was pursued by the SuperSonics, the city's professional basketball team. The team had been founded in Seattle in 1967, but it relocated to Oklahoma City during the 2008–2009 season.[39]

Examples of public–private partnerships range from infrastructure development to marketing tourism. Visit Florida, a public–private tourism agency with annual revenues of $80 million, is Florida's official source for travel planning, and is responsible for promoting the state. In San Diego, California, the city pays eight business groups approximately $1.2 million a year to market the city. In 2004, the San Francisco Convention and Visitors Bureau received funding through a combination of public and private resources.[40] The city of Baltimore, Maryland is considered one of the first urban centers in the United States to pursue the urban tourism strategy. The case study below explores how the Harbor Place emerged as a central development in that quest and showcases the public–private cooperation that was involved in transforming the Inner Harbor of the city.

Harborplace, Baltimore, Maryland

Baltimore's location along an arm of the tidal Chesapeake Bay made it a successful trading center. Like many other industrial cities, the city struggled during the postwar period, experiencing considerable decline. The city was hit particularly hard in 1968, following the assassination of Martin Luther King Jr., with riots lasting more than 10 days and causing millions of dollars of damage.

As early as 1954, local officials and business leaders joined forces to address Baltimore's urban condition. They focused on the downtown and proposed housing and retail development. This was a vast area with extensive vacant space and abandoned warehouses. The nearby Inner Harbor was a focal point for decades; however, by the 1960s, the shipping industry stopped using the port and moved its activities to outer harbor docks. Large commercial vessels now required deeper waters and more space to load and unload their cargos.

Despite some construction during the 1970s, the Inner Harbor was neglected, many buildings were abandoned, and the waterfront remained open and ripe for development. The huge success of the "Tall Ships" display in 1976, and the Inner Harbor setting, as a potential draw for tourists, proved effective factors in the redevelopment of the site along the lines of tourism, leisure, and entertainment.[41]

A dizzying infrastructural program began in the area, first with the construction of the Baltimore Convention Center in 1979, Harborplace in 1980, the National Aquarium in 1981, and the Baltimore Museum of Industry in 1982. During 1992, Oriole Park at Camden Yards for the Baltimore Orioles professional baseball team and other attractions solidified the area's identity. For example, Harborplace and The Gallery, which opened in 1987, is an urban retail and restaurant

Figure 2.5   An aerial view of Baltimore Maryland and the Inner Harbor which is credited with the revival of the city. Camden Yards, home to the Baltimore Orioles professional baseball team, is nearby and is visible on the left edge of the photo (Courtesy Dobresum, Shutterstock Images).

complex that helped the city's revitalization efforts. According to one Baltimore official: "Harborplace & The Gallery put downtown Baltimore on the map. It signaled to the world that Baltimore was coming back after decades of disinvestment. It will always remain a critical asset of downtown Baltimore."[42]

Sport is also key to Baltimore's tourism strategy. In addition to Camden Yards, which cost $110 million with a 48,000-spectator capacity, the Baltimore Ravens of the National Football League host visiting teams at the nearby M&T Bank Stadium. Completed in 1998 for $220 million, the facility has a 71,000 spectator capacity. Both of these stadiums, designed by the HOK architectural firm, pursue an urban stadium concept. They maintain adjacent warehouses and replicate the feel of venues from a bygone era.

The public sector heavily invested in Camden Yards, contributing 96 percent of the financing. The M&T Bank Stadium received 90 percent of its costs from taxpayers. Other publicly owned sports facilities include the 1st Mariner Arena where more than 800,000 guests cheer at 120 events annually. The Baltimore Blast, the city's professional soccer team in the MILS is just one of the events sponsored at the arena. Over the years, city tourism increased considerably from 9.2 million visitors in 1992, to 13 million visitors in 1998 to 17 million visitors in 2005.[43]

Baltimore is considered one of the first cities in the United States to pursue the tourism economic development strategy to such a degree. For more than 30 years, officials focused on developing a massive infrastructure and recasting the city's image. Has this proved to be a successful approach? It is clear that the physical reorganization turned Inner Harbor into a very attractive space. While the degree of this success can be measured through various indicators, the larger question concerns the impact of this approach on alleviating the social problems that are still ravaging the city's inner neighborhoods. This is a complicated issue and one that is often at the heart of these types of public policy initiatives. But the potential benefits from tourism are so extensive that cities have to brand themselves accordingly so they can take advantage of the returns.

Marketing Cities and New Urban Identities

The demand for tourism in the United States from 2008 to 2018 is expected to increase by 3.5 percent and the visitor exports by 4.9 percent. Furthermore, government expenditures are calculated to grow by 3.1 percent and capital investment by 4.3 percent. The travel and tourism industry contributed 3.8 percent to the Gross Domestic Product (GDP) in 2008 ($542.4 billion) but will be rising to $881.4 billion (3.7 percent of total) by 2018. The travel and tourism contribution to the United States economy (percent of total) should increase from 10.0 percent ($1,442.8 billion) to 10.3 percent ($2,480.0 billion) during this same time frame.[44]

These forecasts hold the promise for economic revival. Urban mayors and governors turn to this industry, viewing it as integral to their broader economic development strategy, a way to reviving their struggling cores. While many states had to decrease their total expenditures following September 11, post 9/11 tourism revenues surpassed the pre-9/11 levels. Florida reported more than 47 million travelers in 1997 and more than 83 million travelers in 2005.

The current economic crisis placed pressure on many legislatures that were facing shortfalls. In Florida, 2009–2010 budget proposals included reduction of $13 million in tourism advertising spending. Similarly, because of a projected $1 billion budget shortage, Utah is

Table 2.4 Tourism Spending among States (2007–2008 Budget Year)

1. Hawaii	$85.1 million
2. Texas	$63.2 million
3. California	$58 million
4. Illinois	$50.4 million
5. Florida	$42.1 million
6. Pennsylvania	$31.8 million
19. Kentucky	$15.8 million
25. Michigan	$12 million
37. Ohio	$8.2 million
38. West Virginia	$7.9 million
41. Indiana	$6.75 million

Numbers do not include midyear funding increases or grants funneled to regional tourism agencies.
Source: U.S. Travel Association.

considering dramatic cuts in their advertising tourism budget. Out of a total $10 million spent in that area, the reduction is estimated to exceed $4.7 million.[45]

Hawaii is the current leader in state tourism spending, having invested more than $85 million during 2007–2008. Texas is a distant second, even though they doubled their expenditures to $63.2 million. California, Illinois, and Florida hold the remaining top five positions (See Table 2.4). Regardless of the amount, every government across the country praises the economic benefits of its tourism activities and advocates consistently pursue additional funding opportunities. Colorado maintained a tourism budget of $1 million in 1999. In 2003, the budget increased to $12 million and by 2008, the budget was almost $20 million. According to estimates by state officials, tourism generates $100 billion annually and for every dollar the state spends promoting itself, it should expect to receive up to $13 in return.[46] Even county governments are attuned to the financial ramifications of this sector.

Since cities operate in highly competitive environments they allocate as much money as possible to marketing and advertising. Resources are needed to promote and encourage potential visitors. Increasingly, advertising campaigns often focus on presenting a new urban image.

Patrick Moscaritolo, president of the Greater Boston Convention and Visitors Bureau, recognizes the challenges facing his city by noting: "Tourism is a very competitive industry. With the shift in the visitor mix, you have all the New England states…competing for basically the same market. Now we're all fishing in the same pond."[47]

A review of marketing budgets reveals significant spending patterns. In 2006, Chicago's Convention and Tourism Bureau's annual budget was $14.5 million and Orlando's budget was set at $40.8 million. However, both of these budgets are dwarfed in comparison to Las Vegas, the world's top convention-hosting city. In 2006, Las Vegas maintained an annual tourism budget of $227.8 million. That same year, half of Chicago's budget, approximately $7.7 million, was in the convention sales and marketing category. Los Angeles budgeted $12 million and Atlanta $10.4 million in this category. Orlando spent $5.1 million on convention sales and $6 million for a separate, national advertising campaign to attract business travelers. Chicago's direct spending to promote the city to travelers in 2006 was $3.8 million. Cities sometimes operate satellite tourism promotion and sales offices across the country. Las Vegas maintains six offices and Orlando maintains four branch operations.[48]

Experts argue that urban centers, just like businesses, must become attractive products if they want to revitalize themselves. This places marketing to the forefront of city planning. In the early part of the 1970s, Cleveland, Ohio experienced a number of challenges. Financial decline, decaying infrastructure, failing schools, and poor leadership in the midst of worker strikes gave the city a poor image. Cleveland embarked on a plan to introduce new construction projects in its downtown and promoted the new plan by communicating its activities via direct mail, booklets, and other forms of media. These marketing efforts were recognized with numerous honors in 1982 and 1984.[49]

In 2007, Detroit unveiled a $750,000 promotional campaign to support a new brand identity titled "D. Cars. Culture. Gaming. Music. Sports." As a departure from the 10-year-old "It's a Great Time in Detroit" slogan, officials wanted to project the city as a hip place, focusing on people between the ages of 21 and 35. Research showed that among 11 regional cities, young adults viewed Detroit as offering the most dynamic travel experience. More than 15 million people came to the region in 2004. Officials conceded that the previous campaign proved unsuccessful and via online media such as podcasts and blogs they formally advertised the message, "This is not your father's Detroit." Detroit's goal is to reverse the city's earlier image.[50]

Marketing and promotional strategies linked to tourism are often organized with the view that any of the visitors could be prospective investors. Therefore, in many cases, tourism materials contain a "business message." However, the success is unpredictable, and while some cities are more capable of reimaging themselves through their campaigns, others lag behind. A study of six formerly industrial/ manufacturing British towns and cities (Belfast, Birmingham, Cardiff, Doncaster, Glasgow, and Manchester), which had made a commitment to the promotion of tourism by developing related facilities, reached some interesting conclusions. Specifically, the degree of their previous identity influenced the extent of their newly created external perception. Cities with strong past industrial images that had gone through significant reorganization toward the travel industry, were more successful than those with weaker manufacturing identities that had experienced similar restructuring.[51]

Constructing a new urban identity often goes to extremes and Dubai is an example of a place that has created a tourism market out of nothing. In recent years, the city built islands to accommodate hotels and consumption. One development, the Palm Island megaresort, contains villas, luxury hotels, a marine park, and cinemas and promises visitors a world-class golfing experience. All of these developments aim to attract the rich and famous. In addition, the Dubai Shopping festival is a month long event held every January that transforms the city into a shopping mall, accompanied by other entertainment exhibits and shows. To the east, Macau in southern China focused in recent years on becoming a world-class casino location. Macau refers to itself as the "Monte Carlo of the Orient," and the local economy is closely tied to gaming. Most Chinese come to Macau exclusively to gamble and their spending constitutes the majority of the total government revenues.

Clearly, the advancement of tourism hinges on marketing of new urban images. Urban entrepreneurism is a necessary prerequisite. Overall, whether exercised by political leaders, tourism officials, civic boosters, philanthropists, or marketing experts, the ability of these entities to craft an effective message determines the success or failure of their identity and repositioning efforts. The case of Krakow, Poland provides interesting insights on how that city attempts to manage and market its tourist identity as historic preservation and commercialism collide.

Preserving the Urban Tourist Identity in Krakow, Poland

Krakow, Poland (population 760,000 in 2006) is the second largest city in Poland and one of the best preserved cities in Europe. The Old Town (city center) was spared from the destructive forces of the Nazis and the Red Army. Baroque churches, architecturally unique buildings, cobblestone streets, museums, galleries, and cafés dominate the town. The Rynek Główny (Grand Square) is the largest in Europe. Krakow is viewed as the cultural center of Poland. Its rich history includes the Jagiellonian Dynasty (1385–1572) and Wawel Castle and Wawel Cathedral. Jagiellonian University has the distinct honor of claiming the famous astronomer Nicolaus Copernicus as one of its graduates. Pope John Paul II (1978–2005) served as Archbishop of Krakow before his appointment to the Vatican.

With all these assets, it is no surprise that Krakow was always a center of tourism, attracting foreign visitors, especially after the fall of communism. But officials looked for opportunities to further their city's historical identity, solidifying its standing. In the late 1990s, Krakow pursued the European City of Culture designation, a highly desirable title sought after by many other European cities. Launched in June of 1985 by the European Council of Ministers, this award program was expanded by a 1999 Act of the European Council to continue until 2019. A valued designation, the award would benefit both the cities as well as the notion of European unification. According to the Council, "...[the designation] would strengthen local and regional identity and...foster...European integration."[3] European

Figure 2.6   Rynek Główny, Krakow, Poland is the main square of the old town. It dates back to the 13th century and is the largest medieval square in Europe. As the city's major tourist attraction it hosts numerous cultural events annually (Courtesy Rubi Photo, Shutterstock Images).

cities compete for this honor and utilize this recognition to market and develop relevant cultural programs. Proposed and planned activities typically include festivals, the arts, museums, and other forms of artistic expression for the entire award year.

In 1995, Krakow, along with eight other cities, received the 2000 European Capital of Culture designation. Officials immediately embarked on an aggressive five-year program focusing on film (1996), literature (1997), music (1998), and mixed events (1999) with the organization of numerous festivals (2000) as the culmination of the city's artistic celebration. This was an opportunity for Krakow to distance itself from the Eastern European Socialist past and help accelerate Poland's integration into the European Union. The city could also address the environmental impact of industrialization, which threatened its status as a UNESCO World Heritage Site. According to a government leader,

Krakow's cultural policy is closely linked to making progress on the environmental front. If someone wants to come here for culture, they want also to have clean air and water. We have two large programs in place at the moment to make sure we are successful in this area. This is very important for the future of the city and for maintaining its identity. We can spearhead environmental protection policies and gain funding from European and World organizations.[53]

The capital designation was also part of a broader tourist policy. According to a local administrator, "Our future is tied to our image. We want to be an alternative to Prague. That city is too noisy, too large and of course it is a capital city. We must sell ourselves as a smaller version of Prague. Cultural policy and tourist development of Krakow is tied to the development of the region."[54] By all accounts, Krakow's strategy proved quite successful. The total number of guests receiving accommodations in the city increased from 1.2 million in 2005 to 1.3 million in 2006 to 1.4 million in 2007.[55]

Krakow's Bohemian feel is also attracting young people who are interested in the cultural uniqueness of the environment. But as airline service, especially by budget carriers, increased considerably in recent years, Krakow began to develop a different reputation. With more than a dozen weekly flights from London, Belfast, and Newcastle, rowdy crowds gained easy access to the city.[56]

The case of Krakow shows that cultural policy and tourism development can be part of a strategy aimed not at converting, but rather at reinforcing an existing image. However, there are also unanticipated outcomes that accompany the benefits of economic growth. Krakow must balance historic preservation with commercialization, a direction that can potentially damage the city's longstanding cultural identity.

The Entrepreneurial City

This quest by local officials in Krakow to compete against other cities, manage their urban identity, and use tourism as an economic development strategy demonstrates some of the entrepreneurial practices employed by municipal leaders. In a speech at the Manhattan Institute in 1997, then Mayor of New York City, Rudolph W. Giuliani, outlined the reasons for his city's success as reflected in job growth, crime reduction, and increased tax revenues. The mayor noted that the policies he pursued were responsible for this rebound, encapsulated by a return to "the spirit that made [New York City] great in the first place—a spirit that embraces individual initiative, responsibility, and drive: what entrepreneurship is all about."[57]

Giuliani's statement has a variety of political overtones and clearly reflects the outlook of a conservative mayor. But at the same time, regardless of ideological affiliation, an agreement is certain in the following two areas. The first area concerns the fact that New York City did experience a remarkable turnaround in the 1990s, following visible economic and social declines during the 1970s and 1980s. The second area relates to a movement in urban politics that saw a new breed of mayors entering City Halls across the country, trying to reverse trends of substantial social and economic decline.

In the United States, in addition to New York City's Mayor Rudolph Giuliani, Chicago's Mayor Richard M. Daley, Philadelphia's Mayor Ed Rendell, Milwaukee's Mayor John O. Norquist, and Los Angeles's Mayor Richard Riordan would be members of this "Mr. Fix It" or "Messiah" group of leaders. All of them focused on reform policies by embracing what they often termed as "no-nonsense strategies"— operating outside the traditional boundaries of previous governing practices. By the early 2000s, many of them came to be viewed as capable of transforming the cities in which they served.

Chicago's Mayor Richard M. Daley, first elected to office in 1989, is credited with reviving Chicago and aiding the city in its quest to become recognized as a world class urban area. As the United States representative to host the 2016 summer Olympic Games, the mayor aggressively pursued a multiyear, multibillion-dollar infrastructural development program that focused on restructuring the lakefront. Daley's entrepreneurial agenda surprised many, especially when it included the privatization of public assets.

For example, in 2005, the city sold the rights to operate the Chicago Skyway Toll Bridge to a private company. The 7.8 mile stretch will be under the control of an international group for the next 99 years. The deal yielded the city an upfront payment of $1.83 billion.

Chicago also pursued the privatization of Midway Airport for $2.52 billion and numerous parking garages for $563 million. At the end of 2008, officials even privatized 36,000 downtown parking meters for the next 75 years, yielding $1.2 billion. This privatization of public enterprises is criticized as a new mode of free market economics perpetrated by liberal politicians.

In Indianapolis, Mayor Stephen Goldsmith served from 1992 to 2000 and is credited with the revival of that city's downtown. Goldsmith engaged in an extensive infrastructural development program aimed at improving city services by embracing a competitive bidding process, injecting the private sector when appropriate to benefit the public. The mayor supported the creation of new jobs by integrating the voices of business interests while bypassing partisan politics. His approach received national attention, leading him to edit a volume on the subject appropriately titled *The Entrepreneurial City: A How-To Handbook for Urban Innovators.*[58]

Entrepreneurial mayors typically blame municipal bureaucracies as one of the primary reasons for stifling economic growth. Many focus on reversing inefficient government practices. Thomas Menino, current mayor of Boston since 1993, was acknowledged for the creation of the Back Streets program—a one-stop unit that streamlined city licensing procedures and was noted for better serving the city's more than 4,000 businesses.[59]

Los Angeles holds a very special position when considering the rise of the entrepreneurial city. The 1984 Olympic Games was the start of the modern quest for mega-tourism projects that many cities have since aggressively pursued. The Southern California Committee for the Olympic Games (SCCOG), a private, nongovernment group initiated the bid effort. Established in 1939, the SCCOG was unsuccessful at that time in bringing the Olympic Games back to the city after the 1932 Games. The group promoted the 1984 bid by identifying the positive economic impact that would result from the influx of visitors and the opportunity to showcase the city internationally. While this was exclusively a private effort, by advocating the need for Los Angeles to become a global city, Mayor Tom Bradley managed to successfully maintain the commitment of the public sector for this initiative by ensuring city council support.[60]

Interestingly, the 1984 Los Angeles Olympics were the first Games held where we saw the presence of economic impact studies. These were also the first Games to be financed privately, with minimal organizational links to the host city. The United States Olympic Committee revenues covered the $685 million cost, and for the first time, the Games produced a surplus of $380 million. More importantly, the privatization of the 1984 Los Angeles Games revolutionized the staging of future Games, as selling Olympic rights to media and advertising sponsors became mainstream practices.[61]

Given the widespread attention to the restructuring of the cores, these entrepreneurial practices became central to the development of urban tourism. Infrastructural projects supported culture, leisure, and entertainment activities, bringing millions to downtowns across the country. This remaking of the urban environment also received extensive coverage by the media. *The Kansas City Star* has noted "Downtown is welcoming some new urban pioneers to join the empty-nesters and single adults who've dominated its revival."[62] *The Orlando Sentinel* observed that religious organizations and churches benefited from the rebirth of the core,[63] and the *Houston Chronicle* indicated that the return of a popular festival to the downtown area was due to the vitality of the renewed center.[64]

Conclusion

The rise of globalization had a considerable impact on urban centers. The outflow of jobs and capital from cities that traditionally relied on manufacturing to locations abroad meant that new economic development strategies had to be explored and instituted. The emergence of recreational and business visitors fit the entrepreneurial strategies that local officials pursued. Public–private partnerships furthered that direction, in the process opening up the possibilities for needed investment. However, the growth of the tourism industry within a restructured global environment also expanded international travel, encouraging cities to look at foreign visitors as an additional source of revenue.

In order to maximize the effectiveness of tourism, cities also market themselves as destination centers and work hard to alter their image. This process proves to be a complicated proposition since it poses numerous challenges. It often requires extensive and sustained investments in marketing campaigns, physical infrastructure, and the quest for staging major events that offer the desired visibility. Furthermore, the effectiveness and cost benefits of these practices remain questionable.

The utilization of urban tourism strategies, including the growth of tourism precincts, is examined in the next chapter. Local authorities pursue maintaining existing locations and creating new attractions, nationally and in many cities abroad. However, this type of growth often has unanticipated outcomes. On the one hand, it can fuel further development, but on the other hand, it can alter the socioeconomic makeup of existing communities.

Writing, Reflection, and Debate

The commitment of the city of Toronto to the advancement of urban tourism is reflected through the creation of the Economic Development, Culture and Tourism division. Some of the objectives identified by the unit include:

- Advancing strategies to strengthen the tourism sector
- Promoting and supporting new investment and development
- Responding to the needs of local tourism sector businesses
- Providing advice and support to help businesses and operators attract the tourist market and create packages and other forms of cooperative ventures
- Resolving issues detracting from the visitor experience
- Supporting measures creating a tourist-friendly environment
- Forging strong partnerships with other levels of government, agencies, and the private sector

- Helping new tourism businesses and investors access the information needed to find sites in Toronto
- Advocating on behalf of businesses within City Hall to resolve many types of issues and to cut red tape
- Helping businesses develop new markets in the tourism sector[65]

The above goals clearly demonstrate that this local government wants to partner with the private sector in support of this industry.

Discussion Question

Who was/is responsible for "getting things done" in the city where you grew up, or where you live now? Was it a powerful, proactive mayor, another visible community leader, or was there no clear individual or group working to build up the city?

3

Tourism Policies and Urban Growth

In chapter 2 we examined the rise of tourism and the way in which its evolving character as a commodity has been fueled by globalization. Many cities, especially those whose manufacturing economies have experienced decline, have seized on tourism as an alternative source of economic growth. Attracting tourists requires cities to distinguish themselves as distinctive "places." In this chapter we focus on the characteristic types of place that are identified by, or in many instances, have been created by local governments and their business allies to serve as tourist attractions. This analysis will include a consideration of the pros and cons of developing such tourist districts. When hundreds of thousands of visitors flood the streets of a formerly quiet ethnic neighborhood or historic town, the everyday lives of the residents will be changed in many ways. The chapter concludes by discussing an associated form of tourism, the mega-event, whose mechanism for drawing visitors is an organized array of activities—a World's Fair or Olympic competition—that concentrates visitors in time as well as space.

Key resources of urban economic development, marketing, and related destination-planning approaches have produced powerful landscapes that have furthered municipal advancement. Political scientist Dennis R. Judd, a leading scholar of urban tourism, observes how the "tourist bubble" is now the most common restructuring strategy used to depict tourist spaces as destination spots. For example, in the United States, Las Vegas focuses its district on entertainment that emerges from gaming, while New Orleans utilizes its French Quarter by projecting the historical past, as well as its musical connections to jazz.[1]

Tourism districts in old European cities (e.g., Athens, Rome, London, Paris) maintain themselves by drawing from their powerful historical heritages, world famous attractions, and points of interests. The situation is different elsewhere among cities that do not possess these distinctions. Sydney (Darling Harbor), Chicago (Navy Pier), Liverpool (Albert Docks), and Baltimore (Inner Harbor) constructed precincts to complement existing attractions or formulate new ones. But other modes of urban visitor precincts emerge, often unpredictable in their birth and highly specialized in their function.

These observations clearly point to an organized plan of action on the part of local government, civic elites, and business and corporate interests to advance venues that can draw larger numbers of visitors and subsequent profits. Designed to make cities more attractive, these investments often result in highly structured visitor experiences. Some enclaves spotlight ethnicity, some center on sports, while others combine entertainment and an educational/knowledge-based framework.

There are a number of issues facing urban tourism districts given that local authorities and investors attempt to ensure their continued success. For example, concerns about authenticity abound due to the intense commodification of these locales. The rapidly evolving public–private partnerships, and their effect on the future development and management of these districts, can have operational ramifications. More important, tourism districts must be updated to remain relevant and attractive, which necessitates ongoing investment.

Finally, the corporatization of the tourism experience has brought about significant changes. Mega-firms like Disney and Sony have increased their investment in the urban tourism industry, and in the process have restructured the visitor experience to meet their profit goals. This staged authenticity has additional consequences because these entities are able to overwhelm any localized, indigenous efforts in the form of entrepreneurism and job creation.

Sociologist Sharon Zukin's work is quite relevant here because she points out how the shift to a symbolic economy contributes to a detachment from social institutions, even affecting architectural designs. The culture of place conforms to market interests instead of public values. Within the global forces of competition, distinctiveness gives way to the franchised presentation, creating "nonplaces."[2] Some cities are attempting to address this issue of *McDonaldization* (a term used by sociologist George Ritzer). For example, the principles of the fast-food restaurant are dominating more and more sectors, so Chicago discourages franchise eateries from operating in the downtown area of the Loop, and encourages neighborhood restaurants to establish themselves in the city center. These enterprises bring with them their ethnic cuisines, which aid in the configuration of an eclectic atmosphere.

The issues presented above are evident in many cities across the world. For example, competition for tourists helps create specialized districts, like the one in Penang, Malaysia, discussed next. The case of Penang offers some interesting insights into these tourism-driven policies. Here, authorities attempted to use heritage and ethnicity to attract visitors. Focusing on economic growth also meant injecting elements of cultural artificiality, causing strain and conflict within the local community. While these outcomes are often unanticipated, it is through these processes that we can gain a glimpse of the complexities of these practices.

Penang, Malaysia: An Evolving Tourism Strategy

The State of Penang in the northern region of the Malaysian Peninsula dates back to the seventeenth century. Composed of Penang Island (Pulau Pinang) and Province Wellesley (Seberang Perai) on the mainland, the area has evolved into a major tourist attraction. Its capital, Georgetown, increased in population as a result of the various ethnic groups who, over the centuries, settled in this multicultural city. Because of the diverse groups that occupy Georgetown, distinct heritage buildings such as mosques, Buddhist and Hindu temples, synagogues, and Christian churches stand side by side. Over the years, Indians, Armenians, Arabs, Jews, Chinese, Japanese, Filipinos, and immigrants from many other Asian and European countries have given the city a rich cultural base of spirituality and lifestyles.

In October 2008, because of its ethnic history, Georgetown received the distinction of being designated a World Heritage Site. In its announcement, the United Nations Educational, Scientific & Cultural Organization (UNESCO) World Heritage Committee identified multiple religious structures, unique streets, museums, court buildings, commercial areas, a fort, its city hall, and Little India as the rationale behind the designation. The recognition was also an opportunity to further boost the area's tourism, which already was one of the most important sectors of the economy.

Penang Island is a tourist district with multiple geographical thematic zones of attractions. For example, while Georgetown and the central part of the island possess the elements that could designate these areas as an ethnic and culture precinct, the western part of the island focuses more on agrotourism. Penang saw its tourism increase during the 1990s, from 1.8 million visitors in 1990 to 3.5 million in 1999. But in recent years, there has been a decrease in international visitor arrivals and an increase in domestic tourists. For example, in 1990, 400,000 visitors arrived from Malaysia and 1.4 million visitors arrived from outside the country. In 2005, domestic visitors increased to 1.95 million and international tourists dropped to 1.1 million.[3]

Malaysia's modernization plans, under its Wawasan 2020 vision released in 1991, focused on an economic transformation of the country. The role of the tourism sector proved crucial to fulfilling that goal and Penang came to be viewed as an area capable of advancing this vision. In 2008, *Travel & Leisure* magazine recognized the island as one of the top Asian locations to visit.

A process of "imagineering" ensued, which is remaking spaces into themed settings to develop memorable experiences for visitors. The government facilitated related infrastructural investment, but locals felt that this approach removed their voice. Many questioned why

Figure 3.1 19th Century Shop-Houses, in Penang, Malaysia surrounded by modern structures (Courtesy Chris Jenner, Shutterstock Images).

urban conservation focused only on tourist attractions and expressed concern about the large number of building conversions. For example, a survey of Georgetown residents revealed that tourism development has had a negative impact on their community. More than 55 percent of residents noted the loss of identity in tourist areas and 81 percent noted traffic congestion as a major challenge. An increase in pollution (55 percent of respondents) and an overabundance of hotels and shopping centers (65 percent of respondents) were also reported. Most important, 48 percent of those interviewed indicated that they felt treated as "second-class citizens."

These findings were substantiated by another survey of hotel workers, which revealed that 68 percent felt treated as "second-class citizens." The locals charged that the conservation initiatives of temples made them "too colorful, like a zoo for the gods." Because of that, most locals avoided these religious edifices, leaving them to be primarily visited by tourists.[4]

The case of Penang reveals the contested nature of tourism development. Efforts to utilize heritage sites as part of a larger agenda of economic growth often conflict with the vision of local residents. Globalization pressures have helped create an artificial environment. This is especially problematic when it is injected into an ethnic district that celebrates an indigenous culture whose historic roots have been celebrated by generations of Georgetown residents as part of everyday life.

Types of Tourism Districts

This section discusses in greater detail a central element of the urban tourism development strategy—the tourism district. A variety of such entities are examined here, including ethnic, support, sports, entertainment, and historic precincts. The spatial concentration of these settings is not only available to visitors, but also to residents who participate in and experience the available attractions. Many of these locales are positioned within or near corporate, commercial, or residential areas. Integrated into the broader urban landscape, they receive public financial support for their maintenance and further development. Governments often attempt to maximize their uses by promoting them beyond the tourism sector; however, their localized integration proves a major challenge.

Efforts to transform neighborhoods into popular tourism districts must focus on consumption, a direction that raises questions about the legitimacy of both the environment and the experience. Because of this complication, other cultural districts may emerge. These offer a more realistic, uncamouflaged indigenous setting. For example, the *favelas* (slums) in Rio de Janeiro are the recipients of tours by visitors who want to see the everyday life in these environments. Tourists in Los Angeles can pay $65 to join LA Gang Tours through gang-plagued communities. Passengers must sign waivers acknowledging they can become crime victims during the excursion. The goal of the tours is to use the profits from them to create jobs and provide opportunities for the residents of the area. Also, educating people from around the world about the inner-city lifestyle and gang involvement solutions is viewed as a vital step toward a peaceful existence.

Similarly, City Safaris are promoted by the Rotterdam City Council, Netherlands, providing visitors with an opportunity to venture into the deprived ethnic neighborhoods of the city. In the process, visitors gain a glimpse into the life of recent immigrants and asylum seekers. In Berlin, the Kreuzberg working-class district in the 1960s and 1970s attracted Turkish immigrants, artists, and others who were trying to avoid military service. The area was marginalized and developed a reputation as unattractive and unassuming. But, following the fall of the Berlin wall and the city's reintegration to the West, the district evolved as a prime attraction and an example of the bohemian lifestyle.[5]

Sometimes the development of tourism districts creates unexpected outcomes. For example, the Granville Entertainment District in downtown Vancouver stretches for many blocks along Granville Street. In the 1990s, because of its favorable proximity to hotels and the city center, the Vancouver City Council pursued the creation of a concentrated entertainment area. Vancouver had a reputation as a "No Fun City," and this initiative was intended to alter that perception. Bars, dance clubs, and nightlife flourished in the district. Known earlier as "Theater Row," the new direction slowly pushed movie houses out, converting many structures into nightclubs. But serving alcohol until 4:00 a.m. in these new establishments would have devastating effects. Violent crimes, gangs, and other illegal activity enveloped the area. Unable to deal with the complaints, the Vancouver Police Department recently requested more resources to effectively address area problems. The city council is now battling to alter a damaged urban image.[6]

Understanding the dynamics of tourism precincts necessitates placing their investigation within the broader context of the sociology of tourism. There are four elements that must be considered: (1) the tourist; (2) relations between tourists and locals; (3) the structure and functioning of the tourism system; and (4) the social and environmental consequences of tourism.[7] Various aspects of these and other elements are examined in this chapter and the chapters that follow. Furthermore, we must recognize that these spaces maintain a political dimension that influences their evolution. Decisions by local actors to produce these locales for economic development purposes must strive to maintain a balance between the demands of the visitor, which often focus on comfort, with a desire to ensure the protection of the historical and cultural components of the given environment.

We will now discuss various types of tourism districts, which have distinct identities, and present their overall role in advancing urban tourism. We begin with ethnic and historic districts. These are often existing pieces of the urban fabric that are used and transformed for the purpose of attracting tourists. We then focus on entertainment districts, sports districts, and theme parks. These tend to receive extensive attention and are created for a particular purpose, rather than being existing entities that have been adapted for tourist use. This section concludes with support districts, which spring up without much planning, though at some point they do begin to receive attention from local governments and planners.

Ethnic Districts

Ethnic enclaves are synonymous with many urban centers, especially those that have historically been the recipients of large numbers of immigrants attracted by jobs during the rise of industrialization. For decades, these spaces and their inhabitants were isolated from the larger community and served as a refuge from the dominant society. Local officials identified some of these areas as focal points and initiated marketing campaigns and upgraded their physical landscapes and general built environment. Leisure and tourism are closely connected to these reconstituted districts, giving locals an opportunity to financially benefit from the increased attention. Cultural diversity can be celebrated, repackaged, and presented as an asset in the quest for attracting visitors.

The city of Birmingham in the United Kingdom lured immigrants from all over the world to work in its robust economy in the automobile factories and other manufacturing plants. The city continued to maintain a large ethnic population during its economic decline, making it one of the most culturally diverse settings in England. Birmingham City Council's advertising directed at tourists has taken advantage of this distinction by highlighting the multitude of local ethnic groups. These are referenced along with traditional attractions such as cinemas, shopping, markets, and various places of interest, including modern developments (Millennium Point), Victorian era sites, and Digbeth, the location of the city's birth in the 7th century.

The city also declares itself as the "Capital of Balti," a spicy dish popular among Kashmiri residents. Visitors are encouraged to search for the Balti Triangle in south Birmingham. The location not only offers many restaurants with traditional food, but also provides shopping opportunities for ethnic clothing and jewelry.

Chicago's Chinatown, Greektown, Little Italy, Pilsen (Mexicans), Lincoln Square (Koreans), and West Rogers Park (East Indians, Pakistanis, Hasidic Jews, and Russians) are some of the areas that slowly evolved into ethnic tourism districts with city-sponsored guided tours and promotional literature. These neighborhoods also display special signage to mark their boundaries and advertise local museums and other ethnic attractions. The presence of honorary street names in the native language and flags are commonplace.

Toronto's Greektown and Montreal's Chinatown received extensive makeovers as part of this tourism-based regeneration strategy. In the early 1990s, Montreal focused extensively on the "Chinatown Development Plan." Three specific goals were part of the document: (1) creation of boundaries for Chinatown; (2) identification of land use and design guidelines within the area; and (3) improvement of public spaces as well as services such as street cleaning, parking, and garbage collection.

A key outcome of this initiative was the empowerment of the local community, especially of the business owners who proved most engaged in the process. Because of this direction, Chinatown evolved by becoming inextricably connected to the tourist economy. Large numbers of conventioneers who participate at events in the nearby Palais de Congrès de Montréal, the city's conference center, visit the district. While the neighborhood successfully evolved into a mixed-use community, it struggles to maintain a balance between the needs of local residents and the increasingly large number of visitors.[8]

Historic Districts

Historic districts have grown considerably in recent decades to more than 2,300 across the country. The rise of the historic preservation movement helped the growth of these districts. According to the U.S. National Park Service, "a district is a geographically definable area, urban or rural, possessing a significant concentration, linkage, or continuity of sites, buildings, structures, or objects united by past events or aesthetically by plan or physical development. A district may also comprise individual elements separated geographically but linked by association or history."[9] Examples include the Georgetown Historic District in Washington, DC and the Martin Luther King Historic District in Atlanta, Georgia.

Officials have aggressively pursued local preservation ordinances to protect the historic character of buildings and neighborhoods. Slowly these initiatives are integrated into urban tourism policy development. The protection of special landmarks by halting demolition and upgrading streetscapes not only maintains the historic value of these areas, but it also creates growth potential and is central to the economic affairs of cities. Historic districts typically remind us of Athens, Rome, and Beijing. Millions of visitors pour annually into the Acropolis, the Coliseum, the Forum, and the Forbidden City. Smaller centers also transform their quarters and market them to tourists. Charleston, South Carolina and Groningen, Netherlands are two examples of cities that have benefited in this way.

The Charleston Historic District has been a national landmark since 1960. The area expanded its initial boundaries five times following its addition to the National Register of Historic Places in 1966. The last expansion took place in 1986 and today more than 80 properties comprise the historic structures within the district's borders. As the cultural capital of the South, Charleston possesses numerous historic sites, eighteenth century homes, churches, and museums. Hurricane Hugo devastated the city in 1989, but officials viewed this as an opportunity to reestablish Charleston's cultural heritage. By upholding strict architectural guidelines, the city saw its historic district reemerge better than before. Many of the nineteenth and earlier twentieth century renovation and restoration efforts had lacked the necessary detailed attention to the original.[10]

By its investment in expanding its attractions and services, Charleston brought forth a vibrant tourist center. A study estimates the total economic impact of the sector at $3.09 billion (2007), up from $2.37 billion (2003). The earnings from tourism related jobs were assessed at $1.1 billion (2007), up from $0.8 billion (2003). The analysis also reveals that history is Charleston's greatest asset and that 5 percent of visitors come from abroad, mostly from Canada, the United Kingdom, and Germany.[11] But the increased popularity places pressures on the community. In recent years, residents have raised concerns about their quality of life, which they feel has been negatively affected due to the growing number of visitors. In response to these issues, the city formulated the Downtown Charleston Plan. The plan recognizes the importance of tourism for economic development, but seeks to create a balance by aggressively managing future commercial growth.

Many other cities utilize their historic status to pursue tourism. Being able to draw visitors can have additional benefits. The case of the Grote Markt (city square) in Groningen, Netherlands offers some interesting insights. This Dutch city lacks the cultural reputation found in other European centers. With a population of just over 180,000 residents, it attracts about 1 million travelers annually, primarily from Germany. By crossing the nearby border these visitors take advantage of the shopping opportunities offered along the Herestraat, the city's main shopping area. The square and the immediate dense environments contain the major structural attractions, including the town hall and the main cathedral.

After World War II, planning in the Grote Markt focused on promoting commercial office buildings and large-scale retail development. But as the city evolved, a demographic shift was observed. The total population remained fairly unchanged. However, the considerable alteration in its makeup involved sharp increases in the number of younger residents living in Groningen. By the late 1980s and early 1990s, the city center started to shift in its function as an environment that favored culture, entertainment, and leisure activities, and the Inner City Improvement Plan (Binnenstad Beter) was put in place by the local authorities in 1992.

The main focus of this initiative was to showcase the city's heritage through the construction of new and restored buildings. In addition, the planning document revisits existing design parameters in the city center. For example, by examining and altering motorized routes and making them pedestrian friendly, the Grote Markt evolved into having a greater concentration of people. The introduction of a central library and a museum offered a new entry point to the city center. The opening of the Waagstraat complex in 1994 included the re-creation of a pre-1945 street, cafés and shops as well as a new public open-air piazza. An open-air opera house also reinforces the influence of Italians in Groningen. City planners have been long inspired by Italian cities, calling Groningen "the most Italian city above the Alps" or "Sienna of the North."[12]

The case of Groningen reveals the renewal of public space to emphasize the city's heritage via the re-creation of the city center by reclaiming and showcasing its historical past. This strategy is not exclusively intended for attracting tourists, even though that is an additional desired outcome. Rather, it is intended to construct a new image by recapturing the past. This emphasis allows a view of a more balanced approach, which is the creation of a historical district that maintains its focus on the local population as a space of civic pride and indigenous urban identity. Beyond these spatially concentrated environments, mega-events are also pursued as a way to spur urban growth. Issues related to these types of gatherings are further discussed in greater detail.

Entertainment Districts

Entertainment districts are probably the most popular form of concentrated tourism development. Planners and city officials aggressively support these projects. These locales must first undergo significant planning and physical reorganization to meet their new function as tourist attractions. Former warehousing areas are naturally favored because their spatial dynamics can quickly meet business needs, and can also accommodate large crowds. Furthermore, these areas are in great need of upgrades. Their eyesore status is a reminder of a bygone economic period from which the cities desire to divorce themselves.

Navy Pier in Chicago is an example of an entertainment tourist district. Located on the city's lakefront, the pier opened for the first time to the public in 1916 at a cost of $4.5 million. The addition of its own street car line made it a popular destination. In the 1920s, more than

3 million visited the site annually because of its new restaurants and theaters. But attendance declined during the Great Depression, and by the 1980s the pier fell into disrepair. Over the years, its proximity to the city's downtown area encouraged initiatives to revive the pier but these proved unsuccessful. The area had become a symbol of urban decay.

In 1989, the Metropolitan Pier and Exposition Authority began revitalization. The initial boom of the project was so impressive that it fueled a housing boom in the nearby Streeterville community. Over the years, the venue underwent numerous expansions and upgrades. Due to the extensive renovations; however, many of the original structures were torn down and the pier is no longer on the National Register of Historic Places.[13]

Navy Pier is the most popular attraction in the city. According to the Chicago Office of Tourism, Chicago Convention and Tourism Bureau, the attendance was 4.5 million in 1996, over 6 million in 1997, and in 1999 over 7.75 million. In 2002, the number was near 8.4 million, and in 2003, 8.7 million people visited the pier, generating $45.8 million for the year. Attendance remained strong in 2005 with 8.6 million visitors and in 2006 with 8.8 million visitors, just below the all-time high of 9.1 million achieved in 2000. In 2007, Navy Pier was visited by more than 8.4 million people.[14] The site is an entertainment hub and is currently synonymous with tourism in Chicago.

In addition to Navy Pier, there are many examples of these types of districts in cities across the world. Old Market in Omaha, Nebraska and Darling Harbor in Sydney, Australia also falls into this category. Even though they are located in different sized cities, their goals and functions are quite similar. Both anchored downtown revitalization and served as keys to urban revival initiatives.

Omaha has a long history as an industrial center with commercially robust light manufacturing and wholesale meat processing activities. Its location along the Missouri River, in the middle of the country, assisted in the growth of an elaborate railroad network. Omaha was a major stop for goods traveling via the Union Pacific Railroad across the country. This helped the city thrive during the early part of the twentieth century. Later, deindustrialization and the ensuing manufacturing decline left a vast area of the downtown empty.

City officials embarked on an aggressive construction plan, focusing more than $2 billion on tourism and entertainment. Numerous attractions include a zoo, museums, a performing arts center, theaters, and the Qwest Center, a $291 million, 18,000-seat indoor arena that opened in 2003. The Old Market district is a multiblock, cobblestoned street quarter that contains renovated brick warehouses and historic storefronts converted into shops, pubs, and restaurants. Horse-drawn carriages and street performers add to the ambience of the setting. Over the years, the district has become a popular destination frequented by business travelers attending conventions, and tourists.

Similarly, in the 1980s city officials in Sydney, Australia turned to the harbor area. Dilapidated, especially in the southern part, as a result of a declining shipping industry and storage activities, the location once signified the city's powerful status. Its proximity to the Sydney Central Business District made Darling Harbour a very important part of the local economy. In fact, during the nineteenth and early part of the twentieth century, the harbor was a bustling

Figure 3.2   Arial view of Darling Harbour which has evolved into Sydney's top destination for leisure and entertainment. Restaurants, museums, theaters, bars and other attractions helped transform this once derelict environment into a focal point (Courtesy DarkPurple, Shutterstock Images).

transportation hub. Following World War II, Darling Harbour became progressively underutilized and abandoned warehouses dominated the area.

The location was viewed as a prime opportunity for redevelopment. Festivals were the preliminary strategy that injected the first signs of revival. In 1984, officials decided to develop the site around tourism and recreation. The new district focused on consumption. Restaurants, museums, hotels, nightclubs, theaters, casinos, and other attractions ensued. In preparation for the 2000 Sydney Olympics, Darling Harbour saw the addition of entertainment areas, making this a popular space for social gatherings during the Games. It is estimated that 26 million people visit the area annually.[15]

Tourist districts can often become central to further development. The case of Albert Dock in Liverpool, UK illustrates how a small cluster of abandoned warehouses on the city's waterfront contributed to the revitalization of the area. Converted into an entertainment district, the structure came to be viewed as a tourist destination and a symbol of the city's ascendance. In fact, Liverpool was recognized in 2008 as the European Capital of Culture.

Albert Dock and Waterfront Development in Liverpool, UK

Liverpool's waterfront enjoyed global prominence in the eighteenth and nineteenth centuries, given the city's central position in a vast worldwide transportation network. A number of docks bustled with activity as workers loaded and unloaded shipments, storing cargos in the large warehouses that lined the adjacent docklands. The introduction of large steam ships placed pressure on the function of the docks, which had originally been designed to accommodate sailing ships. Consequently, by the latter part of the nineteenth century, only a small portion of sailing vessels used the port. The goods to and from its storage buildings were transferred by barges or rail to boats docked in more modern facilities nearby. By 1920, the commercial shipping activity from Liverpool's waterfront was almost nonexistent.

By the 1960s and 1970s, Liverpool was experiencing the full effects of deindustrialization and the broader manufacturing decline. Many of the area docks were shut down and some were even razed. Albert Dock, for example, having been closed to shipping in 1972, within a few years saw the interior of its structures filled with mud. Interestingly, Albert Dock would lead the revitalization of Liverpool's waterfront via culture, entertainment, and tourism. In the early 1980s, Parliament created the Merseyside Development Corporation, which in cooperation with the Arrowcroft Group, embarked on the redevelopment of the area. Distanced from the downtown area, this project was part of an activist local government agenda that, in partnership with the private sector, was expected to bring about the improvement of local conditions.[16]

The £100 million ($150 million) refurbishment proved extraordinarily successful, slowly helping transform the place into a centerpiece of Liverpool and a sign of the city's economic rebirth and waterfront revival. Albert Dock was now a top heritage attraction. The multitude of entertainment opportunities, which took place within its more than a million square feet of refurbished space, made it the most popular tourist destination in Liverpool and one of the top destinations in the UK.[17] Unfortunately, attendance started to decline at Albert Dock, a common outcome found in similar districts across the world, especially when their attractions become dated. More than two decades following its restoration, Albert Dock entered a second stage of internal upgrading to meet various demands. Meanwhile, the district led a wider redevelopment that has been central to the city's overall renaissance.

A number of infrastructural projects followed. The Leo Casino opened in December 2002 on the Queen's Dock (adjacent to Albert Dock) with live entertainment, a restaurant, two bars, and more than 20 gaming tables. This is currently one of the city's most popular night spots; a broader residential and commercial revival followed. The addition of a new building to serve cruise liners at the recently revitalized Pier Head will bring tourists directly to the city from the sea. Nearby Mariners Wharf, South Ferry Quay, and Navigation Wharf, all part of the Liverpool Marina, have experienced explosive residential growth with newly constructed or converted apartment units and townhouses.

Figure 3.3   Albert Dock (brick structure on the right side of the photograph) is credited with Liverpool's waterfront revival. Numerous area structures, including the Liver Building (center of the photo) underwent restoration in recent years and were key attractions in Liverpool's successful bid for the 2008 European Capital of Culture designation (Courtesy John Hemmings, Shutterstock Images).

In 2003, Kings Waterfront, on Kings Dock, saw 200 new residential units that included luxury penthouses. Ambitious mixed-use development is forthcoming, exemplified by the nearby yacht club. Finally, in the last few years, the waterfront has also experienced commercial office sector growth. Erected in 1998, the Crowne Plaza Hotel was part of a £150 million ($225 million) redevelopment of Princess Dock. Numerous hotels and new office buildings were constructed in the adjacent area attracting tenants that include PricewaterhouseCoopers, KMPG, and the Criminal Records Bureau. According to a recent city report, "the seeds of Liverpool's renaissance were actually planted as long ago as the early 1980's...by [the] transformation of the Albert Dock into one of the city's major tourist attractions."[18]

In preparation for the 2008 European Capital of Culture celebrations, Liverpool continued to invest in the waterfront. A £5.5 billion ($8 billion) revival of the Central Docks with 23,000 new apartments was proposed. Developers, in their quest for planning permission, argued that the project was needed because "Liverpool's front porch to the world is an absolute disgrace."[19] Early in 2008, the city announced the rebuilding of Kings Waterfront. Overall, it is estimated that almost £1 billion ($1.5 million) has been invested in the one-mile stretch of waterfront.[20]

The case of Liverpool shows how Albert Dock, an entertainment tourism district, spurred wider economic development. The precinct is currently struggling to maintain its identity. Yet, despite declining attendance, the dock is still viewed as central to the city's cultural revival. Recognizing the aggressive nature of the redevelopment efforts, the local press in 2007 published a number of stories comparing Liverpool to Manhattan. Another story went even further by asking, "Is Liverpool the new Shanghai?"[21] This belief that cultural development is capable of increasing the international status of a given city, or at least its perceived profile, becomes evident when examining the case of Liverpool.

Sports Districts

Strategies to promote culture, leisure, and entertainment as a way to rejuvenate the urban core have also included sport, which has evolved as a central theme of this approach. Public support for stadium development is commonplace across the world. Organized efforts by local authorities and civic boosters are staged to compete for the opportunity to host events like the Olympics, the Super Bowl, or the World Cup. Various types of international championship competitions, from soccer and track and field to cricket and rugby, are viewed as a way to raise the urban image and generate economic growth.

In Philadelphia, within a very short distance, visitors are drawn to a cluster of sporting venues that brings thousands to the city center. Citizen's Bank Park is home to the Philadelphia Phillies (MLB). Lincoln Financial Field is the new home of the Philadelphia Eagles (NFL). The Legendary Blue Horizon hosts boxing events. The Wachovia Spectrum Complex houses the Philadelphia Flyers (NHL) and the

Philadelphia 76ers (NBA). In addition, college sports are played at the McCarthy Stadium (La Salle University), Liacouras Center (Temple University), and The Palestra (University of Pennsylvania and Saint Joseph's University). This clustering of sporting venues gives the city a unique status

In Pittsburgh, the opening of Three Rivers Stadium in 1970 at the location where the Allegheny, Monongahela and Ohio rivers converge received praise for its central location. The state-of-the-art facility was home to the Pittsburgh Steelers (NFL) and the Pittsburgh Pirates (MLB). But the pressures by professional teams for newer facilities were experienced across the United States. In the 1990s, Pittsburgh was influenced by these demands for a replacement stadium. With a lifespan of only 30 years, Three River Stadium was demolished in 2000. At the same site, two new facilities emerged, which were both owned by the city. In 2001, the $281 million, 65,000-spectator Heinz Field for the Steelers and University of Pittsburgh opened. Adjacent, PNC Park opened for the Pirates the same year at a cost of $216 million. Across from Heinz Field, UPMC SportsWorks, a large permanent exhibit of the nearby Carnegie Science Center, is a popular attraction. With more than 40 exhibits spread over 36,000 square feet, this is the largest science and sport exhibition structure in the world. The attraction's huge success aided the construction of a new $5 million facility that opened in 2009.

In Kansas City, a debate is being played out regarding the city's downtown revitalization. In 2004, the Kansas City Civic Council engaged in a process to update the Downtown Corridor Development Strategy, initially released in 2001.[22] The conceptualization of various districts includes the construction of a new stadium for the Kansas City Royals (MLB) at a proposed cost of $357 million.[23] In addition, officials discussed the addition of a downtown stadium for the Kansas City Chiefs (NFL). Both professional teams now play at the Truman Sports Complex, which is composed of twin stadiums built in the early 1970s. The belief in Kansas City is that a sports district will accelerate the plan to revive the core and help create a new downtown.

Theme Parks

Theme parks evolved from the amusement industry that dates all the way back to 1583 when Bakken opened north of Copenhagen in Denmark. In 1766, Prater debuted in Vienna. Both of these parks are still operational and Prater currently boasts more than 250 attractions. In 1893, the amusement industry experienced a significant boost during the Columbian Exposition in Chicago when the Midway showcased the first Ferris Wheel, along with rides, concessions, and unique exhibits. The introduction of trolleys was critical to the growth of amusement parks, offering easy transportation to the grounds. Coney Island in New York was a very popular amusement park during the early twentieth century. At that time, more than 1,500 of these parks were operating across the country. The Great Depression, as well as urban decline and massive postwar suburbanization, reduced the popularity of these attractions. By 1935, the number of amusement parks was reduced to 400.[24]

Three general trends in theme-park development can be observed during the second half of the twentieth century. The first trend relates to the rise of Disneyland, which focused on staging multiple environments for its visitors—a highly successful concept. Disneyland in Anaheim, California and Walt Disney's Magic Kingdom in Lake Buena Vista, Florida led the way as the most popular attractions since their openings in 1955 and 1971, respectively. The second trend relates to the growth of additional parks. For example, Six Flags Over Texas opened in 1961 at a cost of $10 million in Arlington, Texas, and the corporation currently operates facilities in California, Colorado, Georgia, Illinois, Louisiana, Kentucky, Maryland, Massachusetts, Missouri, New Jersey, New York, Ohio, Oklahoma, Texas, and Washington. The third trend relates to globalization and the internationalization of theme parks during the 1990s. In 2007, more than 187.6 million people visited the top 25 theme parks worldwide. Attendance at the top 20 parks in North America was 122.8 million, a 4.1 percent increase from 2005. The same year, the top 20 European parks served 60.9 million visitors while the top 10 parks in Mexico and Latin America attracted 11.3 million people. Total attendance at the top 10 Asian/Pacific Rim parks was 65.8 million. In 2007,

Figure 3.4   Grona Lund in Stockholm, Sweden, is a popular theme park that opened in 1883 and continues to attract thousands of residents and visitors annually. A fashionable concert venue it is Sweden's oldest amusement park. The venue is built around an old residential community, making it a unique destination (Courtesy Tom Tsya, Shutterstock Images).

worldwide attendance at the top 20 water parks was 19.4 million, an increase of 11 percent from 2006.[25] In 2009, 185.6 million people visited the top 25 theme parks worldwide (see Table 3.1).

The Walt Disney Company, the largest entertainment corporation in the world, led the internationalization of theme parks with facilities in Tokyo and Paris. But there are other companies that recently entered this lucrative business environment. For example, Tropical Islands in Germany, an artificial tropical resort, is a 1,170-foot-long, 683-foot-wide, 350-foot-high dome that includes a swimming lagoon, a beach, a water park, a rain forest, and an island with 500 living species of exotic plants and trees. The facility serves 8,000 visitors daily. In Dubai, Ski Dubai, the first indoor ski resort in the Middle East, is a man-made winter that can accommodate more than 1,500 skiers at a time. But Disney, recognizing that cities are undergoing rapid reorganization, is looking for additional opportunities in urban cores. According to an executive, Disney's future strategy will focus on exploring the creation of "urban hotels in cities that are major tourist

Table 3.1   Top 25 Theme Parks—World (2009)

RANK PARK AND LOCATION	2009 ATTENDANCE
1 Magic Kingdom at Walt Disney World, Lake Buena Vista, FL, USA	17,233,000
2 Disneyland, Anaheim, CA, USA	15,900,000
3 Tokyo Disneyland, Tokyo, Japan	13,646,000
4 Disneyland Paris, Marne-La-Vallee, France	12,740,000
5 Tokyo DisneySea, Tokyo, Japan	12,004,000
6 Epcot at Walt Disney World, Lake Buena Vista, FL, USA	10,990,000
7 Disney's Hollywood Studios at Walt Disney World, Lake Buena V	9,700,000
8 Disney's Animal Kingdom at Walt Disney World, Lake Buena Vista, FL	9,590,000
9 Universal Studios Japan, Osaka, Japan	8,000,000
10 Everland, Kyonggi-Do, South Korea	6,169,000
11 Disney California Adventure, Anaheim, CA, USA	6,050,000
12 SeaWorld Florida, Orlando, FL, USA	5,800,000
13 Universal Studios at Universal Orlando, Orlando, FL	5,530,000
14 Ocean Park, Hong Kong, China	4,800,000
15 Nagashima Spa Land, Kuwana, Japan	4,700,000
16 Islands of Adventure at Universal Orlando, Orlando, FL, USA	4,627,000
17 Hong Kong Disneyland, Hong Kong, SAR, China	4,600,000
18 Hakkeijima Sea Paradise, Yokohama, Japan	4,500,000
19 Universal Studios Hollywood, Universal City, CA, USA	4,308,000
20 Lotte World, Seoul, South Korea	4,261,000
21 Europa-Park, Rust, Germany	4,250,000
22 SeaWorld California, San Diego, CA, USA	4,200,000
23 Busch Gardens Tampa Bay, Tampa Bay, FL, USA	4,100,000
24 De Efteling, Kaatsheuvel, Netherlands	4,000,000
25 Tivoli Gardens, Copenhagen, Denmark	3,870,000

Source: Themed Entertainment Association and Economics at AECOM.

destinations for families. We could build destination resorts in exotic locations or boutique, branded hotels at a variety of price points."[26]

Support Districts

As indicated above, ethnic tourism districts gained popularity and can be found in many cities across the world, from Little India,

Chinatown, and Arab Street in Singapore to Irish, Italian, Armenian, and Caribbean precincts in Boston. Most recently, however, we can observe the buildup of what can be termed support districts. These are areas that spread slowly, largely because of a popular nearby attraction. In some cases, these locales develop intentionally, but others evolve by chance to serve a specific function. An examination of these districts reveals that these entities can also exist on their own, separated from the main attraction. Two examples are noted below: the International Drive in Orlando, Florida and Plaka in Athens, Greece.

The International Drive or I-Drive is a tourist enclave in Orlando, Florida, which was developed following the construction of the Walt Disney Resort. The opening of that complex in 1971 required the creation of support services. Martin Marietta, which owned the adjacent land, pursued the making of a tourism corridor to serve the millions of visitors pouring into the area. Deregulation and lack of appropriate public planning drove the development of the I-Drive at a time when Walt Disney World saw its popularity rise dramatically. The result is a sprawling array of hotels, restaurants, and related services.[27]

The I-Drive complements the nearby precinct of Disney World by making available, within a 14-mile stretch, 226 eateries and 102 hotels and motels, with more than 30,000 hotel rooms. In addition, three entertainment complexes and three stadium-style movie cinemas offer 41 movie screens. More than 485 designer brand-name outlet stores afford visitors abundant shopping opportunities. But this intense concentration of services means considerable traffic congestion. In 1992, officials formed the International Drive Master Transit and Improvement District, a public–private initiative (county, city, and business owners) to improve transit service with the goal of further promoting tourism in the corridor.

An increasingly distinct tourism district, the I-Drive has its own identity and is undergoing additional development. In 2007, 27 new projects were announced as part of a new construction initiative that will cost $6 billion. Once completed, the plan will introduce more than 14,000 new accommodations and double the existing meeting space. A 1,200-seat performing arts center, more upscale dining restaurants and shopping, as well as a large water park are planned.[28] The economic downturn is expected to reduce the size and scope of the proposed project. Yet, in time, given an eventual economic recovery, I-Drive is likely to be the recipient of many of these services which will enable it to increase the number of tourists.

Plaka in Athens, Greece is another district that would fall in this support tourism district classification. It lies at the foot of the hill on which the Acropolis is built. Because of its position, Plaka is an entry point to the archaeological site above. Before the major increase in tourism in the 1980s, Plaka was another community that offered its residents close access to the city center. The area is also rich in history since the Greeks, Romans, Ottomans, and Christians all occupied the area over the centuries. Archaeological excavations are constantly in progress, signified by entire city blocks protected by fencing.

But as the Greek tourism industry evolved and became better organized and marketed around the world, Plaka evolved into the most convenient location for visitors. Hotels and restaurants increased, traditional taverna and cafe owners saw a potential for profit. Souvenir shops selling shoes and sunglasses, small stores offering antiques, jewelry and leather products lined the streets. Cobbled street roads were established and new signage helped create a quaint setting. In fact, Plaka slowly developed an identity as the traditional Greek community, though there are many questions about its authentic presentation. Nonetheless, as a support tourism district for the Acropolis, Plaka slowly transformed itself into a unique urban environment.

Tourism and the Clash of Urban Functions in Plaka, Athens, Greece

Plaka is an old neighborhood that served as a gateway to millions visiting the impressive Temple of Athena on the Acropolis. In recent decades, the community evolved in a variety of ways, maintaining a vibrant commercial, cultural, residential, intellectual, and tourist identity. But as noted earlier, Plaka also serves as a support district to the adjacent Acropolis. More recently, it has been promoted as representative of traditional Greek life.[29] Plaka is struggling to negotiate these multiple images.

The commercialization of Plaka raises questions of authenticity and threatens the very core that has been responsible for the district's success. Its fluid composition and representation, as well as the coexistence of contradictory and conflicting identities within its boundaries, make this a unique tourism environment. Plaka combines the traditional and the contemporary, the ancient and the modern. It promotes local culture, yet it also expresses a strong desire to embrace its newly bestowed pan-European identity. Religious institutions and secular practices coexist and cheap souvenir shops are located next to expensive art galleries. There is a strong sense of neo-Bohemia, but upon closer examination this gives way to an area of structured and mass-produced consumption.

Similar to the Granville Entertainment District in downtown Vancouver, a vibrant nightlife environment emerged in Plaka during the 1970s as clubs and discos offered entertainment for young people. This also brought increased incidents of violence and drug use. In the 1990s, the government protected the district from these occurrences as well as from the rapid conversion of historic structures to updated residential uses. As a result, Plaka gradually became a tourist

Figure 3.5 The ruins in the area of Plaka in Athens, Greece can be found in the middle of the neighborhood, amongst neoclassical residential structures visible in this photo. Plaka is a unique tourist district since it combines numerous functions due to its long historical standing (Courtesy S. Borisov, Shutterstock Images).

destination as a result of its geographical location. Small souvenir and gift shops lined the pedestrian route to the Acropolis. Boutiques and jewelry and antique stores specializing in mass-produced and hand-made icons were added to older leather stores and textile stores that had operated in the neighborhood for decades. Tavernas and restaurants, small motels and larger hotels, as well as the implementation of longer shopping hours, furthered the development of the area into a tourist precinct with a vibrant commercial function.[30]

In addition, Plaka contains a number of churches, including Kapnikarea Church, a relic of Byzantine architecture, built in the 11th century, the Metropolitan Cathedral, and the adjacent Little Cathedral. The distinct Byzantine style of these places of worship also becomes an attraction for locals and tourists alike. Furthermore, the first University of Athens was housed there in the late 1830s and today the Museum of the University of Athens, the Children's Museum, the Museum of Greek Folk Art, the Frissiras Museum, and the Jewish Museum all operate in Plaka. Numerous art galleries also add a cultural aura to the neighborhood.

The tourist identity of Plaka is constructed via the multiple functions the neighborhood manages to maintain. This highly designed community projects traditional culture through commercialization. Its complex and diverse compositional functions allow for the formation of its distinctive characteristics. It is through these contrasting images (residential, presentation of historical epochs, commercial, artistic, religious, and archaeological) that this community comes to construct its unique tourist identity.[31]

Mega-Events and Urban Growth

In addition to the development of tourism districts, cities turn to other strategies, hoping to grow their local economies and improve their national and international standing. Hosting mega-events is one of these preferred approaches. Districts concentrate tourists in particular places; mega-events join concentration of time to space. The Super Bowl, the Olympic Games, the NCAA Final Four, the FIFA World Cup tournament, and a variety of championship events (cricket, rugby, track and field, etc.) are part of this strategy. Fierce competition between cities is involved in securing these large-scale sports gatherings, and cities must showcase their unique advantages to committees that review their bids. Consistent with an emphasis on tourism, entertainment, and sport, as well as on consumption, this direction is central to urban redevelopment efforts.

The desire by cities to hold mega-events can be traced all the way back to medieval times with market festivals and during the eighteenth and nineteenth centuries with the World Fairs. In fact, expositions were similar in intensity to the modern Olympic Games. Chicago defeated Washington, DC, St. Louis, and New York City for the opportunity to hold the Columbian Exposition in 1893. The St. Louis World's Fair in 1904, known as the Louisiana Purchase, also became the location for the Third Olympiad. These science, arts, and technology gatherings were large public exhibitions that helped propel the host city to a unique status as the center of the world.

In recent years, the number of cities vying for mega-events has grown considerably. There has been a major increase in the intensity of the competition. For example, nine cities submitted bids for the 2012 Summer Olympics. For the 2016 Summer Olympics, seven cities assembled applications but fifteen more cities were either eliminated in preliminary rounds, or abandoned their plans for various reasons. Twenty cities have already expressed interest in hosting the 2020 Summer Olympic Games.

There are two basic reasons for the motivation behind the investment of billions to host these sporting events. The first reason is the international recognition that helps elevate the city's image. The second reason derives from an opportunity to focus on urban and regional development. For example, hosting the Super Bowl is expected to have a $300 to $400 million economic impact. In the eyes of city officials and civic boosters, these two factors are also connected. An enhanced image can attract future visitors and potential investors and be an impetus for urban growth.

Questions can be raised about the actual effect of these policies. For example, in the early 1990s, the NBA championships were held in Detroit following successful runs by the city's Pistons. Riots following the team's victories negatively impacted the city's image, further demonstrating its decline. Similarly, the bribery scandals associated with the 2002 award of the Winter Olympics in Salt Lake City damaged that city's reputation.[32]

On the economic front, this mega-event strategy and its urban growth capability are also questionable. Concerns about the use of economic multipliers to pad the impact of the projects associated with these events abound. Economic multipliers are used to show the impact of expenditures on the local economy. For example, how many times does a new dollar circulate? What is its ripple effect? In addition, the community benefits are unclear because much of the infrastructure developed for the Games is so customized that it typically goes underutilized after the closing ceremony. Sydney (2000) and Athens (2004) are struggling to find uses for their sports facilities. It has been difficult to book the Olympic Stadium in Athens and almost impossible to bring events to other venues. For example, the pool complex in Athens has not hosted a major swimming event in the six years following the Games. In fact, like the Olympic Stadium, the Athens Olympic Aquatic Center already shows signs of deterioration and lack of maintenance.[33]

Large-scale events also pose political problems. In the United States, Olympic bid committees are privately organized. Municipal authorities do not have the expertise or resources to launch bids for securing high-profile sporting events. Many of the professionals working on representing efforts by cities for the Olympics have led the previous initiatives of other bidders. Without direct control over the activities of these entities, local governments are unable to maintain effective oversight. Lack of access, accountability, and responsiveness are key outcomes of this public policy process. Regardless, in most cases we can observe elements of an urban growth agenda embedded in Olympic bid campaigns.[34] The case of the Olympic Games in Beijing illustrates how the city utilized that event as a way to boost tourism.

Beijing, China and the 2008 Olympics

When Beijing was chosen to host the 2008 Summer Olympics in the summer of 2001, Chinese officials promised that these would be the most spectacular games ever. It would also be an opportunity for China to project itself to the world at a time when the country was experiencing rapid change toward a market economy. The government embarked on a very aggressive construction program, spending more than $40 billion, the highest amount ever on the Games. To put the extent of this investment into perspective, staging the 2000 Sydney Olympics cost $3.4 billion. The development of the National Stadium, the National Swim Center, and the Wukesong Sports Center in Beijing alone surpassed $1.1 billion.

The infrastructural program contributed to the transportation, housing, and green space needs of the city after the Olympic Games. In addition to meeting these demands, officials focused on two additional goals, the first of which was to accelerate initiatives that sought to expand new growth centers, especially in the northern part of the city. Two of the Olympic districts, the University Area and the Western Community Area, were already located in urban areas. Planners viewed the construction of the Olympic Green cluster as a way to fuel the development of the Northern Tourist District, which remained underdeveloped. The primary goal was to introduce a new commercial and recreational center in this part of the city. One of the major challenges of this strategy proved to be maintaining a balance between development and historic preservation.[35] The second goal was to address the issue of cultural differences through the Olympic Games. One of the key challenges tourism development authorities in China faced historically was potential visitors' perceptions of the country. Research shows that China is viewed by visitors from Europe, North America, and Australasia as the most culturally distant country.[36] Differences in food, language, cleanliness, transportation, recreation, and intimacy among others account for these low-scoring cultural views.[37]

Regardless, organizers viewed the Olympic Games as an opportunity to address these issues and in the process advance Chinese culture. By reducing the perception of cultural distance, it was hoped that tourism would increase in the years following the Games.[38] Even though officials expected to see a considerable increase in visitors due to the Games, the actual number proved disappointing. Beijing had seen an increase in tourism during previous years and estimates from the event included 600,000 foreign visitors and 2.5 million domestic

Chinese. Furthermore, the event was expected to have a lasting impact, ushering an impressive annual tourism growth of 8 to 9 percent for the following 8 to 10 years. But the actual numbers proved considerably lower with occupancy rates at only 77 percent of the city's 22,300 five-star hotel rooms and 45.5 percent of the 34,500 four-star hotel rooms.[39] Seven months after the Olympics, the main stadium was attracting visitors paying $7 to view the empty but iconic Bird's Nest structure. More important, tourist visits to the site decreased from 80,000 per day in October to 15,000 in December 2008.[40]

The outcome of the Olympics in Beijing will likely prove similar to those in other countries. Like Athens and Sydney, city officials will have to deal with unused facilities. In fact, the $450 million Olympic stadium is costing $15 million annually to maintain. A year after the end of the Games, only one major event was held there. Without a viable plan for its future, a proposal to convert a portion of the facility into a shopping mall is currently under consideration.[41] Tourism after the Games in Athens also declined. The Beijing Olympics may have had the effect of transforming the image of the city and the

Figure 3.6   The Beijing National Stadium in China, affectionately called the Bird's Nest, opened in 2008 and served as the main facility for the Olympic Games. Officials struggled to find uses for the iconic stadium following the Games. In 2010 it was transformed into a winter theme park, hoping to attract visitors (Courtesy East Images, Shutterstock Images).

nation while showcasing traditional Chinese culture to a global audience. This familiarity may eventually help generate tourist destination regions beyond Beijing.

Central to the development of urban tourism is agency: the deliberate and organized effort by officials and business leaders to carry out policies that have the capacity to bring about growth. Promoting the tourist economy requires significant planning outreach efforts. Tourist districts and the organization of mega-events are just two of numerous strategies that have been developed. In addition to offering unique experiences to visitors, these also serve as marketing tools, helping position cities within a competitive environment.

Tourism precincts are dynamic and undergo many changes in the design process. Drawing from ethnicity, sports, and even history, these settings evolve as they aim to develop distinctive identities. However, there are two key issues that pertain to their advancement. First, they must be continually updated to remain attractive and relevant and this often means considerable public and private investment. Second, districts must endeavor to attract locals and outsiders. Entertainment precincts especially reproduce themselves in ways that create banal environments, significantly reducing cultural authenticity.

Large-scale events also receive extensive attention and are viewed as being central to developing tourism and promoting economic growth. Focusing primarily on sports, local leaders pursue these national and international gatherings aggressively, in the process investing millions of dollars in needed infrastructure. While these expenditures are often rationalized by pointing to the expected success for the host city and its residents, evidence suggests that the returns are far from being automatic.

The observations above clearly point to the importance of building and financing the facilities necessary to the realization of the urban tourism agenda. The following chapter examines this subject in greater detail and provides insights on key issues of infrastructural development. Remaking cities, especially formerly industrial centers, requires major expenditures in this area.

Writing, Reflection, and Debate

Discussion Questions

What are some of the positive and negative outcomes associated with pursuing mega-events as part of tourism development? Are you familiar with a specific example of this strategy? Did it prove successful?

Think of a tourism district that is located in your community. In which category from the ones listed above would you place that district? When was it developed and who frequents the location? How is that similar to or different from a tourism district that you have visited?

4

THE INFRASTRUCTURE AND FINANCE OF URBAN TOURISM

Tourist districts are the principal building blocks of urban tourism. Drawing on a unique historical past, or concentrating new entertainment or sports complexes, these spaces have become the destination spots that enable cities to upgrade or even transform their national and international identities. Local governments often work very closely with major corporations and local development interests to take a leading role in shaping the new visitor oriented districts. A key aspect of building this type of city is the development of the physical infrastructure needed to transport, entertain, and provide accommodation for visitors. These expenditures do not simply help cities meet their economic development goals; in many cases they result in the thoroughgoing spatial reorganization of downtowns, outlying neighborhoods, and public facilities. Quite commonly, expanded downtowns and other reconstituted tourism zones, which were once physically dilapidated, with the construction of sports stadiums, convention centers, casinos, and waterfront parks become jewel-like civic showpieces.

Since the 1990s, Richard M. Daley and his municipal administration have made multibillion dollar infrastructural investments the cornerstone of an aggressive campaign to enhance Chicago's cultural and visitor profiles. The city is slowly reimaging itself away from its dominant past identity as a manufacturing city and reinventing itself as a city of leisure. During the last 20 years, there has been a considerable construction boom along the lakefront, including extensive projects toward beautification with numerous festivals and related programming. Through his Mayor's Office of Special Events, Daley instituted entertainment-oriented programming that brings millions to the city from the suburbs and across the country and abroad. All this has resulted in a fundamental restructuring of urban space.

Multibillion dollar projects adorn Chicago's "front yard" and include Navy Pier, Millennium Park, Soldier Field, the Museum Campus, massive expansions to the McCormick Convention Center, and Meigs Field. It is estimated that from 1989 to 2003, the City of Chicago expended over $11 billion on public infrastructure investments. Almost $7 billion of that money is invested along a four-mile lakefront stretch. This transformation proved so impressive that in 2008 Chicago became the U.S. representative and emerged as one of four international finalists to host the 2016 summer Olympics, which was won by Rio de Janeiro.

The city's success is tied to an array of visitor-oriented infrastructural projects. At a cost of more than $200 million, officials redeveloped a 3,300-foot pier in 1995 into a leisure destination center. Navy Pier contains numerous attractions, including the Chicago Children's Museum, a 32,000 square foot indoor botanical garden, a 15-story Ferris Wheel, street entertainment areas with outdoor stages, an IMAX® theater, retail concessions, restaurants, food courts, a skyline stage, a festival hall, and a huge ballroom. The new Shakespeare Theatre significantly diversified the overall use of the space. However, the renovations proved so extensive, the location was removed from its prior status on the National Register of Historic Places. The Pier is the most popular attraction in the City of Chicago with nearly 9 million people visiting the site annually. Recent proposals included a $1.3 billion redevelopment of the structure with additional attractions. Today, Navy Pier is viewed by Chicagoans and tourists as a center of entertainment and recreation, and a generator of substantial tax revenue for the city.

Other initiatives in the city include the development of the Museum Campus that connects the grounds of the Field Museum of Natural History, the Shedd Aquarium, and the Adler Planetarium. At a cost of more than $120 million, the project relocated Lake Shore Drive to the west and added 57 additional acres to the complex. Expansive greenways, massive landscaping, raised terraces, sidewalks, and land bridges were designed to cover the old multilane thoroughfare and beautify the new terrain. More than 120,000 cubic yards of dirt were displaced and the ground was lowered by as much as 22 feet to create a tiered lawn.

The case of nearby Meigs Field illustrates how brute political force can come into play as the city, in the middle of the night, destroyed an old infrastructure (with an explicit transportation purpose) to make way for a new leisure infrastructure. Meigs Field was a small airport along the lakefront providing business people with easy access to downtown Chicago. Following the end of a fifty-year airport lease with the Chicago Park District in 1996, Mayor Daley presented a proposal to create a 91-acre park at a projected cost of $27.2 million. Currently in progress, the park will include playgrounds, wetlands, a nature center, and a sensory garden for the visually or hearing impaired. Adjacent Soldier Field, home of the Chicago Bears (NFL), underwent a massive renovation at a cost of more than $680 million in 2003. The investment also added more than 1,300 trees of 45 different species and the configuration of a sledding hill, as well as the creation of a children's garden.[1]

The Lakefront Millennium Project can be characterized as the most impressive culturally based development effort of the Daley administration and a powerful expression of public–private partnerships. Initially estimated to be constructed over an unsightly railroad yard for $150 million, the actual cost ballooned to $500 million because the project was finished four years behind schedule. The park includes numerous privately funded attractions, including the BP Pedestrian Bridge, the Chase Promenade, the Wrigley Square, the AT&T Plaza, the Crown Fountain, the Exelon Pavilions, the McCormick Tribune Ice Rink, and the Harris Theater for Music and Dance. More than $230 million for the park was derived from private donors.[2]

Figure 4.1   The Pritzker Pavillion at Millennium Park in Chicago, Illinois. Designed by noted architect Frank Gehry, the Great Lawn can accommodate more than 11,000 spectators for performances. The Pavillion cost more than $60 million and the bandshell's stainless steel pedals attract the attention of visitors (Courtesy Author).

Daley's commitment to advancing the tourism industry persisted over the years through the previously mentioned infrastructure developments. The mayor managed to push aside any opposition in order to meet his goals. At a 2006 inaugural address, he reaffirmed this position: "And we must continue to enhance the competitive advantage of our tourism and convention industry, which attracts 30 million visitors to Chicago each year, pumping some $8 billion a year into the Chicago economy."[3]

Chicago is just one of many cities across the world that embraced similar development strategies. The section below identifies different types of cities that have enhanced their tourism business. While all of them look to either maintain or solidify their existing identity, it is the "rebranded cities" that often make the greatest investments in infrastructure. These are the cities that typically have strong manufacturing histories and use this sector as a strategy to craft a new direction. But there are also those cities, without a distinct previous identity, that declare the visitor industry as central to their future.

Types of Tourist Cities

Thousands of municipalities attract tourist and convention business, but in essence, there are three broad categories of tourism city: resort cities, tourist-historic cities, and rebranded cities. Resort cities serve vacationers, attracted by their appealing weather and related natural environments. Tourist-historic cities take advantage of their unique past and organize themselves around themes pointing to their role in the nation's history. Converted or rebranded cities are attempting to reposition themselves within the complexities of a new, postindustrial urban context. They utilize tourism as a strategy for economic development and generating a reformatted urban identity.[4]

Resort cities rely on their favorable location and work to utilize emerging travel networks to grow their appeal. Many develop an appropriate infrastructure that is capable of supporting a great number of visitors. For example, numerous of resort cities can be found in Mexico: Cabo San Lucas in the Baja Peninsula; Cancun in the Yucatan Peninsula; Puerto Vallarta and Acapulco, Mexico's oldest resorts.

Cancun, Cabo San Lucas, and other Baja California resort cities receive extensive funding from the government, which invests heavily in marketing these attractions. All local tourism agencies are part of the country's Ministry of Tourism that oversees tourism research and boards. Mexico has also embraced and promoted public and private tourism alliances. Luxury beachfront hotels, as well as less-costly accommodations away from the waterfront, dominate these cities. They focus on outdoor activities such as water sports, deep-sea fishing, and other, all-inclusive hotel amenities. Mexico's tourism grew considerably in recent years, reaching more than 21 million international visitors in 2005 and 2006, ranking it second to the United States. The total annual receipts from this sector are estimated at $12 billion.[5]

Resort cities feature a robust nightlife and, as a secondary strategy, promote variations of traditional culture as a way of convincing visitors that they are more than about just sun and beach. This presentation

Figure 4.2 This Mexican Caribbean resort hotel in Cancun, Mexico is the midst of the tropics surrounded by swimming pools, beach, and the ocean. Cancun developed this type of tourist infrastructure for visitors lured by the all-inclusive amenities (Courtesy Chad McDermott, Shutterstock Images).

of indigenous cultures is usually inauthentic. For example, as part of the evening hotel activities, Greek resort cities may include "villagers" performing early twentieth century folk dances. In Mexican resorts, one can find performances of Meso-American culture in an attempt to mirror real local entertainment experiences. In Hawaiian resort cities the luau and presentation of leis are tourist experiences that seek to present traditional culture.

Tourist-historic cities promote a different type of amenity, their past, in order to attract both recreational and business visitors. Athens, Rome, Boston, and Jerusalem are examples of such cities. Millions of visitors crowd the Acropolis and the Forum every year. These cities look for ways to take advantage of showcasing antiquities. For example, Greek authorities supported the construction of a new museum. Established in 2008, the $178 million New Acropolis Museum opened in 2009 and it is positioned just 1,000 feet from the historic site. Officials hope that the 226,000 square foot museum and its 4,000 displays will triple the current number of visitors to the Acropolis to more than 3.5 million annually. The increase is expected to benefit the national economy.[6] Similar efforts can be found in American cities.

In recent decades, Boston recognized the importance of its history as part of a broader tourism and convention development agenda. The city halted urban renewal efforts in the 1970s and 1980s that had the capacity to destroy historically significant areas. With the support of Mayor Raymond Flynn (1984–1993), community activists embraced a preservation agenda that aided Boston. Officials attempted to balance attention to preservation with new construction. Achieving that meant integrating new development projects into existing structures of historic value. Faneuil Hall Marketplace (also known as Quincy Market) is a good example of this approach. The area evolved as a central meeting point in Boston, combining the rich history of the location with a vast array of shops and restaurants. With a robust outdoor schedule of street performers and other attractions, this concept is credited with ushering the genesis of a new type urban public space that has been replicated in many cities across the country. This unique integration of old and new may have hindered Boston's short-term tourism growth. Despite this, Boston faired very well. According to one observer, "History is what truly distinguishes the city and provides its competitive advantage in tourism."[7]

Rebranded cities undergo extensive investment in their physical presentation as well as in the way they are conveyed to both residents and visitors. For example, many Frostbelt urban centers engaged in significant infrastructural investments starting in the 1990s. As noted earlier, Chicago spent billions of dollars on the lakefront to construct new public spaces, improve existing attractions, and add new destinations. Cleveland, Cincinnati, and Detroit refocused on their downtown areas, aggressively marketing themselves both internally and externally.

Beyond the physical remaking of the newly built environment, the rebranding process also proves critical. Many British cities have undergone considerable reimaging since the 1990s, especially the former industrial strongholds that suffered from urban decline. In the 1990s, Manchester embraced a new motto, "The Life and Soul of Britain," and Bradford used "Bradford's Bouncing Back." Glasgow currently utilizes "Scotland with Style," which conveys that, beyond its main competitor Edinburgh, this is another city that possesses an array of civic amenities for leisure and entertainment. In 2004, Philadelphia embarked on a highly successful "The Place That Loves You Back" campaign and Pittsburgh considered a number of branding slogans, including "Urban Beauty Surrounded by Rivers & Outdoor Adventure."

The competition is fierce and cities pursue their plans to convert their spaces into visitor destinations—a strategy that necessitates a continual introduction of attractions. Furthermore, it is not just the medium-sized or large cities that are trying to rebrand themselves. Feeling the pressure and the potential of losing visitors' disposable spending, global cities must ensure their leading status. For example, London, between 1993 and 2000, added nineteen new visitor attractions. In 2000 alone, city officials created five new attractions.[8]

Building and Financing the Tourist City

The quest for developing an urban tourist economy is ushering in a new era of city building in America. By the late 1980s and early

1990s, we begin to see major construction programs in downtown areas that focus on attracting and retaining visitors. Convention centers, amusement parks, stadiums, casinos, waterfront developments, and riverboat gambling complexes have reshaped the urban landscape and helped restructure hundreds of urban cores. The financing of this rapidly advancing urban infrastructure is primarily driven by a combination of private and public sources of funding. Some centers utilized tax increment financing techniques to support construction projects that, directly or indirectly, promote tourism growth.

The U.S. economy experienced considerable expansion in the 1990s. The introduction of new technologies in the latter part of the 1980s brought popular electronics and telecommunications into the consumer market. The computer industry grew rapidly and the Internet not only entered American households, but also helped businesses function more effectively. The end of the Cold War also allowed for new trade opportunities in Eastern European countries, which rushed to grow their economies. In addition, the federal government's reduction of expenditures on the military furthered the robust economic climate. Low inflation and low rates of unemployment dominated the 1990s. Rapid increases in the stock market and expanded tax revenues gave local governments considerable resources at their disposal.

Economic performance between 2001 and 2007 in GDP, job creation, investment, and wage and salary growth was overall weaker when compared to equivalent years during the 1990s. The only exception was in corporate profits. During the 2001 to 2007 cycle, corporations averaged an annual growth of 10.8 percent, compared to 7.4 percent during other comparable postwar periods. It should also be noted that the expansion of the 1990s continued in the early part of the 2000s, whereas the 2001 to 2007 expansion gave way to a recession.[9]

These conditions in the 1990s translated to urban growth. One study found that, when compared to previous decades, the bigger cities in the Northeast and Midwest that had experienced serious declines in the postwar era did considerably better in the 1990s. According to the analysis, during the 1980s not one Midwestern city grew in population by more than 12 percent. Six Midwestern cities experienced greater percentage growth in the 1990s. The increased sale of consumer goods is considered one key contributing factor.[10]

It is within this broader framework that cities pursue the construction of tourism infrastructures. A national survey of 463 cities across the United States released in 2000 reported that 96 percent of them had a historic district or site; 76 percent had a museum; 69 percent operated a farmer's market; 62 percent maintained a performing arts center; and 48 percent of cities indicated the presence of a cultural district. Interestingly, 41 percent had a convention hotel; 40 percent possessed a convention center; and 39 percent had a sports stadium. Arts, entertainment recreation, and tourism (54 percent) represented the most important economic sector in central cities, followed by manufacturing (47 percent) and retail and wholesale trade (40 percent). Conversely, suburbs ranked retail and wholesale (73 percent) as the most important economic sector followed by manufacturing (42 percent) and arts, entertainment, recreation, and tourism (34 percent). The majority of the cities (78 percent) indicated that tourism and entertainment were "extremely" or "somewhat" important to their future development.[11] The findings of this survey further substantiate an interesting point that suburbs, as a rule, do not attract tourists, though suburbs in adjoining major air hubs attract business travelers. It is central cities that draw large numbers of recreational visitors.

The financial mechanisms employed to advance the tourism, convention business, and entertainment infrastructure vary, though local authorities generally favor some approaches. Asked to indicate the most common methods of public financial support, cities identified local infrastructure support (57 percent); local bond financing (50 percent); and local land/facilities donation (49 percent) as the preferred methods. Others included tax increment financing (29 percent); federal CDBG funds (23 percent); and local tax abatement (21 percent). The majority of the public financial assistance was derived from local sources. This in turn makes the office of the mayor central to the promotion of this strategy.[12]

The development of an urban tourist infrastructure can be divided into three specific categories: (1) primary facilities and services that include historic, cultural, or entertainment districts, convention centers and convention hotels, stadiums and performing arts centers; (2) secondary tourist facilities and services that entail the availability of accommodations, such as motels or hotels, restaurants, major convention hotels, as well as travel and tour services; (3) tertiary tourist and business traveler facilities and services such as financial, safety, and emergency-care services.

Regarding primary facilities, the dynamics behind the finance and construction of convention hotels offer some fascinating insights. Officials in Austin, Texas were very active in getting the Austin Convention Center Hotel built; it opened in January 2004. The 800-room hotel is managed by Hilton Hotels. As a full-service, first-class, convention-oriented hotel, it offers two full-service restaurants, ample meeting space, and underground parking for more than 600 vehicles. Austin Convention Enterprises, Inc. was formed by the City of Austin to be the municipal owner.

The financial plan for its development included $110 million in senior lien current interest bonds, $135 million in subordinate lien bonds, and $21 million in third-tier subordinate manager and developer bonds. Bonds are issued to raise funds for one time capital projects and are generally repaid, with interest, within three to five years of issuance. The city of Austin's financial contribution was about $15 million. During its first year of operation, the hotel exceeded the predicted profit of $10.2 million by posting an actual profit of $12.9 million. Austin's aggressive spending on the visitor industry included an impressive $1.3 billion between 1998 and 2004. More than $15 million allocated for the promotion of the convention hotel contributed to the success of its operation, which in turn allowed Austin Convention Enterprises to renegotiate the bonds.[13]

Houston, Texas followed a similar financial strategy to complete its 1,200-room convention center hotel. The facility opened in 2003 and it includes two ballrooms and 28 meeting rooms. A 1,600-vehicle parking garage connects the hotel to the George R. Brown Convention Center. The funding scheme for the Hilton Americas-Houston also entailed the issuing of bonds via the Convention and Entertainment Facilities Department under its municipal sponsor, the City of Houston. A total of $626 million was issued ($476 million fixed rate, and $150 million variable rate). The city provided a general obligation pledge to these hotel bonds. Some of the sources of debt service payment include 5.65 percent of the 7 percent hotel occupancy tax and revenues derived from large city-operated parking facilities in the central business district. However, the project proved to have a negative impact on the other major downtown hotels. Due to competition, the 972-room Hyatt Regency Houston's occupancy dropped considerably and it went into foreclosure. Similar trends have been observed in St. Louis, MO, Myrtle Beach, SC, Overland, KS, and Sacramento, CA.[14]

A number of common themes emerge when assessing the building and financing of the tourist city and the examples offered above substantiate these observations. First, special purpose authorities increasingly play a greater role. This is the most popular approach to developing and operating these structures. Second, the private sector is involved and plays a key part in the development process. Third, the localized/municipal nature of this strategy places mayors' offices at center stage, further intensifying the competition between cities.

Sports and Stadium Development

Immense sums of public money are used to construct sports stadiums and arenas in cities across America. The rationale behind these policy considerations is economic and social. By employing economic impact studies and multiplier calculations, advocates note the positive direct and indirect outcomes. At the same time, sporting events are widely seen as having community building and cultural identification benefits. However, there is widespread uncertainty concerning the utility of these construction projects as tools for economic development and urban regeneration because of the emerging corporatization of sport.

As sport slowly became part of the tourism development strategy, stadium development proved a critical means for retaining/attracting professional franchises. From 1970 to 1990, there was an increase from 70 percent to 80 percent in publicly owned facilities used by professional sports teams.[15] From 1993 to 1996, more than $7 billion was spent on the construction and renovation of major league facilities. The public sector provided 80 percent of these funds, which resulted in the introduction of 50 new stadiums across the various U.S. professional leagues.[16] Even smaller cities aggressively pursued minor league sports franchises by offering stadiums to team owners.[17]

From 2000 to 2008, 11 new stadiums were constructed in the National Football League (NFL) at a cost of $4.43 billion (average of $402 million per project). Five new stadiums are currently either under construction, planned, or just completed at a staggering total cost of $4.10 billion. Two of those opened in 2009 at a cost of $1.3 billion (Dallas Cowboys) and $1.6 billion (New York Yankees).[18]

The financial benefits of upscale sport attendance contributed to a new type of athletic arena. The expectation of private boxes and the ability to deliver a range of foods, beverages, and other commodities dictated various design innovations. Today's dominant trends in stadium design favor facilities dedicated to one sport and with room for restaurants and taverns, gift shops, and, in some cases, overnight accommodations.

The drive to attract teams is consistent with, and indeed integral to, the municipal growth ideology. Cities compete with each other to

Figure 4.3 Great American Ballpark, home of the Cincinnati Reds in Cincinnati, Ohio opened in 2003. Cities support the development of new stadiums in downtown as a way to revitalize the area and spur residential and commercial development (Courtesy Stephanie A. Miller, Shutterstock Images).

attract existing sports clubs or to host expansion teams. Subsidies to profitable professional teams constitute a form of capital investment, and as such, are akin to other urban redevelopment outlays. Furthermore, project proponents outline the potential for creating adjacent entertainment districts with retail shops, summer outdoor music, and other recreational opportunities.

Table 4.1   Urban/Suburban Stadium Locations in the NFL, 2008 (Construction year in parenthesis. Cost in millions)

Downtown/Urban
- Atlanta Falcons: Georgia Dome (1992) at $210 million
- Baltimore Ravens: M & T Bank Stadium (1998) at $220 million
- Carolina Panthers: Bank of America Stadium (1996) at $248 million
- Chicago Bears: Soldier Field (2003) at $425 million
- Cincinnati Bengals: Paul Brown Stadium (2000) at $453 million
- Cleveland Browns: Cleveland Browns Stadium (1999) at $290 million
- Denver Broncos: Invesco Field (2001) at $364 million
- Detroit Lions: Ford Field (2002) at $500 million
- Green Bay Packers: Lambeau Field (1957) at $1 million
- Indianapolis Colts: Lucas Oil Stadium (2008) at $625 million
- Jacksonville: Jacksonville Municipal Stadium (1995) at $134 million
- Minnesota Vikings: Metrodome (1982) at $68 million (currently under negotiations for a new $954 million stadium)
- New Orleans Saints: Superdome (1975) at $134 million (currently under negotiations for a new $450 million stadium)
- Pittsburgh Steelers: Heinz Field (2001) at $281 million
- St. Louis Rams: Edward Jones Dome (1995) at $281 million
- Seattle Seahawks: Quest Field (2002) at $450 million
- Tampa Bay Buccaneers: Raymond James Stadium (1998) at $168.5 million
- Tennessee Titans: LP Field (1999) at $292 million

Suburban
- Arizona Cardinals: University of Phoenix Stadium (2006) at $455 million
- Buffalo Bills: Ralph Wilson Stadium (1973) at $22 million
- Dallas Cowboys: Texas Stadium (1971) at $39 million (Cowboys Stadium to open in 2009 for $1 billion)
- Houston Texans: Reliant Stadium (2002) at $352 million
- Kansas City Chiefs: Arrowhead Stadium (1968) at $43 million
- Miami Dolphins: Pro Player Stadium (1987) at $115 million (upcoming renovations are expected to exceed $300 million)
- New England Patriots: Gillette Stadium (2002) at $325 million
- New York Giants/Jets: Giants Stadium (new stadium will open in 2010 for $1.3 billion)
- Oakland Raiders: McAfee Coliseum (1966) at $200 million with recent renovations
- Philadelphia Eagles: Lincoln Financial Field (2003) at $512 million
- San Diego Padres: Qualcomm Stadium (1967) at $27 million (currently under negotiations for a new $400 million stadium)
- San Francisco 49ers: Monster Park (1971) for $24 million (currently under negotiations for a new stadium)
- Washington Redskins: FedEx Field (1997) at $300 million

The commitment to employing sport as an economic development strategy can be seen in the construction of new stadiums in downtown areas. As Table 4.1 shows above, more than half of the 32 NFL teams have downtown or urban stadiums, and a similar trend can be identified in Major League Baseball.

As with convention hotels, cities and states typically rely on special purpose agencies to construct stadiums. For example, in Chicago, the Illinois Sports Facilities Authority (ISFA) was charged with the development of New Comiskey Park for the Chicago White Sox (now U.S. Cellular Field) and the renovation/expansion of Soldier Field (Chicago Bears). In Washington, DC, the District of Columbia government created an independent agency, DC Sports & Entertainment Commission, which oversaw the construction of Nationals Park for $611 million in 2008 (Washington Nationals). The commission is also responsible for the management and operation of the Robert F. Kennedy Memorial Stadium (Washington Redskins).

Property taxes and bonds are the most common methods employed to finance public investments in stadium development. In addition, there is the utilization of motel/hotel taxes, rental car surcharges, sports lottery revenues, and ticket taxes to assemble the needed revenue stream. The economically regressive impact of sales tax collections means that the poor and underprivileged pay more than their fair share of stadium costs. Furthermore, the corporatization of sport is playing a major role in this area given that naming rights of stadiums are almost exclusively tied to conglomerates and large corporations. The case of Cleveland shows how this city is utilizing a sports facility strategy to rebrand itself away from its prominent past as a manufacturing city.

The Gateway Project in Cleveland, OH

Like other older industrial cities of the rustbelt, Cleveland experienced heavy job losses in the 1970s and 1980s as a result of progressive deindustrialization that began in the 1950s. The ensuing population growth in the suburbs also meant persistent declines in the city core. In fact, over half of the older industrial cities across the country lost manufacturing jobs between 1947 and 1972; Cleveland fit that profile.[19]

Mayor George Voinovich (1980–1989) attempted to address many of the major economic problems facing the city by focusing on revitalizing the downtown area. By supporting the construction of office buildings, Cleveland received national attention and was noted for its comeback approach to its economic problems. In fact, in some circles, the city would be referred to as an "All-American city." However, the redevelopment of the Gateway Project in the downtown area under the administration of the next mayor, Michael R. White (1990–2002) showed a greater commitment to the urban tourism strategy.

Historic Gateway District was one of the first areas to receive attention. Formerly a produce market, the 28.5-acre site was abandoned and in disrepair. Surface parking dominated the location. The not-for-profit Gateway Economic Development Corporation was organized in 1990 with the goal of financing and building a new sports complex, which it was hoped would help to jumpstart the revival of the city's downtown.[20] A public–private partnership, which was split almost equally between the two sectors, supported the construction of two facilities. The public investment was derived from a 15-year tax on cigarette and alcohol sales, allowing the issuance of public bonds totaling $118 million. Amenity seating added $31 million in bonds, Cuyahoga County loaned $120 million, and the State of Ohio contributed another $12 million in loans. The private funds came from naming rights, sponsorship of other facilities, and leasing of suites and club seating.

When completed, the complex included Jacobs Field (now Progressive Field) for the Cleveland Indians of MLB at a cost of $175 million and Gund Arena (now Quicken Loans Arena) for the Cleveland Cavaliers of NBA at a cost of $100 million. Both opened in 1994. The Quicken Loans Arena also hosted the Cleveland Rockers (defunct Women's National Basketball Association team), the Lake Erie Monsters (American Hockey League), and the Cleveland Gladiators (Arena Football League). The two structures attract more than 6 million people to the downtown area annually. Between 1994 and 2007, the Quicken Loans Arena reached single-game attendance sellouts of 20,562 on 148 occasions.

The development of this sports-oriented infrastructure also proved critical to fueling additional construction, most of which has been by the private sector. For example, within a few years following the new stadiums, a number of new hotels appeared in the vicinity, including the Radisson (1998; $13 million), the Holiday Inn Express (1999; $11 million), the Hilton Garden Inn (2000; $16 million), and the Marriott (2000; $30 million). New commercial structures also include the privately funded Pointe at Gateway (2000) at a cost of $12 million, which city officials considered key to the future of the downtown area. In addition, from 1994 to 2001, a publicly funded program distributed more than $14 million that resulted in 176 storefront renovations. The initiatives are intended to improve the streetscape and provide more services to residents and visitors.[21]

In recent years, Cleveland supported a robust array of entertainment options, including concerts, restaurants, destination shopping, comedy clubs, and ice skating. The city received national attention for

Figure 4.4 The boardwalk on the Cuyahoga River in downtown Cleveland, Ohio is one of the recently added amenities that is part of a strategy to attract residents to the area (Courtesy Shannon Workman, Shutterstock Images).

its progress in revitalizing its core, and publications like the *Economist* noted the city's revival, claiming that it has experienced a physical renaissance.[22] The new amenities helped promote the city, which in the process increased the number of tourists, injecting a new energy into the core. In addition to the sports infrastructure, convention centers are also viewed as an investment that complements the tourist-city strategy.

The Convention Center Construction Craze

As far back as the early part of the twentieth century, cities organized to attract business visitors. In 1907, the Chicago Association of Commerce identified a subcommittee to work on attracting conventions. Following Chicago's lead, many other cities formed agencies out of loosely defined civic or business groups whose agendas focused on promoting and attracting business people to their locales.

Convention and visitor bureaus appeared across the country: San Francisco (1909), St. Louis (1909), Atlanta (1913), Kansas City (1918), Minneapolis (1927), Washington (1931), Cleveland (1934), New York (1935), Philadelphia (1941), Las Vegas (1960), New Orleans (1960), Anaheim, CA (1961), Orlando (1984), and Miami (1985). The Chicago Convention and Visitors Bureau (CCVB), founded in 1943, eventually expanded in 1970 to incorporate the Tourism Council of Greater Chicago, forming the Chicago Convention and Tourism Bureau. The management and operation of the massive McCormick Place Convention Center became part of the responsibilities of the CCVB in 1980. These entities are very important since they spearheaded the building of tourism and business visitor facilities, including their management and maintenance.

In recent years, the same rationale that drives the construction of stadiums also fuels public investment into convention centers. Viewed as contributors to local economies, there are huge expenditures in this area, especially among former manufacturing cities. The first tier of convention cities includes the most successful, historically active centers—Las Vegas, Orlando, Chicago, and New York. The second tier focuses on developing their economies by investing heavily in their convention facilities—San Francisco, San Diego, Anaheim, Atlanta, and Washington, DC. The third tier includes Seattle, Reno, Nashville, and Portland. This last set is the most aggressive in its convention development and aims to strip convention market share from the first two tiers.

These policies sometimes run the risk of becoming unfocused, often lost in the haze of intense competition for visitor expenditures. Specifically, the total financial proceeds from conventions are not large enough for dozens of cities to make money from these activities. Even in the middle of an economic downturn, Philadelphia is currently pushing ahead with a $700 million Pennsylvania Convention Center (PCC) expansion, aiming to rank in the top twenty convention centers in the country. When completed, the project will increase meeting and exhibit space by nearly 60 percent, which will allow two conventions to be held at the same time.

In 2001, Chicago city officials approved an $800 million addition to McCormick Place. The McCormick Place West building, opened in 2007 at a cost of nearly $900 million. Beyond the noted budget escalation, it is increasingly unclear whether or not the additional 250,000 square feet of meeting room space and 470,000 square feet of exhibition space will produce more convention activity.

In 2007 alone, 93 new or expanded convention centers opened across the country. That is in addition to the greatly increased construction in the 1990s. For example, the total amount of exhibit space from 1990 to 2003 increased 51 percent from 40.4 million square feet to 60.9 million square feet, doubling the public spending on this type of infrastructure to more than $2 billion annually. In this intense environment, cities are often forced to reduce their rental pricing, compelling numerous facilities to operate at a loss. And the craze continues. In the first part of 2009 alone, city officials announced the grand openings of 15 new expanded or renovated venues.[23]

An examination of the top U.S. convention cities reveals the fierce nature of the competition. In 2007, the three top convention cities included Las Vegas, Orlando, and Chicago. In 1980, the top cities hosting meetings with exhibits included New York (ranked no. 1), Chicago (ranked no. 2), and Atlanta (ranked no. 3). Las Vegas was ranked no. 4 and Orlando was ranked no. 27. A decade later, in 1992, the three top convention cities included Chicago, Orlando (from no. 5 in 1991), and Dallas, respectively. Las Vegas ranked no. 13 that year. In 2004, Chicago, Las Vegas, and Washington were the three leaders. More interestingly, San Antonio, TX (ranked no. 12), Tampa-St Petersburg-Clearwater, FL (ranked no. 17), Austin-San Marcos, TX (ranked no. 18), Seattle, WA (metro area; ranked no. 20), and Riverside-San Bernardino, CA (ranked no. 23) did not even make the top list ten years earlier. Securing conventions, especially the 200 largest trade shows (referred in the industry as the Tradeshow 200), has direct and indirect economic ramifications for the local economy and is a key indicator of convention activity. While the competition is very intense, few cities are able to support these large events. In 2007, Las Vegas controlled 22 percent of the total market share with Orlando (12 percent), Chicago (10 percent), and New York (8 percent) hosting some of the largest trade shows.[24]

The building boom is rationalized by projected job creation, increased tax revenues, and direct and indirect opportunities for financial growth. At the same time, this strategy left municipalities wondering if the benefits outweigh the extensive renovations, maintenance, and unfavorable lease agreements. Clearly, adding convention space does not guarantee success. The recent woes of Chicago's McCormick Place's—diminishing shows, attendees, and square feet of utilized space over the last five years—were heightened by the loss of the National Association of Realtors' 100th-anniversary convention to Las Vegas.

Even after considering the cyclical booking patterns of events, Chicago experienced a decline in the overall number of shows (82 in 2000 to 71 in 2005), square footage of exhibit space utilized (16 million in 2000 to 10.3 million in 2005), and attendance (3.32 million in 2000 to 2.17 million in 2005). Like other cities, Chicago is also experiencing competition from nearby smaller cities such as Rosemont and Schaumburg. Suburban Rosemont, which in 2006 ranked ninth in total exhibit space, and the opening of the 100,000 square foot Renaissance Schaumburg Convention Center that same year both aimed to strip away the Second City's dominance in taking in visitor dollars.[25]

Interestingly, booster committees for these convention centers often form at the regional scale, but the competition takes place at the sub-regional level, with benefits accruing to specific municipalities.

Casinos, Entertainment, and Waterfront Development

Casinos and waterfront development have also emerged as significant tools for urban economic development. Connected to broader entertainment opportunities, both of these strategies are viewed by local officials as having significant growth potential. Expanding the tax base through these attractions and utilizing these revenues to provide public services is the long-term objective.

During the 1990s, casinos (riverboat and land) were a popular way to attract tourists. The extraordinary success of Las Vegas proved inspirational for many urban leaders across the nation. The city managed to successfully transform itself from a hamlet in the middle of the desert to the most popular U.S. destination. In December 1946, Bugsy Siegel had opened the Flamingo at a cost of $1 million, which paved the way for the introduction of additional casinos from the 1950s to the 1970s. In 1969, the $65 million International was the world's largest resort hotel, and in 1973 the MGM Grand Hotel and Casino became the world's largest hotel. In 1975, Nevada's gaming revenues surpassed the $1 billion mark. The 1980s and 1990s saw a rapid increase of revenues from the casino industry. This upward trajectory continued in recent years from $18 billion in 1995 to $36.2 billion in 2008.[26]

However, the early financial success of Las Vegas also proved to have negative consequences for the city's image. The presence of organized crime and illegal activities in the gaming industry threatened to hurt the city's reputation. To combat this perception, Las Vegas embraced a strategy that focused on converting itself into a family destination. The corporatization of the gaming industry greatly contributed to this direction. New ownerships invested billions of dollars in this transformation by promoting family amusement opportunities and more accommodations, and in the process reducing the space devoted to gaming in their casinos.[27]

Figure 4.5   New York, New York in Las Vegas. In an attempt to offer something for everyone, the strip strives to recreate major tourist attractions, all in one place, from around the world (Courtesy Charles Zachritz, Shutterstock Images).

For its part, the local government spent more than $1 billion in 2000 to modernize and enlarge the McCarran International Airport. That same year, more than $113 million was committed to the expansion of the Las Vegas Convention Center. During the second half of the 1990s and the first part of the 2000s, a major construction program invested billions of dollars into new resorts and massive additions of hotel rooms with a renewed focus on leisure. Today, the Las Vegas strip not only is a center for gaming, but also has been reborn into an entertainment district with global drawing power.

This transformation brought a major population increase as economic opportunities and jobs became plentiful. But with explosive growth came many social challenges in education, housing, and transportation. Las Vegas successfully shed its image as a seedy underworld Mecca and managed to project itself as an "All-American city," beyond its image as the gambling capital of the world. [28]

Currently, Las Vegas is home to 15 of the 20 largest hotels in the world. The annual number of visitors increased from 21 million in 1990 to 30.6 million in 1998 and to 39 million in 2006. McCarran International Airport is undergoing another $4 billion makeover, and officials are exploring the development of a second airport to handle the increasing number of visitors. In 2006, tourists spent $15 billion in the various casino resorts located on the Strip. Sixty percent of that revenue, approximately $9 billion, derived from noncasino sources.[29]

Las Vegas serves as a model for many other cities when they consider reworking their image. However, this approach necessitates huge investments, and local officials must support extensive infrastructure and public services. Ensuring positive outcomes also involves labor force development and subsidies for educational training. The competition is intense. In 2009, 443 commercial casinos, 44 racetrack casinos, 456 tribal casinos, 588 government sanctioned card rooms, and 11,215 electronic gaming facilities operated across the country. The consumer spending on commercial casino gaming was significant, estimated at $30.74 billion nationally. Nevada ($10.39 billion), New Jersey ($3.94 billion), and Indiana ($2.79 billion) led the states with the highest revenues. Las Vegas ($5.55 billion), Atlantic City ($3.94 billion), and the Chicago/northwest Indiana region ($2.09 billion) were the largest casino markets. Job creation and tax revenue, generating tourism and economic development, as well as additional entertainment and dining options are viewed as the reasons why communities support casinos.[30] The presence of casinos can also have significant social consequences, however, which include gambling and drug addiction and crime. Cities must assess these issues comprehensively before making the casino industry part of a long-term tourism development policy.[31]

Just as investment in casinos anchors entertainment activities, waterfront development evolved in a similar manner. Many decades ago urban waterfronts served as significant centers of commerce, most often for manufacturing, warehousing, and transportation. Since the 1970s, cities have looked to alter these properties and transform them into tourism locales. As we noted earlier, Baltimore, Sydney, and Liverpool are three cities that converted their waterfronts as part of their broader plans for economic growth.

A restructured built environment typically includes activities that are geared toward leisure, often in water-based recreation, and involves sightseeing boat tours, swimming and fishing, as well as other water sports. Cities along waterfronts also support large projects to attract visitors. In 1999, Cleveland invested in a new football stadium for the Cleveland Browns of the NFL along the lakefront at a cost of $283 million. The Rock and Roll Hall of Fame and the Great Lakes Science Center are also located nearby. In San Francisco, the city owns and operates Candlestick Park for the 49ers, which is located on the shore of San Francisco Bay.

Retail shopping, residential development, parkland and open space, restaurants and mixed use development are also employed by cities. An excellent example of this comprehensive strategy can be found in Boston Harbor. This unique urban setting is a popular destination, offering various entertainment opportunities, including boating, waterfront walks, and tours to observe marine life. Similarly, in San Diego more than 27 miles of waterfront were developed with parks, marinas, shopping centers, and cultural activities. Interestingly, in addition to cities located along the seaboards and the Great Lakes, active redevelopment also takes place along riverfronts. Portland, as part of its strategy to revitalize the Willamette River, in 2001 endorsed the River Renaissance Vision. The plan includes a variety of projects. For example, the South Waterfront Plan integrates nature into an urban mixed use community. The Vera Katz Eastbank Esplanade provides 1.5 miles of pedestrian paths and a biking route with art and historic displays. Chattanooga also invested millions of dollars on reviving its downtown area with numerous attractions along the Tennessee River.

Attention to the waterfront is found across the world. For example, the city of Copenhagen in Denmark has engaged in an ambitious plan to transform its harbor area. High-end architecture converted two massive silos into apartment buildings with a circular atrium at the center of each. Three public buildings nearby bring large crowds to the waterfront, shifting the city's perspective toward the harbor

Figure 4.6   The new Copenhagen Opera House in Denmark next to the harbor on the island Holmen opened in 2005 at a cost of more than $500 million. It is part of a larger waterfront redevelopment effort (Courtesy Alan Kraft, Shutterstock Images).

area. Other attractions include the Black Diamond, an extension to the Royal Library; the Royal Danish Playhouse, an architecturally distinctive theater, and the Operaen, an opera house constructed in 2005 on a former military pier. Copenhagen attracts public officials from across the world who are interested in learning how to duplicate these efforts.[32]

Waterfront development will continue to be central to urban tourism and private–public partnerships will be critical determinants regarding the success of these projects. Connected to the physical transformation of downtowns, this strategy provides cities with numerous options and lake, river, and ocean fronts are recipients of this new amenities-based urban economy.[33]

The Arts, Festivals, and Urban Parks

The arts are another central part of urban tourism development with cities positioning themselves to take advantage of their community benefits. The advancement of the arts also necessitates appropriate investment in related facilities and decisions regarding which city government office will be responsible for them. For example, Providence, RI placed the administration of the arts in the same office as the management of tourism—the Providence Department of Art, Culture and Tourism. In addition to enriching the quality of life of its residents, the city views art as an industry, capable of having a significant economic impact. In fact, Providence created an arts and entertainment district in its downtown area and provided tax incentives to those living within the district who were involved in the sale of various forms of art. As an economic zone, the city also promotes the availability of live–work units and rehearsal spaces.

In 2003, the State of Connecticut merged the Tourism Division, Arts, and Film Office with the Historic Commission to create a new unit, the Connecticut Commission on Culture and Tourism. Karolyn Kirchgesler, then executive director of the Greater New Haven Convention & Visitors Bureau, noted that the plan "could certainly benefit the industry, especially in New Haven where arts and cultural activities are such a major staple of our visitor product."[34] Officials across the state shared the belief that art and tourism are connected and the pursuit of a comprehensive approach could benefit the local economies.

Public art is also directly associated with the promotion of urban tourism. The City of San Antonio organized the Public Art and Design Enhancement Program to support artwork in civic spaces with the goal of creating an attraction that encourages visitor attendance. In 2007, Arlington, Washington supported the acquisition of new art for public areas by setting aside 1 percent of the cost for each planned municipal construction project. Also in 2007, the Seattle Convention and Visitors Bureau (SCVB) attributed the record of 9.5 million visitors and the record spending of $5.16 billion (up 8.6 percent from the previous year) to the SCVB's cultural tourism program. The theme and events of that year focused on the arts.[35]

Festivals are another economic strategy to support urban tourism and the remaking of downtown areas as places of entertainment. Knoxville, Tennessee stages numerous festivals throughout the year with the goal of attracting visitors. These range in outreach and scope from the Dogwood Art Festival, the Knoxville Opera's Rossini Festival, the Kuumba Festival, Cherokee Heritage Days, the Tennessee Valley Fair, Christmas in the City Festival, and the nation's largest Labor Day weekend fireworks display. This array of events is complemented by the Italian Street Fair and Civil War reenactments. Nearby Chattanooga organizes the annual Riverbend Festival along the Tennessee River. The music event features more than 100 performances and attracts 600,000 attendees to its multiple stages. New Orleans offers the free French Quarter Festival and the Satchmo Summer Festival to aid local businesses, while solidifying its reputation as a premier tourist city.[36]

Urban parks also help drive the tourism industry and offer the needed spatial dimension for art exhibits and large festivals. They can accommodate temporary structures without major disruptions and can be employed to showcase attractions. Urban parks host sports tournaments, which in some cases are major sources of local revenue. This proves especially beneficial for smaller cities that lack the capacity or resources necessary to stage events. These urban spaces contain attractions such as museums, zoos, memorials, and other artifacts. They can create a critical mass of visitors, encouraging them to stay longer, thus spending more money. Hermann Park in Houston and Balboa Park and Mission Bay in San Diego offer cumulative attractions. Finally, urban parks can contain impressive landscaping, which in and of themselves can be outstanding works of art: Prospect Park in Brooklyn, Golden Gate Park in San Francisco, and Grant Park and Millennium Park in Chicago possess natural and planned lawns and trees that bring millions of people to their respective cities.[37]

It is clear that the arts, festivals, and urban parks play a major role in encouraging people to visit urban areas. Focused attention on promoting these activities and their settings meant the reinvigoration of the built environment as visitors and locals took advantage of these leisure opportunities. Beyond that, the associated infrastructural investments breathed new life to tired urban cores.

The Importance of Urban Beautification

Cities also focus on urban beautification by expending considerable resources on creating visually pleasing environments. A revival of the City Beautiful Movement, which flourished during the 1890s and early part of the twentieth century, is once again part of downtown investment. On the one hand, reorganized physical spaces and attractive landscapes are central elements of this outlook. On the other hand, economic development opportunities, image building, and location marketing and enhancement are key characteristics of this planning directive. These programs have the capacity to create new urban physical terrains, often geared toward municipal advancement and the presentation of the city as a postindustrial environment geared toward encouraging both recreational and business visitors.

Chicago provides some interesting insights on this strategy. Large stone and concrete planters now define the medians of main thoroughfares. Bright flowerbeds and newly planted shrubs dominate open spaces. The presence of wrought iron fences and old-style street light posts are attractive for locals and visitors alike. A 1999 Landscape Ordinance emphasized the importance of increasing the aesthetic appeal in city streets by requiring investment in trees and streetscapes. Numerous amendments include landscaping islands and hedges for new parking lots and shade foliage for every 25 feet of new building frontage. The effect of this policy was dramatic and the private sector shared in the expenditures, sharply accelerating the "greening" of Chicago, a direction reminiscent of the city's sought after identity in the nineteenth century as "Urban in Horto."

Funding in this area from municipal and federal government sources surpassed the $1 million mark annually in the early part of the

1990s. Chicago's budget from 1997 to 2003 incorporated $2.4 million for greening efforts. As part of the mayor's efforts to further enhance the aesthetic quality of the areas located throughout downtown Loop, River North, and Printers Row included in 2001 the installation of 950 hanging baskets in city streets. The number of trees planted since Daley entered office in 1989 is now close to 600,000.

Other beautification projects include the restoration of the Roosevelt Road Bridge in 1995 and the renovation of State Street in 1996 and Wacker Drive in 2007. The bridge ornamentation of Roosevelt Road contains sculptures of dolphins, as well as books and navigation instruments representing the cultural institutions of the city. Similarly, State Street has been transformed from an urban transit mall to an eye-catching public space following the installation of historic streetlights, wrought-iron planters, shrubs, flowers, and old-style signage.[38]

Paralleling Chicago's initiatives, Las Vegas invested $13 million on the beautification of the Strip by planting more than 76,000 palms and bushes. The city of Houston, in preparation for the 2004 Super Bowl, turned to beautification. During the six months prior to the game, landscapers planted more than 20,000 trees. City officials felt this was the best way to showcase their city's changing image.[39] Houston continued these efforts, and in 2006, $28.5 million funded beautification efforts that resulted in the planting of 20,000 additional trees.[40] Overall, these activities are a central part of the renewed effort by cities to provide tourist attractions and increase their residents' quality of life. The case of Bogota, Colombia shows how considerable investment in tourism, including urban parks and beautification, helped not only alter the image of the city, but also made it more livable and inviting for its residents.

Urban Tourism Development in Bogota, Colombia

Government Web sites across the world warned visitors about the dangerous environments in the capital of the Latin American country of Colombia during the 1980s and 1990s. Plagued by violence and crime, which was fueled by drug cartels and included killings and kidnappings, Bogota developed a bad reputation. This condition negatively affected the city's ability to grow its economy and encourage foreign capital investment, including tourism.

In response, the city embraced an aggressive security policy and a robust public works program of infrastructural projects. Strong leadership by the local government helped slowly reverse this previous identity. Consequently, Bogota also benefitted from policies enacted by the federal government that embraced the importance of tourism, placing this sector at the center of the country's economic future.

The creation of a federal program in 2003 titled "Live Colombia, Travel Her" included tourist caravans inviting holiday travelers to use the highways once again. Protected by police, caravans departed from major cities, using once dangerous thoroughfares. Aimed at reclaiming public spaces, the number of travelers began to slowly increase. Within months of its implementation, the number of travelers increased by almost 90 percent. The government utilized 3,500 highway police and 22,500 support personnel to protect 6,200 miles of road.[41] Just a few years later, the progress was so profound that travel guides identified the country as one of the 10 top hotspots in the world. Bogota tourism industry officials continued to promote the city by introducing a highly successful campaign titled "Colombia is Passion." As many as 130 tour operators from across the globe were exposed to the message. According to recent tracking data, the number of international visitors to the country increased from 557,000 in 2000 to 925,000 in 2006.[42]

By reclaiming public spaces and focusing on civic life, a number of mayors during the 1990s and 2000s contributed significantly to remaking the capital. The mayoral leadership of Jaime Castro (1992–1994), Antanas Mockus (1995–1996 and 2001–2003), and Enrique Peñalosa (1998–2001) helped transform Bogota. The Mockus administration intensely focused on the creation of initiatives aimed at the promotion of tourism. The Enrique Peñalosa tenure spearheaded massive infrastructural investments. These included the planting of more than 100,000 trees and the creation of pedestrian zones, including more than 1,200 parks and 300 kilometers of bicycle paths and pedestrian streets. More than $100 million were expended on the greening efforts via tree plantings. By refurbishing parks, Peñalosa created the largest network of bikeways and the longest pedestrian street in the world. Removing motorists from sidewalks infused a new sense of urban identity. As people started to engage with their surroundings, crime decreased, opening up a plethora of recreational opportunities.[43]

In recent years, Bogota, sometimes referred to as the "Athens of South America," has been bustling with outdoor festivals, street performers, fairs, and exhibits that provide unique experiences for both visitors and locals. Within this emerging framework, the urban core is undergoing a cultural and touristic revival. La Candelaria, located in the city center, is an example of a historic tourist district that draws thousands of people each year. Attracted by the cobblestone streets and colonial period buildings that crowd the area, churches and clock towers, historic streetscapes and building facades, La Candelaria represents the cultural renaissance of Bogota. And while the precinct maintains a formal area with Plaza de Bolivar, the Palacio de Justicia,

Figure 4.7   Streetscape of colonial houses in La Candelaria, Bogota, Colombia, near downtown. The historic district is credited with the revitalization of this city and is a main tourist attraction. The presence of universities in the neighborhood has aided in the cultural revival of Bogota (Courtesy Gary Yim, Shutterstock Images).

the Palacio de Narino, the Alcaldia, the Lievano Palace, and many other architecturally significant structures, it also maintains a bohemian side. A cultural area, it is occupied by several universities, a library, and museums; students add diversity to the vicinity.

The future success of this colonial district will largely depend on the fragile security issues that are of paramount importance and continue to dominate the local and national government's agenda. For example, a bomb explosion in the early part of 2009 outside a Blockbuster store caused major damage, killing two people. These types of activities are likely to threaten future development of urban tourism in Bogota. The fragile and unpredictable nature of this situation can negatively impact the continued popularity of La Candelaria, which has made excellent strides in recent years. But the case of Bogota also reveals that a tourist campaign, plus local infrastructure investments can indeed improve the quality of life for local residents.

Conclusion

The ushering of urban tourism as an economic growth strategy required the addition of an infrastructure that could provide the needed attractions and accommodations. Private-public partnerships led the way with local governments stepping up in most cases to initiate and support the completion of the necessary facilities. As a result, entertainment districts, waterfront development, new and refurbished public spaces, museums, stadiums, convention centers and hotels sprung up in cities all across the world. Accompanied by investments in urban beautification and outdoor festivals and events, urban cores slowly became transformed into centers of leisure, often showcasing a multitude of destination spots.

The available infrastructure coupled with the intense marketing efforts and promotional practices exercised by municipal governments, corporations, and business leaders has lured thousands and in many cases millions of visitors to cities. Interestingly, the investments in creating the tourist city would slowly prove to have additional benefits. The newly introduced amenities would also be important for current and prospective residents. In fact, cities would aggressively use these attractions to entice the type of human capital that is capable of bringing about economic growth. This would be a young, college educated labor force that is entrepreneurial and capable of adding another unique and vibrant dimension to urban life. A strong connection is evident in the development of urban tourism and its effect on the culture of the city.

Writing, Reflection, and Debate

Discussion Questions

Identify a city near your place of residence that falls into one of the three types referenced above (resort, tourist-historic, or rebranded). How has that city reach that status? What investments have been made to achieve that position?

In the last twenty years, many cities across the country invested in the development of stadiums in or near downtown areas as a way to revitalize their urban cores. Identify a few cities that embraced this approach and reflect on its effectiveness. Are these public expenditures worth it or are they simply a form of corporate welfare?

Have you noticed investment in urban beatification in your community and is it more prevalent in areas where tourists and other visitors congregate?

5

URBAN TOURISM, AMENITIES, AND HUMAN CAPITAL

Visitor-oriented urban development and associated investment in the infrastructure of play transforms cities not only from the vantage point of visitors. Such development can also enhance the attractiveness of a city for its longstanding residents and serve as a magnet for newcomers intending to settle permanently. The overall physical character of a city, as well as its array of public spaces and neighborhoods, can attract businesses from out of town, increase private investment, and ultimately enhance the quality of the local workforce.[1] Urban tourism and desirable cultural amenities are also tightly linked. Whereas culture often played a secondary role in local industrial economies—as Charles Dickens noted more than a hundred years ago in *Hard Times,* his satire of early urban industrialization—in our globalized, postindustrial world, cultural production is often a mainstay of thriving local economies. Urban visitor development can fuel growth via the production of local amenities, transforming the city into what sociologist Terry Nichols Clark calls an "entertainment machine."[2]

The pursuit of tourism as an urban development strategy clearly affects local employment patterns. Specifically, job growth opportunities, as well as the mix of economic sectors and workforce attributes, are increasingly connected to consumption and lifestyle experiences.[3] Many analysts have highlighted the growth of low-paying, part-time, and otherwise marginal work in the visitor and "hospitality" sectors. However, restructured spatial landscapes and the widespread participation in leisure and entertainment activities can also attract an in-demand workforce with wide-ranging locational options. Regional economic expert Richard Florida has identified the relative presence of the "creative class," highly trained, self-motivated, entrepreneurially oriented professionals, as a primary determinant of a city's future economic trajectory. In Florida's view, urban centers that are able to attract and retain talented, well-educated workers will be positioned for success.[4] A 2009 study by the Pew Research Center identified Denver, Colorado as the most desirable metropolitan area in the United States.[5] This survey explored numerous respondent attitudes and preferences including the presence of cultural amenities. Denver's popular LoDo (Lower Downtown) neighborhood is one of the city's leading tourist magnets. Nevertheless, the recent transformation of LoDo has also enhanced Denver's store of human capital even as it has yielded an urban neighborhood prized by locals and visitors alike.

Neighborhood Development in LoDo

The LoDo district in Denver is an outstanding example of tourist-oriented development that has managed to preserve a sense of place and attract a new, youthful residential population. Because of its unique urban character, LoDo is one of the key attractions that make Denver a desirable place to live and work. As an old industrial district, the area has played a key role in the city's development. A combination of public support and private entrepreneurial investment spearheaded the area's revitalization. Several sports teams are also located in the district: construction of Coors Field in 1995 for $300 million, home of the Colorado Rockies (MLB), and of the Pepsi Center in 1999 for $160 million, home of the Colorado Avalanche (NHL), the Denver Nuggets (NBA), and numerous other minor league sports teams have also enlivened the district.

Denver's 1986 Downtown Area Plan called for the preservation of the existing, architecturally distinctive buildings in LoDo. The area had developed as a major manufacturing and warehousing center during the nineteenth century, but it experienced significant decline in the midtwentieth century. In the 1960s, the Latimer Square project brought about some retail establishments, but did not prove capable of sparking residential redevelopment. Urban renewal initiatives in the 1970s did not focus on LoDo, an act that helped the district survive the destructive nature of these programs.

By the 1980s, the architectural value of the various buildings was recognized, leading to the historic district designation in May 1988. Public expenditures in infrastructure and beautification improvements, along with dedicated funds for loans, slowly drew some early urban pioneers. The establishment of brewpubs and breweries helped the area develop a reputation as a recreational district. In fact, the 1996 Denver Downtown Area Plan update identified LoDo as an entertainment center. The area's aesthetic value lay in its muscular warehouses and loft buildings, properties that drove the ensuing

Figure 5.1   Rooftop dining at LoDo Bar & Grille near Coors Field in historic LoDo district in Denver, Colorado. The 26 block neighborhood in downtown Denver is filled with 90 sports bars, brewpubs and restaurants (Courtesy of the Denver Metro Convention & Visitors Bureau).

housing development in loft conversion. Retailers took advantage of the setting's potential by opening art galleries, hip clubs, restaurants, and bars. Younger professionals found this type of setting inviting—a trend that accelerated following the construction of Coors Field.[6]

According to one real estate professional, the success of the LoDo district's alluring atmosphere and its improved aesthetics attracted individuals possessing "creative eccentricity...a spark that makes them interesting."[7] However, the success of this mixed-use development is one of the greatest challenges currently facing the district. The large sporting crowds threaten the neighborhood's balance between the business and the residential sectors. Coors Field intentionally included 3,800 on-site parking spots, but the majority (46,000 spaces) are positioned away from the facility with about 18,000 within walking distance. This not only leads to considerable foot traffic, which is not appreciated by residents, but it also attracts more retailers, which can be an economic plus. So, it is an example of the uneasy balance that often exists in urban areas between different users of a particular neighborhood.

The historic district currently houses about 3,000 residents, organized through numerous community organizations such as the LoDo District, Inc. and the Lower Downtown Neighborhood Organization (LoDo NO). Both organizations are working to protect the neighborhood interests while promoting the area's continuous vitality. For example, the LoDo District, Inc. aims to maintain the integrity of the historic designation while marketing the local businesses to residents and visitors. One member of the standing subcommittee of the LoDo District, Inc. is the LoDo Young Professionals Committee. The group exists to provide residents between the ages of 22 and 35 with opportunities for civic engagement, mentoring, social interaction, and networking. The LoDo NO spearheaded a campaign that led to the creation of a children's playground and it also promotes public art.

The case of Lower Downtown in Denver reveals how preexisting infrastructure and a broader strategic plan composed of various initiatives can spur development. Conversions of former warehouse, microbreweries, stadiums, museums, and one of the largest performing arts centers in the nation has given LoDo a distinct identity that entices the creative class while advancing the city's economic tourism. The interplay between state and local governments with commercial interests and residents is largely responsible for this outcome.[8] Furthermore, the revitalization of this district is due to a unique residential base that is able to support the new entertainment and retail services and is part of a broader connection that exists between human capital and urban growth.

Human Capital and Urban Growth

When social scientists use the term *human capital*, what in fact do they have in mind? Some of our foundational social theorists, including Adam Smith and Karl Marx, addressed and disagreed about the meaning of this concept, but in recent decades a consensus has emerged regarding the importance of human-possessed knowledge and skills as key components of the complicated processes involved in producing economic value. A local or national population's mean level of educational attainment—years of formal schooling completed—often serves as a basic indicator of the accumulation of human capital.[9] Additional research also shows that economic growth can even positively influence a variety of social conditions. Specifically, increased educational levels in a given population result in lower rates of crime, greater participation in civic affairs and reduction of political corruption.[10]

A study by Christopher Wheeler of the Federal Reserve Bank of St. Louis addresses the question of how human capital is distributed across U.S. urban areas.[11] Wheeler's analysis of 1980, 1990, and 2000 Census data focuses on understanding the relationship between human capital (expressed via educational attainment) and urban growth. Wheeler examined more than 200 metropolitan areas and found that cities with larger populations experienced a greater rate of increase in human capital. Yet surprisingly, this did not necessarily translate into wage increases for the residents of these urban centers. Wheeler concluded that growth in levels of education also increases competition among workers, which tends to hold down earnings growth. In individual cases, increasing one's store of human capital might actually depress earnings.[12]

One might expect that such human capital/wage impact relationships would discourage better educated people from moving to urban centers, but in fact, this appears not to be the case. For instance, individuals seek to enhance their human capital by interacting with others who possess specialized knowledge, advanced training, or in-demand skills. Due to the dense institutional environment of cities, the transmission of these human capital attributes is greatly amplified. As such, the local availability of a greater diversity of specialized human skills helps communities grow via the attraction of young people searching for human capital-enhancing interaction opportunities. Learning thus becomes a central driving force of urbanization and a primary determinant of human capital as well as other markers of economic well-being. Educated workers desire to reside within settings that promote and support learning experiences.[13] Cities with significant population growth typically attract disproportionate numbers of younger persons.[14] Data from the 2000 Census reveals a clear relationship between a city's prosperity and its attractiveness to college graduates.[15] Additionally, research shows that highly educated married couples are drawn to urban centers due to the concentration of educational institutions.[16] Not surprisingly then, during the 1990s cities with strong human capital attributes grew faster than cities lacking a broad base of persons possessing specialized skills or advanced training.[17] Furthermore, a number of analyses reveal that this is a historically consistent pattern that can be traced back as far as the 1940 Census.[18] These findings have substantial public policy implications. The correlation between human capital and metropolitan productivity means that cities must seek ways to attract the college educated.

While level of educational attainment is the characteristic indicator that social scientists have used to measure metropolitan areas' relative concentrations of human capital, recent scholarship has begun to specify a new form of human capital, which is expressed by the concept of "creative capital." In the view of researchers such as Richard Florida, cities whose population includes large numbers of technology workers, skilled professionals in fields such as finance, marketing, and the media, and visual/performance artists are likely to exhibit especially dynamic local economies.[19]

Creative Capital and Urban Growth

Although Richard Florida coined the term *creative class* in just the last decade, there has been an extended debate among scholars seeking to understand the relationships between leisure pursuits, the broader cultural attributes of contemporary society, and the capitalist economic system. Sociologist Daniel Bell's *Cultural Contradictions of Capitalism,* published in 1979, is a critical link in this debate. He derived his argument from the insights of the influential early twentieth century German sociologist, Max Weber. Bell claimed that the bourgeois self-discipline Weber had concluded was intrinsic to capitalist society and its expansion, with rising levels of prosperity, gave way to an ethos of pleasure-seeking, self-absorption, and intemperance. According to Bell, by the middle of the twentieth century, delayed gratification had been overtaken by self-centered, immediate actualization.

This reconstituted culture has produced numerous challenges for the society and economic order that has been its source. According to Bell: "On the one hand, the business corporation wants an individual to work hard, pursue a career, accept delayed gratification to be, in a crude sense, an organization man. And yet, on the other hand, in its products and its advertisements, the corporation promotes pleasure, instant joy, relaxing and letting go."[20] In effect, Bell argued that contemporary capitalism was producing a compulsive consumer culture that, in the long run, would be its undoing. A new social order of narcissistic bohemians was emerging, which shared two largely destructive personality flaws: (1) an overemphasis on "self," and related to that (2) an obsession with "lifestyle."

More recently, journalist David Brooks—focusing on the corporate upper middle class—has offered a sunnier interpretation of the relationship between capitalism and the social world it has produced. Brooks's subjects are the "bobos,"[21] which in his "comic sociology" refers to bourgeois bohemians:

These are the people who are thriving in the information age. They're the people, you go into their homes and they've got these renovated kitchens that are the size of aircraft hangars, with plumbing. You know, you see the big sub-zero refrigerators and you open the door and you think, they could stick an in-law suite in the side. So these are the people who are really making a lot of money.... It used to be easy to tell a bourgeois from a bohemian. And the bourgeois were the straight-laced suburban types, went to church, worked in corporations. And the bohemians were the arty free spirits, the rebels. But if you look at upscale culture, at the upper middle classes, the people in Silicon Valley, you find they've smashed all the categories together. Some people seem half yuppie-bourgeois and half hippie-bohemian. And so if you take bourgeois and bohemian and you smash them together, you get the ugly phrase "bobo."[22]

Brooks further proposes that bobos exercise enormous influence on all aspects of American economic affairs. In contrast to Bell's concern that a culture emphasizing individual fulfillment corrodes the rationally inflected self-denial he equated with capitalist productivity, Brooks finds little or no contradiction between an ethos of hard work joined to ostentatious personal consumption or an open-ended quest for self-realization.

Brooks's bobos seek out foreign-made cars, designer home furnishings, and clothing from high-end retailers Banana Republic and Anthropologie. They purchase organic produce and meats to prepare in their spacious, state-of-the-art kitchens. They spend $4 for a Starbucks chai and simultaneously advocate virtuous spending. They are a countercultural plutocracy committed to authenticity, comfort, and simplicity. They oppose confrontation and extremism, value moderation, believe in meritocracy, and seek community and intimate authority through decentralized power structures. At the same time they are professionally embedded in the impersonality of the corporate world.

Richard Florida's creative class shares much with Brooks's bobos, but in Florida's influential reinterpretation of urban development precepts, the leisure preferences, workplace culture, and ultimately the local "value added" produced by the creative class drives contemporary urban growth. According to Florida, the rapidly evolving contemporary economy necessitates a workforce that has mastered the newest information technology tools, can adapt to an ever-shifting menu of new projects, and pursues self-fulfillment both at and away from the workplace. From the standpoint of local or even national economies, the production and dissemination of new ideas, products, and technologies within a matrix of rapidly evolving economic sectors is crucial to the generation of wealth and the maintenance of "home" economy competitiveness.

The local availability of high paying jobs is but one lure for the creative class. Florida argues that, in addition, a tolerant and diverse local cultural environment is central to enticing these educated, highly motivated, and inventive workers. In his research, he has developed a number of indicators to capture the relative standing of U.S. cities and metropolitan areas. These run from the relatively intuitive to a number that depart substantially from conventional thinking about "local business climate": wage inequality, presence of high tech sectors, diversity, social tolerance, and innovation. Florida's creativity index rankings for regions with more than 1 million residents included San Francisco, Austin, San Diego, Boston, and Seattle (top five) and Memphis, Norfolk, VA, Las Vegas, Buffalo, and Louisville (bottom five). These cities also ranked similarly in other categories including percent of creative workers.

Florida argues that traditional approaches to local economic development must be altered in the face of the emergent information economy, dominated as it is by members of the creative class. Cities must begin to invest in the "lifestyle amenities that people really want and use often...investments in amenities like urban parks, for example, last for generations. Other amenities like—bike lanes or off-road trails for running, cycling, rollerblading or just walking your dog—benefit a wide swath of the population." [23] Florida's linking of urban growth to attraction of the creative class has generated considerable criticism. More than one commentator has pointed to cities such as Las Vegas, which during the 1990s experienced phenomenal growth even as its local economy generated limited "new economy" employment and attracted only small numbers of creative class workers. One study examined economic indicators for 276 metropolitan statistical areas to test Florida's theory as well as the human and social capital models of economic growth. The authors concluded that the relative presence or absence of the creative class is not related to growth and warned about using this strategy to generate urban economic development.[24] Another study similarly concluded that the impact of the creativity variables is weaker than the impact of more conventional factors such industry mix and educational attainment.[25] Some even argued that his argument is irrational.[26] Florida's contention that high technology and population growth can be related to higher percentages of locally residing gays and bobos has, in particular, generated great skepticism.

Nevertheless, Florida's theory has been supported by other social scientists. For instance, a multifactor analysis by sociologist Robert Cushing found the creative capital theory most applicable in explaining rapid growth and consistently high economic performance in Austin, Texas.[27] Irrespective of the controversy generated by Richard Florida's revisionist view of local economic growth, these days few if any local development officials reject the proposition that there is a creative class and that, as a rule, a prosperous city will be the place of residence of a disproportionate share of this occupational group.

Culture, Amenities, and Urban Development

A national survey by the Pew Research Center asked respondents to identify the metropolitan area where they would most like to live. Denver, San Diego, and Seattle ranked at the top of the list of 30 cities. Detroit, Cleveland, and Cincinnati were chosen as the least desirable (see Table 5.1). While this analysis was conducted a few years following the release of Richard Florida's creative class index, it is interesting to note that only San Diego and Seattle make his top-10 listing. Although when considering age, it is important to note that five of the top 10 cities for 18- to 34-year-olds in the Pew Report can be also found in the creative index: San Diego, Seattle, San Francisco, New York, and Washington, DC.[28]

The respondents identified the importance of amenities, a concept that can be defined in various ways. For example, one interpreta-

Table 5.1   America's Most Popular Big Cities, 2009 (Percent Who Say They Want to Live in this City or its Surrounding Metropolitan Areas)

Denver	43
San Diego	40
Seattle	38
Orlando	34
Tampa	34
San Francisco	34
Phoenix	33
Portland	31
Sacramento	29
San Antonio	29
Boston	28
Miami	28
Atlanta	26
Washington, DC	25
New York	24
Dallas	24
Philadelphia	24
Chicago	24
Houston	23
Las Vegas	23
Riverside	23
Los Angeles	21
Baltimore	20
St. Louis	18
Pittsburgh	17
Minneapolis	16
Kansas City	15
Cincinnati	13
Cleveland	10
Detroit	8

Source: Pew Research Center Social and Demographic Trends.

tion explains that "amenity" can mean many things, including good weather, a shoreline, ethnic diversity (or its absence), options for dining and entertainment, cultural offerings, and aesthetically beautiful architecture.[29] Another notes that, "a pure amenity is a nonproduced public good such as weather quality that has no explicit price. In practice, previous empirical studies include some government services such as education and public safety."[30] These definitions consistently place amenities in the realm of public services, presupposing the creation of resources from intangible goods.

The connection between culture, amenities, and urban development is continuing to receive extensive attention, especially from local officials who view these factors as playing a key role in the revitalization of their cities across the country. For example, in addition to smaller cities in the South such as Fort Lauderdale, Key West, and Palm Beach, large cities also market their services to gay and lesbian tourists. The Greater Philadelphia Tourism Marketing Corporation organized a $250,000 promotional campaign and published "The City of Brotherly Love (and Sisterly Affection)," a guide specifically targeted to gay and lesbian visitors. In the 1990s, Chicago identified a north side neighborhood as a "gay business district," calling it Boystown. Rainbow-colored signs and pedestrian improvements at a cost of $3.2 million help define the area's identity. The City of Cleveland formally recognized this community by raising a rainbow flag at City Hall and appointing the first ever openly gay member of the Community Relations Board. Similarly, St. Louis, Washington, DC, and Salt Lake City have attempted to address various community issues by formally reaching out to gay and lesbian residents.[31]

Urban areas' pursuit of diversity and amenities slowly reversed the smokestack chasing of a previous era. Earlier initiatives centered on urban competition for private firms and goods.[32] This newer strategy is viewed as being more economical for taxpayers than past approaches. Sociologist Terry Nichols Clark argues for the need to look beyond the traditional approaches to urban research, since these largely kept the city's economy and culture separate. Cultural activities are keys not only to developing urban identity, but also to jumpstarting plans for economic expansion. Clark and his colleagues place this trend, evident in the postindustrial economy, within the rise of a new political culture. The emphasis on consumption is a central tenet of the new political culture, an approach that also focuses attention on the role of individuals, support for culture and amenities, and the advancement of public goods within a managed growth framework.[33]

Tying urban change to amenities and human capital as a response to globalization and consumerism is a key contribution offered by Clark in his view of "the city as an entertainment machine."[34] An analysis of the impact of natural amenities and constructed amenities in 3,000 counties, between 1980 and 2000, supports his argument that urban amenities drive urban growth. Constructed amenities may include libraries, museums, cafes, Starbucks, and Whole Foods. This research also reveals that population growth, education attainment, and the number of constructed amenities are all positively related.[35]

However, the connection between amenities and urban growth as well as consumption and location decisions are more complicated than initially perceived. Skilled workers, when congregating in a specific location, are capable of infusing two unique, transformative qualities: social tolerance and bohemianism. Even though these two factors can contribute to a climate that favors growth, causality issues are likely. According to one analysis, "high incomes, after all, are not usually exogenously determined, which suggests that the young and well-educated need first to live somewhere where they will be well-paid and only second can pursue their consumer tastes."[36] Econometric research findings also point out this complication. These caution that "a preliminary investigation of several direct measures of quality of life indicates that the effect of college graduates may operate through 'consumer city' amenities such as bars and restaurants, rather than from more politically mediated area attributes such as crime, schools, and pollution."[37]

Often, cities attempt to improve the quality of life of their residents by pursuing macro- oriented policies, which are expected to contribute to the creation of urban amenities through the advancement of culture. An example of this can be seen in the European Capital of Culture competition. Glasgow, Scotland was one of the first cities to receive the designation and use it to alter its historically strong industrial identity. As a result of the distinction, the city invested considerable resources in the development of an infrastructure that has since contributed to its reimaging process. Ironically, the benefits of this strategy proved mixed, even though Glasgow is referred to as the model that candidate cities would need to replicate.[38]

Glasgow, Scotland and the 1990 European Capital of Culture Designation

The competition for the European City of Culture designation and the case of Glasgow, Scotland offers an opportunity to view the injection of elements of cultural amenities. Numerous cities vie for this recognition, and while the award is made annually by the European Commission, the organization does not provide any subsidy to the winner. In recent years, as many as 50 cities from Britain alone have considered bidding for the accolade. Many city councils view this as an opportunity to infuse civic prestige and alter the image of their community for both residents and potential recreational and business visitors.

Glasgow served as a model for this transformation, primarily because that accolade was conferred at a turning point in the competition. Up until that time, cities like Athens, Paris, and Florence held the designation. All of them had a long cultural history to be celebrated. However, the identification of Glasgow signaled a new direction. When the city was awarded the 1990 cultural distinction, it managed to use the opportunity to recraft its previous identity, which until that time revolved around heavy manufacturing. By the 1970s and 1980s Glasgow had become synonymous with deindustrialization. The "city of culture" honor could infuse a new image centered on art and fashion. On the economic front, the success was extraordinary. A bid official for the city of Newcastle, UK said: "[Glasgow's] tourism numbers increased by 81 percent in one year, and its conference business increased by 45 percent."[39]

Glasgow's city center experienced a considerable property boom. The area saw more than £1 billion (about $1.5 billion) particularly in cultural infrastructure in preparation for the 1990 events.[40] Many

Figure 5.2   The Clyde Auditorium, known as "The Armadillo", is a concert hall on the bank of the River Clyde in Glasgow, Scotland. The iconic structure is a central part of the city's new strategy to reimage itself along cultural and entertainment lines. The facility is also part of a second, $1 billion redevelopment effort to include an exhibition, conference and arena complex (Courtesy Iain McGillivray, Shutterstock Images).

buildings were converted into theaters and concert halls. New art galleries, museums, and exhibit venues sprouted up across the city. The planning strategy also included modern art as a central theme for the event, an apt signifier and a fitting departure from the industrial era.

Following the celebration, Glasgow struggled to maintain its facilities and continue to fund the cultural programs introduced during the European capital of culture year. For example, the Scottish Opera in Glasgow barely avoided bankruptcy in 2000 and the McLellan Galleries, which reopened in 1990 after a £3 million (about $4.5 million) restoration, survived a near closure caused by limited funds. Luckily, the boom of institutionally supported cultural activities during the award year led to the founding of numerous cultural organizations, many of them by the private sector. This helped give Glasgow a long-lasting identity as a city of culture.

The findings of a qualitative longitudinal study regarding Glasgow's identity from 1986 to 2003 reveal that the 1990 European City of Culture designation proved to have limited economic and physical impact. Job creation was evident because it was imperative to meet the needs of the tourists during the award year. Unfortunately, the employment opportunities were low paying and not sustainable. The real effect can be found on the cultural front, specifically surrounding the city's image. The study concluded that "if the core objective is attracting tourism rather than enhancing the city's artistic and cultural life, hosting the Capital of Culture could be easily replaced by large business conventions, global sport competitions or any major corporate event, without mattering whether these events are sensitive or not to the character and cultural roots of their local hosts."[41]

The 1990 European Capital of Culture distinction helped Glasgow host numerous exhibitions over the years and paved the way for additional awards, including the UK City of Architecture in 1999, the National City of Sport from 1995 to 1999, and the European Capital of Sport in 2003. The British national media also celebrated the city as a center for the creative industries. According to a story in *The Daily Telegraph*:

> Glasgow's gradual ascent from the economic doldrums after becoming Europe's Capital of Culture in 1990 helped the city to reposition itself as a centre for creative industries, in much the same way as Gateshead, another former shipbuilding giant faced with reversing its post-industrial decline, has done with the Baltic art gallery and Sage music centre. Scottish Enterprise estimates that creative enterprises, with Glasgow as their hub, are now worth £5.3 billion to Scotland's economy.... Like Berlin, whose low rents and stubbornly bohemian outlook also attract artists and musicians from all over the world, the city has a relaxed, out-of-the-way feel, but it is not in any sense provincial.[42]

Civic Tourism and the Creative Economy and Class

So, does the promotion of urban tourism help advance the creative economy? Cities endeavor to construct an infrastructure to encourage visitors, expand their economy, and grow their tax base. In the process, these actions also contribute to producing the needed elements necessary to attract the creative class. A new museum or a new entertainment district increases the urban amenities. Enticing a professional sports team by supporting the construction of a new stadium can position the city in a favorable national light. Similarly, waterfront mix-use development and the promotion of ethnic restaurants and districts not only have the ability to increase tourism, but can also serve as a magnet for professionals who find these amenities central to their lifestyle.

Connecting economic development to quality of life, however, is a complex proposition. In recent years, the organization and maintenance of tourist bubbles has emerged as a typical strategy that can be found in many cities across the country. Notably, these should not be automatically considered a feature that can attract young professionals. In fact, the lack of authenticity and the establishment of "Disneyfied" spaces can prove to have a reverse effect.

Officials in Cincinnati, Ohio embraced the concept of the creative class and endeavored to upgrade the downtown area by investing $1.3 million on a bike path between the downtown area and the Cincinnati airport. In addition, they allocated $2.2 million for arts groups that are expected to assist in the formation of a bohemian and street culture. Cincinnati Tomorrow, a city-backed organization, embraced the concept of the creative class and opposed local black churches because the latter groups spearheaded legislation that would make the city less gay-friendly. All of these municipal efforts were aimed at recasting Cincinnati's image following the destructive race riots of 2001.[43]

Considerable resources, exceeding $3 billion, were invested in remaking the city's riverfront areas on both the Ohio and Kentucky shores. These huge public investments included new stadiums, a new convention center, entertainment areas, as well as new museums and parks. A central goal of this strategy was to attract tourist spending dollars.[44] It is unclear though how these structured environments helped Cincinnati's quest to lure the creative class.

Civic tourism is another strategy embraced by urban mayors who aim to attract the creative class. City Mayors is an international organization composed of professionals who work together to address challenges, share experiences and information, and seek innovative and sustainable strategies to deal with urban problems. The group identified cultural and civic tourism as an opportunity to preserve and enhance urban identity. Civic tourism conceptually focuses on the community and endeavors to protect and improve the residents' quality of life. According to this approach, economic development is just one aspect of the tourism industry. Protecting historic neighborhoods, enhancing local cultures, and upgrading the social and physical aspects of the urban setting are all key aspects of this outlook. Instead of viewing tourism as having a negative impact on the local environment, a rethinking of its role and standing can transform the industry into a tool for community advancement. In fact, this can be an opportunity for public participation and engagement. According to one observer:

> Civic tourism urges your community, beginning with the caretakers of place, to help change the way the public sees tourism: as a *means* and not an end.... It's one thing to talk about tourism as a "means" or "tool," but acting on that talk is a huge and difficult frame flip, and it's not a mission statement you'll find embossed on the letterhead of too many travel and tourism bureaus. Your state office of tourism, for example, is a research and marketing agency, and probably a good one, but it's definitely focused on economic ends and place-making is not its job. But it's yours if you want it, and especially at the local level tourism gives citizens a tool, when held in their hands, to build the kind of place where they want to live, work, and raise a family. Ultimately, a "civic" approach can embolden sense of place, the local economy, *and* tourism's social ties and political standing, a not unwelcome change for an industry that's usually talked about, if at all, as a necessary evil among residents or the Rodney Dangerfield of economic development among planners and politicians.[45]

Mainstream tourism operation practices often contribute to fragmentation. Tourism service providers, public agencies, museums, historical societies, and other stakeholders engage separately and rarely collaborate. As an alternative model, civic tourism calls for the integration of existing resources to build capacity. By utilizing this strength, it aims to address issues of community sustainability, including quality of life considerations.

Interestingly, Carol Coletta provides a related perspective in a 2008 report titled *Fostering the Creative City*. The document is part of the efforts of another organization, CEOs for Cities, and explores how philanthropy can advance arts participation and the cultivation of creative cities. By integrating the philanthropic community, it is expected that communities can go beyond the professionally managed tourist and convention business bureaus. Since the arts have a strong economic impact component, their promotions can induce cultural spending. For this reason, Boston, Providence, and Chicago house culture, tourism, and the arts in the same City Hall department.

Arts districts are also viewed as capable of revitalizing neighborhoods, increasing property values, and stimulating urban development. This strategy can also infuse a climate of progressivism, increased tolerance, inclusiveness, and diversity. Furthermore, beyond money and infrastructure, the traditional drivers in the arts, cultivating the creative industries, can help attract knowledgeable workers who have the necessary skills and talents to jumpstart innovative industries and induce competitiveness.[46] The City of Toronto embraced a creative perspective (see Table 5.2) as part of its efforts to become a first-tier, world-class creative city.

In the United States, Portland, Oregon is viewed as a city that managed to successfully create a culture of creativity. In this Pacific Northwest city, creativity is celebrated as an integral part of economic development, urban design, and tourism. Culturally rich districts evolved to include artist studios, restaurants, performance spaces, and festivals. The coexistence of these urban functions not only provides unique urban living environments, but also attracts visitors. For example, the Pearl District is a popular destination in Northwest Portland. Formerly an industrial section, the area has been transformed into a lively community with a variety of dining establishments, art and framing galleries, creative services, spas, and antique shops and a diversity of retailers. More than 60 furniture stores are housed here, making the Pearl District a major urban tourist destination.

On the other hand, civic tourism does not view restructuring of urban space as being primarily to attract tourists. Rather, from this perspective, tourists are expected to participate and contribute to the

Table 5.2   Developing the Values of the Creative City (Utilitarian vs. Creative Perspective)

UTILITARIAN PERSPECTIVE	CREATIVE PERSPECTIVE
Stretch tax dollars	Make beauty necessary and necessity beautiful
Cost	Benefit
Function	Form in dissociable from function
Generic and predictable	Original and unique
Uses	Outcomes
Homogeneous	Heterogeneous
Ensured Security	Planned Risk
Simplicity	Complexity
Cohesion of similarity	Celebration of Diversity
Efficiency of space	Quality of place
Cost of construction	Returns over lifecycle
Formulaic	Artistic
Delivering on expectations	Novelty of experience
Reducing cost	Adding value
Same as the other place	Unique to this place
Fulfill purpose and minimize maintenance	Enhance economic, social, environmental and cultural capital
Immediate results	Long-term change
Repetition	Innovation
Rigid systems	Ecology
Convenience	Experience
Organization	Culture
Growth	Development
Separation	Integration
Consumption	Condition
Build	Design

Source: City of Toronto.

enhancement of place. The preservation of cultures, support of citizenship, protection of the environment, and upgrading the quality of life are alternative ways to think about the development of urban tourism. In the conventional, mostly boosterish approach, these goals are often secondary to the quest for profit. However, the pursuit of this approach coupled with the making of the creative city is a com-

Figure 5.3   Pearl District market, Portland, Oregon (Courtesy Larry Bennett).

plicated proposition. The city of Brisbane, Australia embraced these planning ideas. The case below identifies some of the issues that relate to the implementation process.

Brisbane, Australia—The Creative City?

The popularity of the creative cities concept among planners and policymakers reached international levels with urban policymakers attempting to identify elements that could give them the competitive edge in a global economy. Australian cities embraced this notion and directly or indirectly worked to advance related policies. City governments in Brisbane, Melbourne, Sydney, Adelaide, and Hobart promoted economic development ideas that were connected to creativity. The degree of engagement among these cities varied, but all of them instituted similar procedures, with Melbourne and Adelaide going further by introducing specific plans. Actually, among all these state capitals, it would be only Brisbane in Queensland that pursued a formal creative cities strategy.[47]

In 2003, the Brisbane City Council released a report titled *Creative City: Brisbane City Council's Cultural Strategy 2003–2008*. The document outlines the city's commitment in this area dating back to 1997 when the Council adopted the cultural statement *Creative Brisbane*. The outcome of this earlier effort included completion of major infrastructural projects such as the Brisbane Powerhouse, a performing arts center, and the Queen Street Mall, a highly successful pedestrian mall. The latter is the city's premier shopping and entertainment hub and attracts more than 25 million visitors annually. Developing Brisbane into a cultural capital, ensuring access and equity, and investing in culture are some of the core principles listed in the 2003 *Creative City* endeavor.

While this initiative communicates support for the development of various cultural industries such as filmmaking, public art, and digital artwork, it also recognizes the importance of tourism in achieving its goals. According to the report, linking Brisbane as a center for creative activity of local artists with continuous outdoor festivals and events helps maintain the city as a national and international tourist destination. Furthermore, by creating the Brisbane City Marketing scheme, the Council brought together a number of agencies that are now part of a coordinated effort and responsible for the new "Brisbane—It's happening" brand. This initiative is expected to advance tourism and lead to key partnerships. On the policy development front, the report called for the making of a creative city map. The goal of this long-term project will be the "mapping and promotion of Brisbane's cultural tourism sites including interesting locations which often remain hidden."[48]

The creative city strategy also endeavors to aid the success of existing cultural and entertainment precincts that are central to the growth of urban tourism. The Queensland Gallery of Modern Art, the Queensland Museum, and the Queensland Performing Arts Centre all are part of the cultural district. The South Bank Parklands and Portside Wharf are entertainment districts that offer access to a variety of restaurants, shops, cafes, and cinemas. Portside Wharf, redeveloped in 2006 for $750 million, showcases waterfront residential living opportunities.

Many of these and other attractions are connected to the creative strategy. A review of the 2008 Official Brisbane Visitor's Guide reveals an abundance of references to all things "creative." The promotional publication includes the following phrases: "creative confidence,"

Figure 5.4   Brisbane Roma Street Parklands, Brisbane, Australia. In 1999, the Queensland government integrated a former rail yard with an existing park to form destination parkland in this self proclaimed "creative city." The new attraction opened to the public in 2001 (Courtesy Holger Mette, Shutterstock Images).

"creative adventures," "creative hands-on place," "creative industries," "a hub for everything creative," "creative menu," "creative crowd," "creative dining," and "creative twist." This commitment raises questions about the meaning and value of this approach. Specifically, is there a creative strategy in Brisbane? What does this strategy entail?

A study on the consequences of the pursuit of the creativity strategies in Australian cities concludes that the concerted effort in Brisbane proved limited and can be even characterized as superficial since it was part of a political process that had ulterior motives. Specifically:

What is particularly interesting about Brisbane's *Creative City* strategy, however, is that the political process has appeared to have stripped it of much of its initial promise and depth...the report lists what is being done and what could be done in each area. As one local government official noted during an interview, these areas became more of a "wish list" of projects than a strategic framework or plan.... In discussions with Brisbane City Council officials, we discovered that when the strategy was being written, the then Mayor had been very supportive...and the final Creative Cities document was released as part of an electoral campaign. With a change of Mayor, the focus on creative cities ideas dissipated. The fact that it was a "wish-list" and not a policy framework appeared to make it easier to ignore, and provided an example of how political processes might erode the promise of some of the deeper elements of any creative cities prescriptions.[49]

At one level, we could surmise that this rhetoric is part of a marketing campaign to help differentiate Brisbane from its competitors, aiding its efforts in building a stronger tourist economy. Visiting a self-proclaimed creative city is in and of itself an attraction. At another level, the policies emanating from this strategy could also have social implications. Specifically, many city projects can be pursued regardless of their intent, camouflaged under the creative cities strategy.

The pursuit of urban tourism as an economic development strategy proved to coincide, in fact complement the efforts by cities to grow their population and further their financial fortunes. The creation of amenities to attract visitors not only altered the physical landscape by constructing new destinations and reconstituted spaces, but it also meant that the culture of the city would undergo significant changes.

For example, public and private investments produced traditional tourist attractions from shopping and dining outlets to sporting events and museums. However, cities also offer unique neighborhoods and distinct settings, steeped in rich history, architecture, and ethnic and racial diversity. These locations received the consideration of local officials and tourism boards, which endeavored to showcase them as tourist sites in visitor guides and promotional materials. This renewed attention and the significant upgrading of the general amenities present in the city also proved enticing to young professionals, attracted by the edginess of urban living reformatted to meet their expensive tastes.

Illustrated in the next chapter, this type of human capital, the creative class, would prove to have a considerable impact, changing the nature of urban cores. Residential development in new construction and converted lofts helped revitalize not only large, but also smaller cities that also saw significant increases in their downtown population. These interrelated forces of urban tourism and downtown residential regeneration would prove vital to their new, reenergized status.

Writing, Reflection, and Debate

Discussion Questions

Social scientists have recently focused on the importance of amenities, linking them to urban growth. Can you identify some cities where this relationship holds true? What type of growth resulted from these investments?

Reflect on the relationship between the creative class and tourism development. Are the two concepts interconnected? If cities aim to attract the creative class does that cause tourism development? Conversely, do efforts to increase tourism invite the creative class?

6

Residential Development and the New Face of Downtowns

Many cities that have emphasized tourism as an economic development strategy have, in turn, begun to experience substantial increases in their downtown residential populations. The transformation of central business districts to "downtown neighborhoods" has occurred in both major metropolitan centers such as San Diego and smaller regional hubs such as Greenville, South Carolina. These new neighborhoods have been carved out of existing commercial and industrial properties via "loft conversion" and built anew by residential developers who once concentrated on suburban tract home development. Concerns over gentrification have emerged as incumbent residents of transient hotels and remnant, working-class enclaves have been pushed out by more prosperous newcomers who are drawn to these areas and their improved amenities. Often, critics of the residential upgrading of downtowns note the absence of affordable housing in local redevelopment plans.

Tourist attraction coupled with upscale residential development is not guaranteed to turn around ailing downtowns. In some cities, the scarring effects of deindustrialization have produced barren cityscapes not easily "rebranded" via investment in sports/entertainment attractions, streetscape improvements, or the hosting of downtown festivals and outdoor markets. Detroit, Michigan, for example, has worked mightily to reimage its downtown core, but in the face of city-wide population loss, the flight of downtown employers and retailers, and much core area property deterioration, attracting a permanent residential population has been very difficult.

Promoting tourism and downtown residential development typically necessitates the involvement of multiple public agencies and private groups. Because of the municipal government's perceived role as the catalyst for local regeneration, the office of the mayor often plays a crucial coordinating role. Other city agencies such as the planning department or—if it is publicly funded—the visitors' bureau routinely coordinate their work with organizations that represent the accommodations industry, tour operators, and other local merchants. The special events and amenities so produced can serve as a lever to induce investments by private residential developers.

The promotion of the downtown as an exciting place to live and play is, in many cases, the designated responsibility of nongovernment promotional groups. Formed as public–private partnerships or alliances, such organizations typically emphasize downtown "place-marketing." In Tucson, Arizona, for example, the Downtown Tucson Partnership promotes the central city as an up-and-coming, 24-hour, 7-day-a-week community. By disseminating information about cultural activities, upcoming events, existing and new residential developments, local arts, history, and architecture information, as well as dining and shopping options, the Downtown Tucson Partnership serves as both a development resource and agent of social change. The Partnership also "makes the case" to prospective investors by advertising unique opportunities for purchase and lease of housing, retail, office, and studio space. Staffed by a CEO, a VP for Community Development, a Downtown Planner, and a small support staff, the group has a diverse board of directors. These include local merchants, representatives of arts organizations, commercial property owners and managers, educational institutions, Pima County, the Tucson Regional Development Office, and even downtown residents.

The residential growth of central Tucson has been facilitated by the downtown's array of culture and entertainment opportunities, the same attractions marketed to visitors. The city's historic commercial core is dotted with loft residential developments, condominiums, apartments, and even newly built single-family homes. Additional construction is anticipated in the Congress Street District. As described in a Partnership publication: "Residents will be able to walk to enjoy professional theater, live music, sidewalk dining, concerts at the Tucson Convention Center, exhibitions at the Tucson Museum of Art, as well as shopping and special events." The case of San Diego, California below offers some interesting insights into how a large city turned to the pursuit of tourism as a strategy to advance residential development in the downtown area. Support for a new convention center and a stadium for a professional team proved to aid the creation of new neighborhoods.

Urban Tourism and the Revival of Neighborhoods in San Diego, California

Even as San Diego thrived following World War II, its downtown area suffered. The increasing numbers of abandoned structures in the core caused declines in property values, and suburban residential development pulled major retailers toward the outskirts of the city and beyond. Between 1950 and 1957, San Diego's population grew 47.8 percent, but the number of downtown residents declined by nearly 10 percent. During the same years, retail sales across the city increased by 76 percent. Downtown, retail sales actually declined.[1]

San Diego missed an opportunity to grow its port like Los Angeles and Long Beach had done during the 1940s and 1950s, but the city managed to maintain itself as a significant economic hub for the shipping industry. It slowly became clear to local officials that a new direction was essential. According to one observer, all the way back in the 1960s, port director Don Nay "saw the future of the port not in cargo and maritime operations but in recreation and tourism through the development of new marinas, yacht repair yards, waterfront hotels, restaurants, and other tourist attractions."[2]

The active redevelopment of San Diego's downtown dates back to the early part of the 1970s when Mayor Pete Wilson committed to the revitalization of a 15-block area as an urban mall and festival market-place. The Horton Plaza, a five-level outdoor shopping mall opened in 1985 for $140 million. Once a transit center, this spot was decaying, attracting homeless people, and was becoming synonymous with the city's standing. Other downtown waterfront infrastructural developments included Seaport Village, which opened in 1980. With 14 acres

Figure 6.1   A view of San Diego's Gaslamp section including Petco Park, Harbor Drive and the trolley (Courtesy Christpher Penler, Shutterstock Images).

of shopping, dining, and entertainment, the complex provides walking access to the San Diego Bay via a boardwalk. The nearby San Diego Convention Center opened in 1989 and underwent significant expansion in 2001. Adjacent hotels include the Hyatt Hotel Towers, Marriot Hotel Towers, and the Hilton Hotel—all of which support the activities of the convention center and serve more than 600,000 visiting delegates annually.

In close proximity is Petco Park, home to the San Diego Padres of the MLB. At a cost of more than $450 million, the construction of this facility proved to be part of a comprehensive strategy to help further revitalize the downtown area. The majority of the funding for this project came from the city. Developed in the East Village area, the ballpark is located close to the Gaslamp Quarter. The restoration of nineteenth century buildings and additional preservation and beautification efforts started during the 1980s in the historic district, and today this area is considered San Diego's premier entertainment hub and a symbol of the city's new urban identity. Since then extensive housing and loft conversions have taken place, with an influx of new residents.

Nearby, the efforts to furnish the Padres with a new baseball home included ancillary plans in the form of retail and residential development, resulting in the creation of the Ballpark District. Like other waterfront investments, this area is refashioning the downtown area along with the tourism industry. The municipal government was an active agent in this process, and went beyond its traditional role to become entrepreneurial. Its aggressive stance not only aided the private sector (the baseball team), but also controlled the redevelopment of the surrounding area by providing considerable initial infrastructure. According to one scholar, the public sector then became a "land speculator, market analyst, and a deal broker"—a behavior that can be characterized as an example of "municipal capitalism."[3]

Since that time, the Ballpark District has been the recipient of more than $3 billion in private residential, hotel, office, and retail investment. The Omni San Diego Hotel and the Metropolitan Condominiums helped add to Ballpark Village, a new San Diego neighborhood. More mix-use development is expected to add $1.5 billion of additional construction activity in downtown. From these trends, Central San Diego saw its population grow from 155,827 in 2000 to 175,240 in 2008, and witnessed a 17 percent increase in the total number of housing units during the same period. Also, demographic data indicate a changing median household income of the residents, which increased by 15.3 percent (adjusted for inflation). This raises public policy questions about issues of diversity given the socioeconomic standing of those living in this new downtown.[4]

Gentrification, Residential Development, and the New Face of Downtowns

Substantial investment in infrastructural facilities, in the form of museums, parks, stadiums, and entertainment districts, not only expanded the availability of services, but also strengthened existing amenities and introduced new ones. The opportunity to experience enhanced cultural attractions, unique urban sceneries, beautified environments, and vibrant and diverse locales has a considerable effect—notably shifting the population makeup of downtowns.

An investigation of downtown household and income trends of 44 cities from 1970 to 2000 conducted by The Brookings Institution revealed that during the 1990s, the downtown population grew by 10 percent, a significant rise after 20 years of decline. There was an 8 percent increase from 1970 to 2000 and a 13 percent increase during the 1990s in the number of households in downtowns. Households of singles, unrelated individuals living together, and childless married couples grew the fastest in downtowns. Downtown homeownership rates also more than doubled during the 30-year period, reaching 22 percent by 2000. During that same year, Chicago's downtown posted a 41 percent increase in households. In addition, downtowns have a higher percentage of both young adults and college-educated residents than other areas of the nation's cities and in the suburbs. In 2000, 25- to 34-year-olds represented nearly a quarter of the downtown population—up from 13 percent in 1970. Forty-four percent of downtowners had a bachelor's degree or higher.[5] As Table 6.1 illustrates, only four of 22 downtowns with a population of at least 10,000 residents experi-

Table 6.1 Downtown Population Change (1990–2000) with 10,000 Minimum Residents

| | DOWNTOWN POPULATIONS CHANGE | | | |
	1990	2000	1970 TO 1980	1990 TO 2000
Baltimore	28,597	30,067	–13.9%	5.1%
Boston	77,253	80,903	–3.0%	4.7%
Lower Manhattan	84,539	97,752	17.8%	15.6%
Midtown Manhattan	69,388	71,668	14.9%	3.3%
Philadelphia	74,686	78,349	–8.8%	4.9%
Washington, D.C.	26,597	27,667	–18.7%	4.0%
Atlanta	19,763	24,931	–21.9%	26.1%
Chattanooga	12,601	13,529	–6.3%	7.4%
Dallas	18,104	22,469	–27.7%	24.1%
Miami	15,143	19,927	–41.1%	31.6%
Orlando	14,275	12,621	–24.7%	–11.6%
San Antonio	19,603	19,236	–21.6%	–1.9%
Chicago	56,048	72,843	–3.1%	30.0%
Detroit	38,116	36,871	–32.4%	–3.3%
Indianapolis	14,894	17,907	21.5%	20.2%
Milwaukee	14,458	16,359	–11.6%	13.1%
Minneapolis	36,334	30,299	– 7.0%	–16.6%
Los Angeles	34,655	36,630	46.7%	5.7%
Portland	9,528	12,902	–2.5%	35.4%
San Diego	15,417	17,894	2.2%	16.1%
San Francisco	32,906	43,531	–19.1%	32.3%
Seattle	12,292	21,745	.7%	76.9%

Source: Birch, Eugenie L. 2005. Who Lives Downtown. The Brookings Institution (November) p. 5 (www. brookings.edu/metro).

enced population decline from 1990 to 2000. From 1970 to 1980, 16 of these recorded population decreases.[6]

Gentrification contributes to the residential restructuring of downtowns. The increased investment in cultural activities attracts younger professionals who transform the population makeup of many neighborhoods. British sociologist Ruth Glass first coined the term *gentrification* in 1964 by writing that "One by one, many of the working class quarters of London have been invaded by the middle class—upper and lower. Shabby, modest mews and cottages—two rooms up and two down—have been taken over, when their leases have expired, and have become elegant, expensive residences."[7]

Recent research points to the evolving nature of gentrification, or the mutation of this process in light of structural changes such as globalization.[8] Scholars observe its maturing stages, including what is referenced as a second/third generation, termed "supergentrification." The term refers to changes in already gentrified neighborhoods that experience significant social changes that cause regentrification due to globalized cultural and socioeconomic forces. Accordingly, a new generation of wealthy residents, which has benefited from the international markets and finance industries, engage in extreme consumption practices that result in considerable community reorganization, leading to a new cycle of gentrification. Barnsbury in north London[9] and Brooklyn Heights in New York[10] would fall into this category.

As noted earlier, the rise of tourism proved to influence residential patterns. Public and private infrastructural investments to attract visitors not only physically renewed the core, but also brought new residents. An unanticipated social consequence of these municipal policies is found in what can be termed tourism-driven gentrification. For example, the construction of Navy Pier in Chicago, an entertainment district that opened in 1995 and has since undergone considerable upgrades, proved to have a direct impact on nearby communities. The revitalization of housing in the adjacent neighborhood of Streeterville, and its thousands of new residents, is attributed, among other factors, to the popularity of Navy Pier.[11]

Twenty-one Battery Park in the heart of Asheville, North Carolina is a luxurious residential development and the city's premier address. The seven-story building is the first high-rise in downtown Asheville in more than 40 years. The project is part of a new condominium construction trend that also includes renovated lofts. Welcomed by the local government, the investment is in concert with the city's *2025 Plan,* which calls for additional downtown housing. The building has close access to the many new area amenities such as restaurants, galleries, and entertainment opportunities, and as a result, unit sales proved brisk. However, the making of an upscale city center has direct implications for Asheville residents since the revitalization caused gentrification. Many of the working-class residents who once lived in downtown neighborhoods are pushed out. Some city officials have criticized this direction describing it as "government-supported gentrification." Others focused on the needed reinvestment and the expanded tax base.[12]

In downtown Los Angeles, the Walt Disney Concert Hall, the Staples Center, and the LA Live district brought about substantial changes. Access to these and other entertainment options fueled residential development as more than 30,000 residents now call the area home. Trendy restaurants and popular nightspots, along with related services such as the first grocery store in the area followed. The new downtown dwellers are young with high disposable incomes, and retailers are rushing to serve this unique demographic.[13]

From 1985 to 2004, Houston's downtown was the recipient of public–private partnerships that included $1.3 billion for public facilities and $2.2 billion for private projects. The creation of organizations such as the Downtown District in 1992, the Main Street Market Square Redevelopment Authority in 1995, the Houston Downtown Alliance, as well as the Downtown Houston Association in 2003 proved vital to the area's transformation process and steered the construction of an impressive new infrastructure.

The *2025 Vision* for the city's core also called for an expansion and refinement of the theater district, promotion and enhancement of the convention and sports district, and the introduction of small-scale cultural and historic attractions. Central to achieving this strategy is an aggressive residential development program that aims to increase the number of people living in downtown neighborhoods from 11,882 in 2000 to more than 25,000 by 2025.[14]

The presence of expanded recreational amenities in the downtown area created strong residential demand, issues of affordability remained. Central Houston, Inc., a group that focuses on the redevelopment and revitalization of the city center, warned of the effects of this direction by noting that new residential construction will likely replace the existing modest bungalows. The ensuing gentrification will bring professionals who will occupy the new townhouses and eventually displace the working-class residents. This will change the essential character and flavor of the neighborhood, since according to a community organization "living opportunities for all income levels should become a major goal of any future vision for downtown and the central city."[15] The new housing stock found in these reconstituted city centers falls into two categories: loft conversion and new construction, both of which are examined below.

Loft Conversion and Revitalized Communities

The extensive investment in promoting tourism eventually led to the creation of considerable housing demand. City officials, real-estate companies, and developers rushed to meet these emerging needs. The lure of a renewed urban romanticism coupled with existing structures in the form of old warehouses and former manufacturing spaces that could be quickly redeveloped and offered for sale proved key ingredients to a new wave of residential growth. Marketing the historic past of these buildings along with their unique landmark designations contributed to transforming urban living into an immediate success.

Loft conversions offer brick and timber exposures, open spaces, high ceilings, and windows with extensive natural light. The opportunity to combine working and living arrangements made them a popular choice for young entrepreneurs, artists, and families in need of additional space. The vast stock of this housing option in cities like Denver, Chicago, Cleveland, St. Louis, and Philadelphia fueled rapid residential expansion.

Beyond private capital investment, the success of this trend also hinges on public commitment and investment in upgrading relevant infrastructure. Planning initiatives that focused on creating, promoting, and maintaining loft districts proved essential. For example, officials involved with the creation of the Washington Avenue Loft District in St. Louis reviewed successful cases on Walnut Street, Broad Street, and South Street in Philadelphia. These areas saw their streetscapes revamped through outdoor arts and crafts stores, high-end hotels and restaurants, decorative street signs, antique lamp posts, and newspaper stands and planters. Cobblestone streets and historic building facades created nineteenth century nostalgia.

Figure 6.2   These warehouses near skyscrapers in downtown Cleveland, Ohio are part of the loft conversion trend that is evident in many cities across the country. These reconstituted spaces offer unique spaces but more importantly are located close to amenities (Courtesy Henryk Sadura, Shutterstock Images).

In St. Louis, state tax credits helped spur the redevelopment of the Washington Avenue Loft District. Millions of dollars in investments transformed the area, which during the 1920s had been a garment district, and in more recent years had served as the city's commercial center. The large number of lofts along Washington Avenue underwent significant restoration. Decorative sidewalks, trees, new lighting, and park benches contributed to the area's renaissance.[16]

Beyond state and municipal support, the federal government also played an active role. One of the largest Missouri loft conversion projects took place in 2004. Federal tax credits helped a private developer, Historic Restoration, Inc., complete a $47 million conversion of a large distribution center on Washington Avenue in St. Louis. The Liggett and Myers Building, constructed in 1889, received a historical landmark designation in 1984. However, the structure had stood empty since the early 1980s and was almost demolished in 2001. Remodeled into 213 loft apartments, the 350,000 square foot building greatly contributed to further investment in the area.[17]

Focus on the revitalization of urban cores through loft conversion can be found beyond the Frostbelt. By the mid-1990s, Sunbelt cities experienced a similar demand for downtown living. The first such residential project in Dallas was the Titche-Goettinger building, which showcases a neo-Renaissance style of architecture. Completed in 1929, the structure served as a major department store. It closed in 1986, and in 1996 it was included in the U.S. National Register of Historic Places. The dilapidated building was purchased for just $100,000, and following an $11 million conversion, it opened in 1997 with loft-style apartments and a first-floor retail space.[18]

Today, downtown Dallas boasts new arts and entertainment districts, restaurants, professional sports facilities, and numerous shopping opportunities. Loft conversions comprise a considerable part of the area's housing market. Due to such housing, the city saw its Central Business District population grow tenfold from 1,654 (2000) to 5,646 (2005) to 10,446 (2010). According to current forecasts, the downtown population is projected to surpass 15,000 residents by 2030.[19]

Houston, Atlanta, and many other smaller cities in the Sunbelt like Little Rock, Arkansas and Jacksonville, Florida experienced similar reorganization. Nashville promotes loft living in the downtown tourist district, and in Birmingham, Alabama the Literacy Council holds an annual Historic Footnotes Loft Tour. However, the success of these downtown conversions requires extensive government subsidies. These come in the form of city tax abatements on the improvements, historic-building tax credits, and low-interest loans offered by the federal government.

New Construction and Emerging Neighborhoods

Demand for housing in the newly reconstituted downtowns proved extensive, and the conversions of old buildings into lofts could not keep up with the high demand and diverse consumer tastes. Developers rushed to fill empty lots with new residential construction. In the process they contributed to the expansion of the area by creating new city center neighborhoods. A 2008 survey of downtown residents in Nashville, Tennessee revealed that the demand for new housing was connected to three reasons expressed by respondents. The urban experience and being close to arts, cultural, and sporting events ranked as the top two factors that favored their quest for a downtown lifestyle. The third factor was proximity to work.[20]

Data released in 2008 by the Greater Nashville Association of Realtors showed that for the first time ever, the median price of condominiums was higher than that of single-family homes. Furthermore, the downtown rental market was shrinking as the ownership percentage rose. Specifically in 2004, 83 percent of downtown housing was rental. In 2008, that number decreased to 40 percent of the total, and in 2010 it is expected that rentals will comprise just 28 percent of the total downtown Nashville housing stock.[21] This commitment to making downtown a place to live helped expand the residential population in Nashville by creating new neighborhoods.

The North Capitol neighborhood in Nashville is a good example. Located between the Central Business District and Germantown, it emerged as a residential area following the recent addition of more than 300 housing units. Historically a commercial district, the housing demand ignited a rapid transition. The nearby Nashville Farmer's Market underwent considerable renovation and emerged as a popular destination, helping the establishment of many new restaurants. In addition, the French Lick Greenway, which leads to the Cumberland River, is part of a bike-trail complex and another neighborhood amenity.

The Gulch is a similarly developed neighborhood nearby. Railroad lines once dominated the area but a robust private–public partnership dramatically gave rise to a new community. The Metropolitan Development and Housing Authority officially declared the Gulch as

Figure 6.3   Farmers market near downtown Nashville, Tennessee. These city efforts add another dimension to urban living and support residential development (Courtesy Kenn Stilger 47, Shutterstock Images).

a redevelopment district, a decision that infused considerable public investment. The rehabilitation of older buildings helped pave the way for new residential construction, which with the addition of restaurants, bars, nightclubs, and other venues turned the area into an exciting place for younger professionals. A major loft and condominium development is currently underway, which is scheduled to add more than 800 condominiums. Once the entire project is completed, it will increase the total number of residents in the neighborhood to more than 3,000.[22]

Tampa, Florida has not experienced the mature neighborhood environment and new construction seen in Nashville; nonetheless, the city wants to pursue the remaking of its core as an entertainment hub. A commissioned report offered the following direction:

> Downtown redevelopment should be viewed as a mix of residential, employment, and entertainment uses, at a variety of densities where the market allows, with ground-floor retail and service uses at key nodes....

The attractions and activity centers are important in creating the concept of downtown Tampa as a regional entertainment center and destination for a wide variety of experiences, while reinforcing its role as the region's primary business center.[23]

New master planned communities in Tampa such as Central Park Village received approval and more than 6,000 residential and commercial units are either developed or are under consideration in the city's downtown. By strategically focusing on public–private partnerships, the city expects to support more retail space and restaurants that in turn will promote further residential development. Existing assets include the Cultural Arts District and the waterfront. These, along with new attractions such as the $27 million Tampa Museum of Art, the $21 million Children's Museum, and the $40 million Riverwalk, will serve as an array of amenities that are expected to enhance the downtown environment.[24] While the cases above reveal that the use of this culture-driven development strategy can have a positive impact and yield good results, this planning approach also has its limitations.

Downtown Rebirth? The Trials of Detroit, Michigan

In 2007, *Money Magazine* published a list of the top 30 largest U.S. cities for retirement. In addition to Hudson Heights and Tudor City in New York, South Loop and Streeterville in Chicago, and the Marina District in San Diego, the list included downtown Detroit. New residential projects and affordability were identified as some of the positive attributes. On the negative side, the magazine noted that the area's incomplete resurgence may make newcomers feel like urban pioneers. The Riverwalk, the Eastern Market, and arenas for professional sports venues were mentioned as some of the unique attractions for downtown residents.[25]

This distinction is a surprise to many because Detroit suffered significant declines following deindustrialization. During the height of industrialization, the city was viewed as a beacon of manufacturing and an emblem of economic success. However, since the 1950s, the city has lost half of its population and more than 40 percent of its job base. In the mid-1990s, under the Detroit Renaissance, Detroit embarked on an ambitious $2 billion redevelopment effort. Entertainment replaced manufacturing as the central focus of the city's policy development agenda.[26]

Sports stadiums emerged as a key part of this new strategy. In 2000, the $300 million Comerica Park replaced the aging Tiger Stadium for the Detroit Tigers of the MLB, and in 2002 the Detroit Lions of the NFL moved back to downtown from suburban Pontiac to a new $430 million state-of-the-art Ford Field—both of these facilities are located adjacent to each other. Over the years, the city sought and hosted various national sporting events, including an NCAA Basketball Final Four, two Super Bowls, and a Major League Baseball All Star Game. The Joe Louis Arena for the NHL Detroit Red Wings is also located in downtown.

Similarly, local officials supported entertainment-oriented infrastructural development in the form of casinos. The MGM Grand Detroit Casino Resort opened in 2007, the Greektown Casino in 2000 with successive expansions in 2008 and 2009, and the MotorCity Casino Hotel in 1999 with additions in 2007 and 2008. The casinos cluster along the riverfront. Other attractions include the theater district and the Detroit Science Center, which in 2001 doubled its space as a result of a $30 million renovation.

Concurrently, an aggressive greater downtown residential development plan added almost 2,500 condominium units from 2000 to 2006. Tax and Neighborhood Enterprise Zone incentives aided the rapid pace of construction. A 2006 survey of downtown residents revealed that "convenience to dining/entertainment" and "proximity to arts and cultural institutions" ranked as the two most influential factors among those who chose to move downtown.[27]

But the redevelopment success of Detroit's downtown is far from secure, and the future remains unpredictable. The city is struggling to meet its goals given the vast physical size of the space waiting to be revitalized. Another major hurdle relates to the image of Detroit. In a recent survey, developers identified the following challenges facing the success of their projects: "perception of crime/weak police presence," "poor condition of surrounding areas/public infrastructure," and "lack of marketing plan/need for better public relations."[28]

Among these observations, the perception of Detroit as a dangerous city proved one of the most difficult to reverse. In recent years, the national media had published numerous stories, often showcasing downtown in a negative light. For example, a widely circulated article on

Figure 6.4   The Renaissance Center is a commercial complex in Detroit, Michigan. Recent renovations constituted significant investments in downtown. Along with the nearby Detroit Riverwalk (more than $1 billion), these projects were hoped to help the city rebound from the decline following deindustrialization (Courtesy Alexey Stiop, Shutterstock Images).

conventions declared the neighborhood outside the Cobo Conference/ Exhibition Center as ranking second in crime risk when compared to similar facilities across the country. Furthermore, the essay indicated that the crime risk in the surrounding area is five times greater than in the entire local county and 10 times greater than the national norm.[29] This forced the city and the Convention and Visitors Bureau to embark on a strategy aimed at reversing this image. A 2008 commissioned report by Wayne State University concluded that "the perception of Downtown Detroit as unsafe is false… [in fact the] crime rate is lower than that of the United States and the State of Michigan."[30]

It is clear that Detroit joined many other cities across the country by infusing billions in supporting a tourism and entertainment infrastructure, which was expected to help revitalize its urban core by attracting visitors and by encouraging new residents to call downtown home. Unfortunately for many cities with crumbling buildings, vacant storefronts, and empty streets, the long-term success of this strategy is uncertain. For example, one of the major problems facing Detroit is the lack of large retail shops and available grocery stores. Recently, all national outlets that sell fresh produce and meat pulled out of the city forcing the local United Food and Commercial Workers union to consider building and operating its own shopping center.[31]

It is becoming increasingly clear that the negative effects of deindustrialization are so extensive in Detroit that a new economy based on leisure and tourism is unlikely to single handedly bring about a complete recovery. Political scientist Peter Eisenberg noted that claims by the city's political elites to position Detroit as a world class city, a center of a thriving metropolitan region, and as a tourist and convention destination are misguided and are likely to fail. Eisenberg concluded that this direction will create a city for visitors not for residents.[32]

The issues surrounding the relationship between urban tourism/ convention business and residential development are also evident in smaller cities. Like larger city centers, many of these communities experienced the negative effects of postwar urban restructuring. Their once thriving downtowns became desperate for capital investment and increased population. As a result of these changes, many view tourism as a viable option.

Downtown Revitalization and the Tourism/ Convention Strategy in Smaller Cities

With the departure of manufacturing, a renewed function was essential for many smaller cities across the country. Cultural policy and practices emerged that focused on utilizing leisure, tourism, entertainment, and business visitors as the fuel for economic development. By aiming to revive the urban core, these strategies would attempt to breathe new life into these distressed communities.

Yet, the transformation of these smaller cities into destination spots that are primed to produce revenues is not an easy task. In addition, it is the larger cities that capture a large portion of the available tourism/ convention dollars. In a consumption-dominated economy, approaches to urban growth must be tied to consumer desires and habits. Local governments must embrace entrepreneurial models if they are to successfully achieve their goals and must search for opportunities within an "experienced economy." In addition to entertainment and culture, this new economy also relies on services and place. Smaller cities then must connect consumption (experiences) with production (infrastructure) as they pursue experience-based strategies that focus on events and branding.[33]

An interesting example can be drawn from the Chicagoland area. Since the mid-1990s, Chicago's satellite cities of Joliet, Waukegan, Elgin, and Aurora embraced an active redevelopment agenda that focused on reviving downtown areas, while attracting visitors to their locales and expanding opportunities for economic growth. According to the 2000 U.S. Census, each city boasts a sizable population. In Illinois, Aurora ranks as the third largest city with 142,990 people; Joliet ranks as the seventh-largest city with 106,221 people; Elgin ranks as the eighth-largest city with 94,487 people; and Waukegan ranks as the ninth-largest city with 87,901 people. These cities also possess a large percentage of minorities: Aurora (32.6 percent Hispanics and 11.1 percent African Americans), Elgin (34.3 percent Hispanics and 6.80 percent African Americans), Waukegan (44.8 percent Hispanics and 19.2 percent African Americans), and Joliet (18.4 percent Hispanics and 18.2 percent African Americans).

All four of these communities share a long history in the Chicago metropolitan area that dates back to the 1850s. Each grew rapidly, benefiting from their independent industrial/manufacturing activities, their proximity to Chicago's robust economic environment, and their position on key transportation routes of regional and national importance. Deindustrialization proved extensive and devastating, forcing their local governments to explore alternative modes of development.

In the 1990s, these cities would revitalize their cores by developing entertainment and recreation opportunities and by investing in residential construction. Riverboat casinos, minor-league baseball, historic preservation, festivals, parades, children's activities, farmer's markets, and outdoor performances became commonly employed strategies. Local officials also attended to an ailing infrastructure by refurbishing old theaters, restoring streetscapes, adding new lighting, and creating attractive public spaces. Musicals, theater productions,

Figure 6.5 Waterfront development in historic Savannah, Georgia. Cotton warehouses along the river have been restored to include trendy shops, restaurants, art galleries, and nightlife destinations. Leisurely strolls and river boating offers visitors and residents numerous recreation opportunities (Courtesy Larry Bennett).

symphony concerts, and free events bring thousands to downtown areas. Private sector investment followed, further upgrading these locations, which also saw their populations increase.[34]

Similar patterns are evident elsewhere across the country. Syracuse, New York, the state's fifth largest city, with 140,658 (2000) residents, experienced unprecedented industrial growth in the nineteenth century. During World War II, Syracuse was a major supplier of products that supported the war effort. The city benefited from considerable industrial expansion with General Motors, Chrysler, Carrier Corporation, and General Electric, which had established major operations in the area. This helped the city's population grow and reach its all-time high of more than 220,000 residents in 1950. Unfortunately, by the 1970s deindustrialization began to set in—a precursor to urban decline. Many of the corporations that aided Syracuse started to move. Rockwell International, a major supplier to the military and the automotive industry, left the state. General Electric and Carrier ended up in new locations across Asia. Population loss followed: 2.1 percent (1960), 8.7 percent (1970), 13.7 percent (1980), 3.7 percent (1990), and 10.1 percent (2000).[35]

In recent years, Syracuse has focused on reviving its downtown, drawing tourists and offering locals an urban culture experience via leisure activities and entertainment. The area experienced considerable change under the leadership of the Downtown Committee of Syracuse, a not-for-profit professional management organization. The creation of a downtown special assessment district reimaged the core by emphasizing art and culture. Wine tasting and silent auctions, lectures, civic morning musicals, gallery exhibits, a downtown farmer's market, festivals, and concerts and an annual jewelry exposition dominate the area's summer activities.

The Syracuse Convention & Visitors Bureau also played a key role in the city's efforts. In 2008, the authority completed a $357,000 integrated destination image marketing campaign. The goal of this initiative was to bring visitors to Syracuse by building an awareness of the city as a destination for leisure travelers. An assessment of the campaign revealed success in categories such as "increase excitement," "suitability for family and adults," an "abundance of things to see and do," "popularity," and "worry-free atmosphere."[36]

Syracuse's promotional literature showcases its unique neighbor-hoods, but it is the downtown area that received considerable invest-ment in mixed retail, office, and residential development. New apartment buildings attract first-time residents who along with tour-ists and business visitors contribute to transforming the area into a nightlife center with numerous restaurants and bars. Infrastructural expenditures on improving the streetscape helped the success of Armory, Hanover, and Clinton, which are three downtown squares that provide lively entertainment throughout the week.

Private–public partnerships and historic preservation tax credits jumpstarted the housing needed to accommodate more than 2,500 residents in downtown. With an occupancy rate of 99 percent in 2006, more housing units in new construction and loft conversions entered the market. From 2003 to 2006, an excess of $180 million was invested in downtown Syracuse. Even in the midst of an eco-nomic downturn, the Downtown Committee of Syracuse determined that between 2008 and 2010 the city center saw more than $300 mil-lion expended in the district.[37]

Another smaller city, Asheville, North Carolina, with a population of 68,889 (2000), also embraced tourism and its perceived economic benefits. A gateway for those drawn by the outdoor activities avail-able in the nearby western North Carolina mountains, the industry is the recipient of extensive attention by local officials who pushed to convert this community into a visitor destination. The destructive urban renewal programs of the late 1960s and 1970s passed Asheville by. This allowed the city to showcase its surviving mix of Art Deco, Beaux Arts, and Neoclassical architectural styles.

By promoting continuous programming of downtown festivals, including Bele Chere, the largest free street festival in the South-east, the city attracts thousands annually. Downtown After 5 and Downtown Countdown are two events that specifically aim to create a vibrant environment for all ages, including families and young pro-fessionals. An urban trail guides walkers through the city, showcasing sculptures, public art, and historical attractions. The sophistication, fine cuisine, art galleries, and unique urban setting earned the city the distinct reference as "Paris of the South."[38]

It is clear that tourism helped develop the city's identity, and as a major employment industry it has seen considerable growth in recent years. In fact, leisure and hospitality ranked third in the total number of jobs during 2006, behind health services and retail trade. From 2006 through 2008, this sector experienced the largest employment gains, placing second behind health services.[39]

As part of its 2008 legislative agenda, the Asheville Chamber of Commerce identified the tourism and travel industry as the generator of more than $15.4 billion in direct visitor expenditures and responsible for contributing more than 187,200 jobs to the local economy. Competing with other Southeastern cities, officials called for more marketing and advertising appropriations to expand the share of business and pleasure travelers.[40]

From a planning perspective, the completion of Pack Square Park surfaced as a centerpiece of tourism development, furthering the focus on the downtown area. At a cost of more than $20 million, the 6.5 acre public park opened in successive stages in 2009 and 2010. With two performance stages, several interactive water features, and public art displays, the site is a key focal point, attracting locals, tourists, and business visitors. According to a Western Carolina University Center for Regional Development study, the park is expected to increase income to the lodging industry by $1,045,222 annually. Its overall impact on the economy is estimated at $24,143,400.[41]

Even the name of the local minor baseball team that is affiliated with the Colorado Rockies of MLB conveys the importance of tourism for Asheville. The Asheville Tourists play in historic McCormick Field and are part of the Southern Division of the South Atlantic League. Positioned on the eastern edge of downtown, the facility underwent significant renovations in 2007 having served in its previous incarnation as the set for the 1988 film *Bull Durham*. The Tourists are very popular, breaking season attendance records in recent years. Just to the south, Greenville, South Carolina followed a similar development plan. Like Asheville, this is another smaller city that in recent decades underwent significant restructuring, focusing on remaking its downtown, and attracting new residents and tourists.

Remaking Downtown in Greenville, South Carolina

Greenville, South Carolina (population 56,006 in 2000) is the largest city in the Upstate. For many decades, it maintained a robust economy based on textile manufacturing. In fact, the city was referred to as "The Textile Capital of the World," and as late as the early part of the 1980s it continued to maintain considerable manufacturing activities in this economic sector. Since that time though textile activities sharply declined, leaving many production facilities and storage warehouses empty.

The focus on the downtown area can be traced back to the 1980s, but it is during the 1990s that we see that effort generate signs of success. A newly created city master plan and municipal support for public–private partnerships resulted in extensive core investment. Over the years, the outcome of this strategy included anchor projects such as the Peace Center for the Performing Arts, the West End Market, and the Greenville Commons/Hyatt Regency, the city's first luxury hotel. Former industrial areas would be converted into art centers while integrating strong elements of historic preservation in the design.

For example, planning for the West End Market initially intended to create a farmer's market. However, this public investment encouraged private sector participation, expanded the project considerably, and eventually converted the location into a historic district. Since 1995, art galleries, office, and retail services, as well as restaurants reconstituted the area. In 1986, Main Street had only four restaurants; by 2006, more than 75 restaurants operated in that stretch. Overall it is estimated that, from 1980 to 2002, $185 million in public investment generated more than $700 million in private capital investment in downtown Greenville. In fact, many smaller cities across the country view Greenville as a blueprint for their downtown development efforts.[42]

A new sports stadium for the Drive, the city's minor league baseball team, opened in downtown in 2006 on a site that once functioned as a lumber yard. The facility, named Fluor Field in 2008, attracts thousands to the area every year. Nearby Reedy River Falls Historic Park along with numerous festivals, outdoor theater and music performances, nightclubs, museums, and art galleries transformed downtown into a center of regional tourism. The city used eminent

Figure 6.6 A look down the Reedy River in downtown Greenville, South Carolina. The city redeveloped its downtown by focusing on the river (Courtesy Cathleen Clapper, Shutterstock Images).

domain to redevelop riverfront structures and engaged in extensive urban beautification. Future plans to link the History Museum and the Children's Museum with the downtown will further market the core as a destination.

A new Downtown Master Development Plan released in 2008 focused on expanding an already notable range of cultural activities and furthering downtown's residential base. In fact, the city views a strong relationship between leisure and entertainment with economic growth. The 2008 Master Plan notes: "rather than targeting industrial development, a downtown-centered, lifestyle marketing campaign should be employed. This marketing campaign should target a broad audience—businesses, retirees and tourists. Capturing any one of these markets translates into economic development."[43]

Even though the city's center experienced considerable population growth, the plan also called for a new direction, cautioning that "while many new housing units have been built, they tend to be targeted toward the wealthy and are not yet achieving the diversity that makes a downtown interesting." Some officials argued that developing entry-level housing would help cultivate the presence of a younger constituency for downtown. While the West End was intended for artists, high residential costs priced out many interested in moving to the area.

The plan also conveys the city's commitment to tourism, linking it to its overall success by noting that "Greenville should continue to develop its role as a visitor destination recognized not only regionally but nationally for excursions."[44] The city has been the recipient of many awards, including the International Downtown Achievement Award for Economic Development and the prestigious American Main Street Award. Furthermore, Greenville has been featured in numerous national publications for its attractive center, including *Southern Living* and *Money Magazine*.

Greenville's downtown residential revitalization is the outcome of a 30-year effort that focused on private–public partnerships and relied on the creation of a thriving center by establishing key anchor developments, maximizing the presence of natural settings, and by aggressively introducing cultural amenities and attractions. In the years to come, sustaining this alliance between private interests and public commitment will be one of the key challenges facing the city. Diversifying the socioeconomic background of downtown residents will likely place additional demands as local officials plan the future direction of the city's core. Regardless, by altering its urban image and by attending to compelling planning and design elements, municipal leaders will improve the quality of life and afford increased residential options. The major boom in Greenville's downtown is the outcome of a persistent policy strategy on revitalization that embraced the public and private sectors while connecting those efforts to the visitor economy.[45]

In addition to being pursued as a form of economic development, the rise of urban tourism proved to have additional effects. These effects contributed to significant changes in the physical and social composition of cities across the country. New residents with higher incomes were attracted by the amenities and the infrastructural investments intended to draw visitors. Residential developers embraced the opportunities presented as local officials pushed for the rebuilding of their once dilapidated and abandoned downtowns. While this strategy worked and transformed many city centers, it should be noted that its mere utilization does not automatically yield successful results. Tourism can be a fruitful economic development policy only when it is combined with other initiatives intended to bring about urban growth. The case of Detroit is a stark reminder of the difficulties municipal governments face in their revitalization efforts. Nonetheless, it is during the past 30 years that we can see the pursuit of tourism as a central agenda item of city councils, a position that is likely to remain unchanged in the future.

Writing, Reflection, and Debate

Discussion Questions

Gentrification is caused by numerous forces. How significant is tourism in restructuring the residential makeup of the urban core? What other factors contribute to the gentrification process and are these related to the development of tourism?

Identify a smaller city or a suburb. How has its downtown evolved over the last decade? What is its focal point (e.g., casino, waterfront development, a stadium, or park)? Has there been nearby residential growth? Are projects currently under development? How do these contribute to the broader tourism strategy?

7

IMPLICATIONS AND DEBATES

Like many other economic sectors, tourism is experiencing significant challenges in the wake of the global economic upheavals that began in 2008. According to a report by the United Nations World Tourism Organization (UNWTO), the number of international tourist arrivals was estimated at 247 million between January and April of 2009, down from 269 million in 2008 and 254 million in 2007 during the first quarters of each year. This downward trend is expected to continue for some time to come. During the first quarter of 2009, most regions of the world experienced substantial visitor declines from the previous year: Europe (10 percent); Asia and Pacific (6 percent); North America (7 percent); the Caribbean (6 percent); Central America (4 percent); and the Middle East (18 percent). Only two world regions experienced growth during that period: Africa (3 percent) and South America (0.2 percent). The authors of the UNWTO report further that "there are possibilities of a moderate recovery, but much will depend on the evolving economic conditions and on the restoration of consumer and business confidence."[1]

The growth of global tourism in recent years has been quite uneven. Short-term periods of rapid expansion, from the mid- to late 1990s and then from 2004 to 2007, flanked a period of slowdown from 2001 to 2003. The UNWTO assumes that the current crisis is likely to be short-lived and thus holds to a long-term positive forecast. Specifically, from 1950 to 2007, international tourism grew by 6.5 percent per year. By 2020 it is expected that international travel will almost double to 1.6 billion arrivals. [2] This future growth will be accompanied by extensive investments in infrastructure to meet visitor needs. Travel and tourism expenditures in infrastructure were estimated at $1,241 trillion in 2010 and are expected to reach $2,757 trillion by 2020. The contribution of travel and tourism to the GDPs around the world is expected to double from $5,751 trillion in 2010 to $11,151 trillion in 2020. By 2020, 9.2 percent of the world's total employment will be in travel and tourism, up from 8.1 percent in 2010. [3] The United States will continue to be a significant player in this industry (see Table 7.1). Because of its status as a multitrillion dollar financial sector, tourism will continue to count as a significant source of revenues for national and local economies across the world. In the view of the UNWTO, these are welcome trends because tourism revenues can be used to support environmental protection programs, as well as to reduce poverty. [4]

Tourism-oriented development represents a complex intertwining of economic and cultural promotion. Tourism impacts the economic condition of cities as local officials embrace it as a tool to stimulate private investment. This quest has been a significant part of the response to the negative effects of deindustrialization and metropolitan decentralization. Tourism has also restructured and expanded various public affairs functions, including government sponsored outreach efforts (festivals, concerts, arts, beautification, etc.) and reconstituted municipal administrative practices. And because tourism development tends to stimulate interurban competition, huge investments in infrastructure projects and place-enhancing attractions have followed. The further result has been a new era in city building, especially across the downtown areas of large and small cities alike.

In the effort to restore their financial health, urban centers have mounted extensive branding campaigns to promote their new or reconstituted amenities, and thus upgrade their reputations as desirable destinations. Much of this rebranding involves presenting these locales as cultural hubs. The results are varied. Out-of-town travelers,

Table 7.1   Long Term Prospects in Tourism

TRAVEL AND TOURISM ECONOMY GDP (2010 AND 2020 IN US$BN)			
Economy GDP 2010		**Economy GDP 2020**	
1 United States	1,375.9	1 United States	2,485.7
2 China	499.9	2 China	1,948.9
3 Japan	459.3	3 Japan	594.8
4 France	284.6	4 United Kingdom	393.3
5 Germany	273.4	5 France	379.9
6 Spain	237.9	6 Germany	377.1
7 United Kingdom	231.1	7 Spain	341.1
8 Italy	217.1	8 India	330.1
9 Canada	136.1	9 Italy	292.5
10 Australia	123.1	10 Russian Federation	258.2
CAPITAL INVESTMENT IN TRAVEL AND TOURISM (2010 AND 2020 IN US$BN)			
Capital Investment 2010		**Capital Investment 2020**	
1 United States	252.8	1 China	688.5
2 China	203.4	2 United States	489.3
3 Japan	59.6	3 Russian Federation	115.9
4 Spain	46.8	4 India	109.3
5 France	42.3	5 Indonesia	75.6
6 Germany	39.0	6 Japan	72.3
7 Australia	38.9	7 Spain	72.1
8 Italy	35.8	8 Australia	70.3
9 Russian Federation	34.8	9 Brazil	63.9
10 India	34.7	10 Germany	61.8

Source: World Travel & Tourism Council.

including day-trippers, search for leisure attractions. Young, central city-residing professionals rush to take advantage of inviting, newly refashioned residential and commercial spaces. In the process, these newcomers have leveraged robust residential development trends. An enterprising private sector has targeted retail developments for what were once rundown commercial areas and abandoned industrial sites. Public–private partnership has been the planning and implementation tool favored by municipal leaders and city councils seeking to advance this new era of downtown building.

The rise of urban tourism as a development tool and a reimaging strategy has also generated its share of criticism. For example, it is often asserted that the city of leisure, culture, and entertainment comes at the cost of downplaying social equity concerns. From this perspective, expending resources on tourism necessarily restricts the ability of the public sector to support key services in schools, housing, and transportation. Political scientist Dennis Judd describes this position by noting that "the trade-offs seem stark: beautification and flowers vs. unpaved streets; downtown amenities vs. neighborhood development; tourist infrastructure vs. adequately equipped schools; gentrification vs. displacement. The result of this direction is said to be two cities, one inhabited by the wealthy and middle-class, the other by the poor."[5]

Many business and civic leaders reject this perspective, pointing to the multitude of benefits the tourism industry brings to local economies. These range from image building to providing needed revenues and employment opportunities. Just like the arguments offered by supporters of stadium construction or major sporting events, tourism advocates assert that without clean downtowns, up-to-date convention centers, and appealing shopping districts, a city's economic competitiveness, and more broadly its reputation, will be reduced. Moreover, so it is claimed, at a time of intense economic competition, individual cities cannot afford to fall behind their peers in the contest to attract visitors, recreational and business-related alike.

A more subtle objection to many forms of contemporary tourist-oriented urban development concerns the loss of local "authenticity." Indeed, the term *Disneyfication* has entered the popular lexicon to characterize tourist districts that offer superficial representations of ethnic markets and cuisines, gritty street environments, or other ostensibly unique urban experiences. What critics have in mind is the marketing of carefully designed "spaces of consumption" whose surface detailing mimics the appearance of "classic" urban spaces. More troubling still to social commentators such as Sharon Zukin or Michael Sorkin is the intrinsic exclusiveness of many festival marketplaces, arts quarters, and gentrified residential enclaves. The urban experience that is sold via such spaces is an experience appealing to prosperous local residents and visitors. Even tax dollars are supporting corporate interests at the expense of the weaker segments of our society.[6] By means both subtle, such as highbrow cultural programming, and unsubtle such as entrance fees and "defensible space" design techniques, the less privileged are turned away.

Tourism and Cultural Authenticity

A commonly leveled charge against tourism is that it has become increasingly responsible for the creation of environments that, in an effort to attract visitors, end up reducing cultural authenticity. Specifically, within a consumption-driven environment that is primarily concerned with profit, we can observe the decline of spatial and cultural distinctiveness. For example, some researchers argue that travelers become progressively exposed to homogenous settings, the result of a replication of culture that disguises itself as traditional tourism. In their quest to reimage themselves and benefit from the economic development possibilities, cities utilize the urban culture they possess and haphazardly convert it into an attraction. Both the physical environments and the experiences that comprise the tourist visit lack rationality and are part of a fragmented postmodern way of life.[7]

As it endeavors to construct exclusivity, urban tourism development slips into banality. City streetscapes become subjected to similarly prescribed methods and the outcome is a culture of serial reproduction,[8] tourist bubbles,[9] or McDonaldization.[10] For example, the concept of McDonaldization has received extensive attention because of its applicability to tourism. Drawing from the Weberian notion of "disenchantment," the idea emphasizes an examination of production. The same principles employed by fast food restaurants are also dominating numerous other sectors of society. In an effort to attain rationality, diverse cultural expression becomes subjugated to the dominance of commodification.[11]

Sociologist George Ritzer extends his idea of McDonaldization to the rise of what he terms the "globalization of nothing," which is a movement away from "something" to "nothing." Social forms are increasingly characterized by a loss of indigenously conceived and locally controlled content. Instead, social realities now maintain conditions devoid of substance. Familiarity with "nothing" thus emerges as the dominant mode of interaction. The key problem according to Ritzer is "loss amidst monumental abundance (of nothing)." Regarding tourism, Ritzer argues that "the proliferation of nothing in tourism leads to boredom as an ever-increasing portion of the world comes to be characterized by the same empty forms (indoor shopping malls, hotel chains, and the like)...the loss of something (in this case, tourist attractions true to local traditions) in the face of the massive expansion of nothing (hotel chains with no ties to the local area)."[12] Recent work by Dennis Judd notes that the study of tourism must move away from the current dominant analytic framework of consumption. Instead, Judd conceptualizes a restructured tourism production system by examining the role and potential ramifications of commodity chains. This is likely to have significant implications since the focus is placed on the structure of the industry, a direction which diminishes the consideration and value of cultural authenticity. The various elements found within what he terms as "investments in place infrastructure" (the museum, the convention center, the domed stadium, and the convention center, and hotel) are examples of an input that can have considerable effects on the tourist experience.[13]

Numerous studies can be found in literature about the homogenization of space. Some even caution of top-down and hegemonic practices that refuse to integrate local voices in the decision-making process. These range from ethnic festivals in urban neighborhoods,[14] branding and promotion of specific spaces via servicescapes and designscapes,[15] as well as the marketing practices of cultural tourism[16] to approaches related to the development of heritage policies.[17]

Figure 7.1   Dam Square in Amsterdam (Courtesy Chuck Suchar).

Not everyone shares this perspective because some argue that tourism has the capacity to showcase and even strengthen the cultural status of a given city or of an urban group to the outside world. A recent study in Australia found that residents living in a coastal area with high tourist activity nearby perceived a higher positive impact of tourism than residents of hinterland areas in the vicinity of high tourist activity.[18] Another study concluded that the Bai people (a Chinese ethnic group) in Dali, China benefited because of tourism development. Specifically, different forms of ethnicity and artifacts promoted in the tourist market have not drowned out the sense of being ethnically Bai. In fact, the tourist industry has become a daily reminder of ethnicity to both insiders and outsiders by making people more self-conscious and reflexive.[19]

The question then remains whether tourism development can be conducted in a way for municipalities to avoid these challenges. Can the potential cultural degradation that is often associated following the creation of tourist spaces with unauthentic environments be avoided? This is very difficult to answer due to numerous complexities. The economic drivers of this sector are so powerful that in many cases even the locals involved in the delivery of tourism place the preservation of identity secondary to financial returns.

For example, the Amana Colonies in southeastern Iowa are seven villages of radical German Pietists who moved to the Midwest from the western part of the state of New York in the 1850s. Amana is a major tourist attraction and is included in the National Historic Landmark list. A study of authenticity and community within this consumption-driven, heritage tourism environment revealed some interesting findings. Specifically, an examination of the social interactions and social structures related to historic conservation and tourism shows that only heritage professionals seem to have a short-term interest in ensuring historical reality through presentation and interpretation. The author concludes that "greater authenticity does not always imply greater profits" and "in communities such as the Amanas, tourist management implies resident management. Residents agree to be managed and controlled if they see a clear profit resulting."[20]

Culturally authentic settings can be successfully developed by employing volunteer tourism. This type of activity focuses on protecting the indigenous environment by immersing the tourist in the specific locale in hopes of producing sustainable outcomes. According to one analysis, "with volunteer tourism, intense rather than superficial social interactions can occur; a new narrative between host and guest is created, a narrative that is engaging, genuine, creative and mutually beneficial. The narrative and traditional interaction between host and tourist is thus potentially rewritten as the tourist experience is actively constructed by the host as well as the tourist."[21]

A variation of this approach is found in creative tourism that advocates the active engagement of tourists. Specifically, "creative tourism involves not just spectating, nor just 'being there,' but reflexive interaction on the part of tourists."[22] Regardless of these proposed solutions, the relationship between tourism and cultural authenticity is complex and the subject of continuing debate. What is certain though is that because of globalization, a reconstituted system of production has given rise to new concentrated consumption patterns that are highly influential. In the process, these come to place considerable pressure and possibly alter previously held community values and cultural practices.

Economic Development Debates: Priorities in Jobs and Expenditures

Economic development arguments in favor of the tourist city typically focus on job creation and a healthy business climate. Both are expected to contribute to an expanding tax revenue base that can then be employed to further social services to local residents. Public expenditure and private investment are rationalized in this manner by local officials and business leaders. For example, the Department of Housing and Urban Development promoted historic preservation as a powerful force in stimulating heritage tourism, economic development, and job growth by noting that "heritage tourism is an economic development tool designed to attract visitors to an area based on its unique history, landscape and culture. This not only boosts regional and local pride but also can be a good source of revenue and employment for a community."[23]

Linking historic preservation efforts to economic growth is just one example of many similar claims that we can see in urban centers across the country. In Detroit, the Tourism Economic Development Council aims to encourage public and private leaders to pursue various aspects of tourism development, mostly in the area of infrastructural development. Specifically, the goal of the council is to increase tourism spending in the region from $5 billion to $8 billion a year. It is expected that this will not only make the city more attractive, but it will also provide needed jobs from construction to service positions.

These types of declarations are regularly reported in mainstream media reports. The Quad Cities Convention and Visitors Bureau is responsible for promoting and managing the tourist activities of the Quad Cities along the Mississippi River. Its jurisdiction includes Davenport and Bettendorf, Iowa and Moline, East Moline, and Rock Island, Illinois. An effort to better understand the travel habits of potential visitors revealed the possibility of more jobs for nearby Chicago. With 300,000 travelers expected to come to the area from Chicago annually, officials are exploring the restoration of passenger rail service. In Michigan, a Centers of Regional Excellence Grant in 2008 focused on the Eastern Upper Peninsula maritime experience. The plan was to create awareness of key maritime-related and cultural tourism attractions. These attractions would help expand the job base.

Even corporations showcase this relationship between tourism and job creation. The following claim by VISA Corporation aptly captures this belief, a position also expressed by local policymakers who believe that it is necessary to induce public and private expenditures if these outcomes are to be achieved. The general idea is that the greater the investment, the bigger the return. The VISA Corporation notes: "Tourism is an important factor to economic growth, job creation and the stimulation of infrastructure development. In the United States, the $1.3 trillion travel and tourism industry generates $116 billion in tax revenue for state, local and federal governments and an estimated 7.7 million direct travel-generated jobs."[24]

There is another view regarding these investments and their celebrated returns. Research analysts and community group advocates point to major discrepancies that often overestimate the extent of the purported economic benefits. This, in turn, ignites extensive debates that often play out in the "Letters to the Editor" section of local and national newspapers. The following commentary by a resident about a publicly subsidized baseball stadium proposed for a new minor league baseball team illustrates this perspective. In 2004, in an effort to bring minor league baseball to Southern Maryland, supporters of the initiative in Charles County identified the city of Hughesville, Maryland as the preferred location for a 4,500-seat stadium. In addition to upsetting the rural character of this small community, opposition to the plan centered on the needed municipal funding necessary for the construction of the facility. Pauleen Brewer, a Hughesville resident submitted the following opinion to *The Washington Post*, outlining the reason why she is rejecting the proposal. Brewer made her point by primarily focusing on the weak job prospects of these expenditures:

> I have no problem with public money being spent to grow existing local businesses that will ultimately benefit local residents. I do have a problem with this "field of schemes"—and a team that, in all reality, will probably be replaced, sold, etc., after two or three years, with the sports team owner moving on all the richer. An already-wealthy sports team owner getting wealthier on taxpayer dollars—none of that money will benefit Charles County. Peanut vendors and concession workers are not the types of jobs we should be putting this money forth to create. The fact that the county administrator included the team players' salaries in the average pay figure for jobs this project will create to boost this number to $33,000 a year is insulting to our intelligence. Enough taxpayers' dollars have been spent on this endeavor. It doesn't have to go any further.[25]

The effort to develop the stadium eventually collapsed, only to reemerge a few years later in nearby Waldorf, Maryland. The Regency Furniture Stadium, completed in 2007 for $25.6 million, is home to the Southern Maryland Blue Crabs of the independent Atlantic League of Professional Baseball.

Benefit claims made by local authorities on the positive returns of tourism are often challenged by independent analyses. A study of downtown infrastructure development in Baltimore reports contradictory findings. Since the 1970s, as part of that city's tourist strategy, municipal leaders have spent $2 billion in constructing and maintaining complementary facilities. Furthermore, hundreds of millions of dollars subsidized tourism businesses, providing visitor services in the popular Inner Harbor area. These were mainly in the form of stadiums and convention and waterfront hotels, which were touted to have significant positive returns for the local economy. In fact, because of the massive downtown investment, Baltimore experienced an increase in available jobs, with the majority of those connected to the tourism industry. Downtown employment grew by 80 percent between 1970 and 1995. Instead of focusing on creating quality jobs, critics assert the tourism economic development plan produced nonunionized, mostly part-time positions. Waiters, cashiers, janitors, and food service workers are not offered health and retirement benefits, making it difficult for workers to support their families. An analysis concluded that the benefits derived from tourism are exaggerated. The report noted that "Baltimore's economic development efforts reveal a recurring history of high costs, low benefits, and a lack of safeguards to ensure that taxpayer investments really pay off in family-wage jobs and an enhanced tax base. The city neglected to enact standards to ensure that the new tourism jobs were of high quality. As a result, low wages and part-time hours are so prevalent that all but three of the city's non-managerial tourism job titles pay less than the federal poverty line for a family of four; many pay far less."[26] As Table 7.2 illustrates below, the majority of the job categories listed in this sector are below the federal poverty line for a family of four ($17,650 per year in 2001).[27]

Similar observations and conclusions are drawn by academic researchers in other cities. For example, Durban, South Africa (the third largest city in South Africa) placed strong emphasis during the 1990s on local economic development strategies by advancing the Trade Point Programme. This effort included considerable infrastructural investment that intended, via the promotion of tourism, to help

Table 7.2   Average Wages for Non-Managerial Tourism Jobs in Baltimore, 2001

	AVERAGE	ANNUAL SALARY FOR AVERAGE HOURS WORKED IN OCCUPATION	PER CENT OF WAGE POVERTY-LINE FOR A FAMILY OF FOUR
Amusement and Recreation Attendants	$ 8.10	$ 11,667	66%
Baggage Porters and Bellhops	$ 7.40	$ 14,007	79%
Bartenders	$ 8.60	$ 13,237	75%
Cashiers	$ 7.80	$ 11,762	67%
Concierges	$ 8.20	$ 13,176	75%
Cooks, Restaurant	$ 10.40	$ 18,171	103%
Counter and Rental Clerks	$ 9.10	$ 14,243	81%
Counter Attendants	$ 7.80	$ 11,762	67%
Dishwashers	$ 7.40	$ 10,120	57%
Food Preparation and Service Workers	$ 7.70	$ 11,892	67%
Janitors and Cleaners	$ 7.90	$ 13,269	75%
Maids and Housekeeping Cleaners	$ 8.10	$ 14,531	82%
Parking Lot Attendants	$ 7.40	$ 12,352	70%
Security Guard	$ 10.30	$ 18,318	104%
Tour Guide	$ 12.40	$ 19,473	110%
Ushers, Lobby Attendants/ Ticket Takers	$ 6.80	$ 6,506	37%
Waiters and Waitresses	$ 7.10	$ 9,931	56%
Average Tourism Job	$ 8.38	$ 13,201	75%
All Occupations	$ 18.40	$ 34,253	194%

Source: Davis, Kate and Chauna Brocht. 2002. "Subsidizing the Low Road: Economic Development in Baltimore." Washington, DC: Good Jobs First (September) 27, p.27 (www.goodjobsfirst.org).

disadvantaged communities and create jobs. However, the focus on the formal economy proved problematic with limited outcomes. In fact, an extensive analysis concluded that it was incapable of meeting the publicized objectives and rationales offered to justify the vast expenditures.[28] Interestingly, one of the key threats facing the growth of tourism in Durban is that even with high levels of unemployment, locals do not seek employment in this sector because of the industry's reputation for offering low-paying jobs. Some have argued that linked tourism, connected to existing or new attractions in neighborhoods, may help renew the commitment and jumpstart local urban revitalization efforts.[29]

Beyond these assessments in direct employment, tourism advocates also argued that the process of creating the needed infrastructure will produce new construction jobs. This would be especially helpful to minority groups that are often in greater need given that they experience higher levels of unemployment and general dislocation. The cases of three cities in Great Britain provide some insightful findings. In recent decades, Birmingham, Sheffield, and Manchester embraced progrowth strategies as a way to recover from the effects of deindustrialization. In Birmingham, from the latter part of the 1980s to the early part of the 1990s, the city council expended an estimated £331 million (about $450 million) in projects related to business tourism and sport. During that same timeframe, Sheffield invested £147 million (about $220 million) on sports and leisure facilities, and Manchester unsuccessfully pursued hosting the Olympic Games following the development of world-class venues. All three cities endeavored to leave behind their manufacturing past and become centers for culture, leisure, and tourism. Given their larger size, history, and status, Birmingham and Manchester also aimed to attract substantial numbers of international visitors.[30]

Job growth proved to be one of the major rationales for this policy direction and a key justification for the substantial public expenditures. The local governments expected that the construction projects would provide jobs for disadvantaged groups and made specific plans to set aside a certain percentage of employment positions for that purpose. One analyst who examined these policies in all three cities concluded that in Birmingham, the construction of the £180 million (about $270 million) International Convention Centre "provided access to low-skilled and low-paid occupations and few inner-city residents obtained jobs at the end of the programme. Whilst a target of 180 jobs was originally identified by the city council, only 80 places were made available (primarily in lower-skilled and lower paid occupations) with only 19 inner-city participants obtaining jobs. Of these 19 successful trainees, 14 were allocated employment within security, cleaning and catering services."[31] Birmingham also experienced considerable construction job leakage outside the city to regional and national firms. The outcome in Sheffield, according to the same analysis, proved similar since "despite these claims, relating to the local economic benefits accruing from Sheffield's massive investment in prestige projects there is some evidence that city residents, and disadvantaged groups in particular, failed to receive substantial economic benefits from them. There are a number of factors that highlight this distributional outcome: first, the need to 'fast track' the construction of the facilities in order to meet the World Student Games timetable, mitigated against the use of smaller local construction firms, with only 37 percent of construction expenditure (£39m—about $60m) retained within the local economy."[32]

In Manchester, the city council adopted an Employment in Construction Charter. The purpose of this initiative was to link the public sector with private companies to support the distribution of jobs to locals. However, the effort once again proved limited in its impact since the study found "the Charter managing agents identified 836 employees working on the prestige project development and other area-based regeneration initiatives within the city, of whom 36 percent were Manchester residents. Additionally, the Charter database held the names and skills of nearly 1,000 individuals of whom only 61 percent has been placed on a construction site. As of December 1994, only 165 people (27 percent of those who had been placed) remained in employment on a construction site."[33] It should be noted that the studies commissioned by the city councils in all three cities, whether conducted internally or by external consulting firms like KPMG Peat Marwick offered very different findings and conclusions. Their assessments focused on the importance of these prestige projects by outlining how they helped meet the differentiated demands of capital caused by globalization. According to these analyses, without these investments, the cities would be unable to compete, grow their local economies, and convey the active nature and dynamic image of their locales.

The Tale of Two Cities: Urban Tourism and Uneven Development

Another major area of debate and criticism that follows large investments in urban tourism relates to the uneven development conditions that it creates. There is a general agreement that postindustrial urban patterns of growth brought about fundamental changes in metropolitan America. The increasingly popular relocation of businesses to the periphery of the central city, and the robust decentralization after World War II had significant social implications. The rapid ascendance of a new service economy resulted in the creation of two communities, or cities. One community comprises educated, highly trained, and well-paid professionals whose skills are central to the increasingly international nature of commerce. The other community comprises low-paid service workers who are needed to help maintain the activities of the reformatted production functions. The latter group is made up of nonunionized, working-class poor who are struggling to make ends meet. These class divisions are reflected in residential patterns and other spatial arrangements within the built environment.

A "dual city" is formed, characterized by affluence and poverty, leading to social polarization and intense division. Separated and disconnected from each other, the two types of communities reflect the formal and the informal economies. Urban injustices are visible and social problems ravage the trapped residents of the poor neighborhoods.[34] Uneven development ensues in the form of disparate social services, private investment, and public attention to community needs. Are these conditions inevitable and an outcome of late capitalism? The following interpretation by sociologists Gregory Squires and Charis Kubrin reflects the foundation of this critique, namely that "uneven development of metropolitan America is a direct result largely of a range of policy decisions made by public officials and policy-related actions taken in the private and non-profit sectors. Policy decisions could be made to alter that pattern of development."[35]

These patterns are identifiable in many cities. The rapid rise of Las Vegas, for example, is attributed to the power of urban tourism. Put on the international map by this sector, the city is often celebrated as the ultimate example of a successful postindustrial economic transformation. It is the envy of municipal leaders and civic boosters from across the world. The Brookings Institution in a 2008 report ranked Las Vegas seventh among the country's 100 largest metropolitan areas for strong trading clusters. The report noted that the geographic concentration of entertainment facilities creates an industry cluster that "represents a potent source of productivity" and one that can "produce more commercial innovation and higher wage employment."[36]

However, the creation of a concentration of employers and a healthy labor market from casinos and leisure activities in Las Vegas is not a pattern of growth to be celebrated. In fact, these conditions can serve as the ultimate scenario of coordinated forces leading to uneven development. On the one hand, you have developers and real estate investors who benefit from the growth of tourism in the city. On the other hand, according to one observer, you have "a growing number of blue-collar Las Vegans, both longtime residents of minority communities and new immigrants of all backgrounds, scrape for a living on the low-rent fringes of the Strip…here the forces of economic marginalization and urban development have united in a sinister compact to displace some of the Strip's poorest residents."[37]

The recent emphasis on building the city of culture and tourism is a part of policy decisions that can have direct and uneven development consequences. Urban core investments cause restructuring with considerable socioeconomic implications for the neighborhoods. A recent study on leisure amenities and urban growth moves operationally away from the use of the Central Business District (CBD) as the basic analytic framework. Instead, this analysis proposes the investigation of the Central Recreation District (CRD). In the past, the CBD served as the main geographic characteristic of urban locations; however, it is argued that the CRD may offer a deeper understanding of demographic change and economic evolution of city neighborhoods.[38]

The CRD is defined "as the locations within a metropolitan area that are close to recreational and leisure-oriented amenities." Two measures for locating these settings are employed. The first measure includes "access to recreational leisure opportunities and aesthetic consumption externalities based on the distance of each census tract in an MSA [Metropolitan Statistical Area] to the central city's tourism information offices," while the second measure is "based on accessibility to historic sites and recreation centers."[39]

An investigation of CRDs between 1990 and 2000 focuses on the top 100 tourist destinations. Of them, 88 are located in metropolitan areas. The total number of census tracts that contain a historic and recreational classification is 2,573. Referenced as "beautiful neighborhoods," the CRDs grew faster than the CBDs during the 1990s, an observation that caused the researchers in this study to reach the following conclusion:

> "Beautiful cities" disproportionally attracted highly educated individuals and experienced faster housing price appreciation, especially in supply-inelastic housing markets. Local government investments in new public recreational areas were associated with increased city attractiveness. Despite worse initial economic conditions, CRDs managed to grow faster than other comparable areas. Rents, incomes, and educational attainment increased faster in such "beautiful neighborhoods," but at the cost of minority displacement. While the American central city generally did not "come back" in the 1990s, the "beautiful city" within flourished.[40]

City center growth through infrastructural development, at the expense of the neighborhoods, receives extensive criticism, sometimes even by local government representatives. A member of the Kansas City Council expressed the following observation as the city pursued a downtown development plan that focused on residential and entertainment renaissance. The official urged that "we should take the same momentum and commitment that's been taken toward downtown, and apply it to neighborhoods; it's the neighborhoods' turn now."[41] But it is not only academics and politicians that express these concerns. Residents who convey their dissatisfaction with public expenditures on leisure also echo this perspective on tourism-oriented activities. The potential consequences of these actions for the disadvantaged are often assertively included on the pages of newspapers across the county. For example, taxpayer support for stadium development tends to ignite intense emotions and negative responses. A Kansas City resident took the following position in a letter to the editor:

> There are many blighted neighborhoods in Kansas City, Mo. I live in one. We have potholes big enough to damage a car tire.... We hear daily about our leaders' plans for new sports arenas and stadiums, refurbished stadiums, rolling roofs and other multimillion-dollar plans that they

want me to vote for and to pay for with my tax money. I don't think so-not until they can use the money we are all paying now to provide some basic services for neighborhoods. Most of the people in Kansas City can't afford to attend the events that take place at these arenas and stadiums anyway. Why should we pay for a playground for the well off?[42]

The debate is fueled further because of the trickle-down approach taken by public leaders who see the success of the downtown linked to the future condition of the neighborhoods. Spokane, Washington experienced considerable recent investment in its downtown, attracting visitor spending and a renewed confidence. However, the city's long-term comprehensive plan to create more livable neighborhoods hinges on the continued viability of its city center. According to the mayor, "we must also focus on the positive since the downtown has been a key to the success of Spokane."[43] City officials hope that the popularity of the $110 million River Park Square shopping mall and entertainment complex will spread into the neighborhoods, since that development proved central to the revitalization of the downtown. Similarly, in Kansas City, a recent mayoral candidate conveyed her support for the neighborhoods and described her commitment to combating blight as a natural outgrowth of the success found in the recent resurgence of the downtown. One political observer described her leadership approach in the following manner: "Among her priorities is the need to extend the downtown renaissance into the neighborhoods or else risk squandering that investment."[44] In that regard, investment in tourism-related infrastructure and programming at the city's core is expected to aid the entire metropolis.

Gentrification and Displacement

The restructuring that follows the promotion of urban tourism as an economic development tool also generates conditions of gentrification and displacement. This spatial transformation is accompanied by changes in the social composition of the residents, a process that receives extensive coverage by sociologists and other social scientists. Urban tourism gentrification is comparable to other types of gentrification, since its general effects relate to remaking both commercial and residential areas. The infusion of entertainment and leisure activities introduces a consumption environment that in turn necessitates the formation of appropriate production processes to meet the increased demands. The genesis of these consumption demands and visitor desires do not just happen. Rather, they are part of the dynamic nature of the built environment within which the quest for growth brings about spatial and socioeconomic changes. An analysis of the Vieux Carré (French Quarter) district in New Orleans, Louisiana shows the ramifications of tourism gentrification. Plans to expand and fortify the tourist-oriented configuration of that area, with the goal of maximizing profit, reduces the past avant-garde and free-spirited qualities found in the neighborhood. These banal representations inject an essence of safety that in turn helps drive capital investment. This then leads to gentrification that also causes displacement.[45]

Much of the debate about urban tourism gentrification draws from the number of positive and negative effects of this process (see Table 7.3 below). For example, displacement through price increases, loss of affordable housing, loss of social diversity, and speculative property price jumps can be identified as some of the problems urban tourism gentrification brings to city neighborhoods. These criticisms are countered by positive outcomes, which include stabilization of declining areas, rising property values, and reduced vacancy rates, increases in municipal revenues, and further investment. Regardless, urban tourism gentrification has fundamentally restructured urban areas. It breathes new life into tired and distressed localities, but it also contributes to the creation of culturally monolithic environments and a general sense of sameness.[46]

Pilsen, Chicago's largest Latino community, powerfully conveys this process. Located on the Lower West Side, the area saw an increasing number of Mexican residents in the late 1950s and 1960s. During the 1970s, Pilsen emerged as a major port of entry for Hispanic immigrants, and in the subsequent decades it developed a very strong ethnic identity. Over the years, the surrounding district maintained a large percentage of foreign-born residents. In the 1980s, the neighborhood became home to the Mexican Fine Arts Center Museum, which was renamed in 2006 as The National Museum of Mexican Art.

Table 7.3   The Positives and Negatives of Urban Tourism Gentrification

POSITIVE	NEGATIVE
	Displacement through rent/price increases
	Secondary psychological costs of displacement
Stabilization of declining areas	Community resentment and conflict
Increased property values	Loss of affordable housing
	Unsustainable speculative property price increases
Reduced vacancy rates	Homelessness
Increase local fiscal revenues	Greater take of local spending through lobbying/ articulacy
Encouragement and increased viability of further development	Commercial/industrial displacement
	Increased cost and changes to local services
Reduction of suburban sprawl	Displacement and housing demand pressures on surrounding poor areas
Increased social mix	Loss of social diversity (from socially disparate mix to rich ghettos)
Rehabilitation of property both with and without state sponsorship	Under occupancy and population loss to gentrified area

Source: Rowland, Atkinson and Gary Bridge. 2005. *Gentrification in a Global Context: The New Urban Colonialism.* Routledge, p. 5.

In recent years, the residents experienced some significant forces, which have threatened their current status. As part of a larger, ethnically based promotional strategy, Pilsen was identified by the city as a tourist destination and the center of Mexican culture and life in Chicago. This unique distinction helped propel the development of related initiatives such as walking tour maps, trolley routes, bus visits, and new signage. These initiatives altered the flavor of the local environment. Furthermore, both the establishment and subsequent expansion of the nearby University of Illinois at Chicago campus, along with the construction of the adjacent University Village, a massive new residential and retail development introduced in the early 2000s, placed considerable pressure on the Pilsen community.

Local community groups organized to address the incoming gentrification that was threatening the community's ethnic character. The Pilsen Alliance embraced a number of mottos as a way to rally the

Figure 7.2 University Village residential development in Chicago, Illiois. The battles over gentrification in Pilsen (Courtesy Chuck Suchar).

residents, including "Pilsen is not for sale" and "Protest gentrification." However, different visions exist on the future development of the area. The local alderman embraced and actively pushed the commodification of Pilsen's culture. By promoting its reorganization as a tourist attraction, it is a strategy that in the end may prove conducive to opening up and gentrifying the neighborhood.[47]

The nearby community of Bronzeville, on the south side of Chicago, offers some related insights. Bronzeville has a long history as the port of entry for African Americans from the Southern states during the late nineteenth and the early part of the twentieth century. By the 1920s, the "Black Metropolis" was nationally recognized and evolved into a major social, cultural, and intellectual hub. However, the immense post-World War II public housing developments and aggressive urban renewal programs in the area created large pockets of poor residents, concentrated on streets where brownstones once housed middle- and upper-income African American residents. In fact, during the 1960s and 1970s, Bronzeville contained some of the poorest census tracts in the entire country.

By the latter part of the 1980s and early 1990s, Chicago's downtown and surrounding residential areas started to experience considerable physical and social changes. Like Pilsen, leaders of community
organizations in Bronzeville, fearing gentrification by white residents,
engaged in efforts to restore the area. A renewed racial nostalgia introduced heritage tourism. Redevelopment projects by African Americans contributed to this larger goal. Deemed capable of reinventing
a racial tradition, these projects received quick support; however, an
analysis of this unique process found that:

> Cities and neighborhoods that create racial heritage tourist districts
> are involved not only in the processes of economic regeneration; they
> are also engaged in the construction and transformation of ethnic and
> racial identities.... Neighborhood residents in the process of reinventing
> their community cannot help but reinvent themselves. And these new
> found collective identities could be used to try to control the process
> of redevelopment. Like other global economies that rely on the com-
> modification of difference, heritage tourism has the potential to change
> patterns of neighborhood revitalization.... In Bronzeville, residents
> were able to disrupt the traditional pattern of racial displacement, both
> by making race a valuable commodity, and by portraying themselves
> as the rightful recipients of the Bronzeville heritage.... Racial heritage
> tourism provides an alternative justification for development and under-
> mines established policies that legitimate more conventional forms of
> gentrification. But it does not give the black community control over the
> decision-making apparatus in development politics.[48]

Gentrification and displacement caused by urban tourism often
extends beyond the residential realm. For example, in Cusco, Peru
the planned displacement of informal traders from the city center is
part of an effort to reorganize the local environment and help grow
tourism. The removal of informal trading is an example of what can
be termed as "policy-led gentrification." Similar trends can be seen in
other urban centers of developing countries.[49]

However, rejecting gentrification and its negative effects is not
embraced by all communities. Harrisburg village is a residential area
west of downtown Augusta, Georgia that desires the infusion of gen-

trification as a way to revitalize itself. Identified as the Harrisburg-West End Historic District by the National Park Service, the location includes the 1797 Ezekiel Harris House, a distinctive structure built by a tobacco merchant that is listed in the National Register of Historic Places. The historic nature of this location presents numerous opportunities for aiding the development of tourism, but in recent decades, poverty, crime, and drug trafficking made the district unattractive. Run-down properties and inattentive landlords turned many neighborhood streets into a nuisance. Two community organizations recently partnered to address these social issues. The Harrisburg West End Neighborhood Association and HONGKONG (Harrisburg Organization Networking for Gentrification to Keep Our Neighborhood from becoming a Ghetto) joined together and held marches. As a way to revive many of the dilapidated homes and take advantage of its historical status and tourism potential, HONGKONG not only welcomes gentrification, but also advocates it.[50]

Public Support of Private Enterprise: Does Urban Tourism Fit the Mold?

Another criticism of urban tourism relates to the close relationship it cultivates between the private and public sectors. This charge has its merits, especially since the potential of future economic growth is closely tied to the advancement of this industry. The local government's pursuit of this strategy as an effective model of economic expansion and improvement furthers this complication, revealing the extent of the association. However, there is a long history of taxpayer assistance of private enterprise. A review of the forces that gave rise to the Sunbelt cities following World War II shows that government spending in support of profit initiatives, undertaken by the private sector, greatly contributed to business relocation and job and population growth. Aggressive federal funding of defense programs and a reconstituted federal tax code favored the Sunbelt. In 1954, the introduction of depreciation allowance deductions encouraged corporations to develop new facilities. Between 1954 and 1980, this subsidy was valued at $30 billion in reduced taxes. Similarly, a 1962 federal subsidy in corporate taxes for new plants was valued in 1982 alone at an impressive $20 billion. The economic growth of cities and states in the South was, in addition to favorable conditions, also the outcome of extensive government support.[51]

Furthermore, the politics in Sunbelt cities underwent significant changes during the postwar era. The culture and practice evolved from being generally centered on a race-based orientation and a conservative outlook to the development of coalitions that connected municipal governments with corporate/business organizations. The quest for growth brought these entities closer together under reform movements such as the Phoenix Charter Government League and the Good Government League in San Antonio. During the 1980s, the latter group spearheaded considerable infrastructure development programs, leading to the remaking of the city's core and adding an expanded freeway system. These programs helped San Antonio experience significant economic growth.[52]

Urban tourism fits this mold. Civic boosters and tourism providers, connected to corporate and business interests, such as hotel and shopping center operators and entertainment providers, find themselves as the recipients of a government framework that aggressively pursues the revitalization of their declining central districts. In the process, public support of these private enterprises generates an outcry of criticism. Stadium subsidies are always in the forefront of these debates. A letter to the editor in Tampa, Florida asked: "My question is this: ...why do the taxpayers of Hillsborough County have to pay $2 to $3 million for a new training room and other ongoing operations at James Raymond Stadium for the Tampa Bay Bucs when they are a for-profit corporation?"[53] In Miami, the proposal for public support of a new baseball stadium elicited the following commentary:

> Such corporate welfare and outright fleecing of taxpayers for the sake of building an already-over-budget baseball stadium is especially dangerous during these foul economic times. Increasing the tax burden on tourism, a key industry for the Miami area, absolutely will hurt the local economy. While local officials and taxpayers might believe that residents will not have to bear these tax burdens, they are sorely mistaken.

Increased hotel taxes result in reduced demand for hotel rooms, which means fewer jobs and a weakened overall business climate.[54]

A related concern surrounds the lack of democratic engagement in the decision-making process. For example, the construction of facilities necessary to create the needed tourist infrastructure rarely includes referendums. Stadium development offers once again interesting insights. From 1984 to 2000, 70 teams on the four major professional leagues built new stadiums.[55] In 2001 and 2002 alone, 10 new stadiums were developed in the NFL, NBA, and MLB.[56] The public sector funded two-thirds of the estimated cost of $17 billion. Between 1990 and 2000, municipalities conducted 26 stadium or arena referendums. Of these, 20 passed and 6 failed.[57] In all of these cases, the teams and their supporters expended considerably more money to ensure passage of the proposed stadium subsidies. In 2004, the Dallas Cowboys and stadium proponents spent $6 million for a stadium subsidy to help fund a new facility for the team. Antisubsidy activists contributed only $43,000 to the opposition effort. By a 54 to 46 percent vote, Arlington, Texas voters approved a .5 percent sales and property tax that allowed the city to contribute $325 million toward the facility's cost.

The use of Tax Increment Financing (TIF) is another practice that is employed extensively to build the tourist city. Here too, critics charge that this strategy benefits the private sector at the expense of the public. Municipalities use TIF revenues to finance conditions that promote the upgrading of the built environment. The first step in the use of TIF is to designate a geographic location in need of special assistance. Generally, this means that the district must be underdeveloped or experiencing blight. The strategy became popular in the 1980s and 1990s and emerged as a significant component of economic development efforts, helping cities replace the limited flow of federal funding.

Officials can accumulate property tax revenues from the increased assessed value that derives from the investments in the TIF district. Instead of these funds going to the traditional taxing units (e.g., schools, city or county governments), the redevelopment district is now the recipient of these monies. Local authorities then use the money to finance debt and complete public projects, which are viewed as being capable of helping the long-term revitalization of the area. Beyond developing the infrastructure, TIF is also used to create a favorable environment for the private sector, inducing capital investment. By using eminent domain to clear residential or commercial areas, private investors are often offered prepared land to complete various projects. This process is conducted at considerable fiscal stress, making it difficult for local authorities to support public services, especially in education, which relies heavily on public resources. Chicago created many such districts, including the Loop, which is now transformed into a tourist Mecca. City officials in Indianapolis employed TIF to develop Circle Center, an indoor shopping mall in the downtown. Greenville, South Carolina used TIF districts to invest in its downtown beautification, and in Austin, Texas, the construction of flood control improvements, under a TIF, is expected to result in parkland enhancement and promote tourism by convention visitors.

An interesting variation and a more focused approach can be found in the Tourist Development Zone (TDZ). As part of its Convention Center and Tourism Development Financing Act of 1998, the State of Tennessee assembled a number of TDZs. This state-administered program authorizes sales tax revenue for financing tourism- and business visitor-related public use facilities such as convention centers and stadiums. Municipalities that fall within the district boundaries receive new sales tax revenues from within the TDZ following the construction of the tourist-related facility. Revenues then are used to pay off the debt of the project with additional monies flowing to the coffers of the local government. The extra disbursements expire after 30 years. According to the Tennessee Department of Revenue, during fiscal year 2006, Chattanooga received $427,823 from this program, $319,835 went to Sevierville, and $7,084,764 was distributed to Memphis.[58]

These types of practices are viewed as bad public policy. For example, a recent report by the National Education Association concluded that:

Too often, these poorly monitored subsidies have gone to low-density industrial parks; tourist, convention, and shopping destinations; and other enterprises that may not really need special public support, do not create long-term jobs with decent wages, and contribute little to community infrastructures as a whole. Moreover, paying businesses to shift their operations from one location to another or even just to stay put—as has happened most visibly with the financing of some sports stadiums—is likely to offer no net benefit for the economy as a whole. What one area may gain, another may lose. That is poor policy at any level.[59]

But the popularity of these local economic development strategies is continuing to gain favor. Cities in the United Kingdom, including Edinburgh, Newcastle, and Birmingham, are looking to regenerate their urban spaces and promote tourism. For many of them, Chicago's 158 TIF districts, which cover 29 percent of the city's territory, serve as a model. *The Economist* published a story quoting an official from that city's community-development department who commented "businesses were leaving Chicago's Loop before it became a TIF district in the 1980s; now the zone is thriving."[60]

Future Directions: The Promises and Challenges of Urban Tourism

A number of issues can be identified regarding the promises and challenges of urban tourism. The first issue concerns the implications that arise from tourism as an industry. In many cases, public officials over-commit public resources in this area, since they view it as an urban savior strategy that on its own could revive their dilapidated core. The fact is that this sector is subjected to fiscal expansions and contractions, conditions that place pressure on municipal leaders who want to see this economic development policymaking as a success. The second issue concerns the changing dynamics of downtown politics. City centers are remade as places of leisure and entertainment, which introduces a different set of political actors into downtown affairs. In the process, this is impacting the nature of urban politics. The third issue concerns the prevalence of access and gentrification, as the revamped residential cores also alter the socioeconomic composition of these reconstituted spaces.

Like other industries, tourism is subjected to larger cycles of boom and bust. Broader economic growth is likely to encourage consumption and expand the number of travelers searching for the products and experiences provided by this sector. These conditions help increase tax revenues, introduce additional jobs, and assist the private interests that can thrive and benefit within this reconstituted environment. Yet, declines in the overall health of the economy will also signal shrinkage and a slump in this area.

A review of tourism reveals the close relationship that exists between this industry and the general status of the economy. These cyclical characteristics are evident in lodging and other subsectors. Room demand and average hotel rates are positively correlated to the GDP and employment growth. In the United States, recessionary periods from 1973 to 1975, 1980 to 1983, 1989 to 1991, and 2001 to 2002 also meant declines in the airline industry. Given this relationship, more research is needed to determine the dynamics of tourism's economic structure. According to one researcher, it is important to understand how spending patterns relate to broader economic forces. In turn, this information can influence policy decisions. Specifically, "how tourism demand is affected by the level of disposable income, the price of commodities, foreign exchange rates, deregulation, and marketing expenditures...could lead to the development of government policies and business strategies that could avert decline, and foster and generate greater tourism activity."[61]

The most recent economic recession though is having slightly different effects. During the 1990s, all types of cities—large and small, urban, suburban, and ex-urban—embraced the tourism agenda. These cities invested billions of dollars to remake their environments and market themselves to visitors in pursuit of tourism as a means of economic growth. In the process, downtowns not only underwent physical transformation, but also experienced residential investment as new neighborhoods emerged in stressed quarters. The expanded tourism supply and reduced demand will mean winners and losers. Some cities will prove unable to recoup their investment, while others will experience a very slow recovery.

It is within these circumstances that one of the major challenges facing urban tourism development is evident. The quest for tourist dollars will intensify at a time of an economic downturn. Due to this, the immediate success forecast by some officials will never be realized. The cities that are likely to fare better within a highly competitive environment are those that:

- Possess an existing tourist infrastructure that has been in recent years augmented with newer attractions
- Possess a larger immediate or surrounding population base
- Have existing natural amenities
- Have strong historical roots
- Already have in place a diversified economic development strategy

The cities that maintain some or all of the above characteristics are likely to be more successful in their tourism marketing efforts. Furthermore, during recessionary times these centers can endure economic decline, and even benefit once the markets revive.

Cities also need to address another challenge inherent in tourism development, one that is present even during good economic times. The resort cycle model conveys a key characteristic in the evolution of tourism.[62] Specifically, new attractions go through stages of maturity. Initially, attractions undergo exploration and discovery by tourists. This is followed by government involvement that eventually fuels precinct development and rapid growth in the number of visitors, which creates a successful draw. As time progresses, the novelty begins to diminish, a condition that generates stagnation and places pressure on the district. Consolidation of services is often employed as a first strategy and a way to sustain the success of the location. Eventually the attraction is forced to follow two different evolutionary paths. It will decline and disappear, or it will persist. Survival though requires rejuvenation. That revitalization process is critical if the community can experience continued visitor growth and sustainable development. Entrepreneurship and the use of private–public partnerships emerge as critical components in the future success of these efforts.[63] This places considerable pressure on local government, which given that it has already made extensive public investments cannot avoid becoming reengaged and committing additional resources.

In addition to the physical remaking of central cities, the political dynamics of downtown development undergo changes. The rise of urban centers as hubs of consumption intensified in the last 30 years and the transformation of tourism and entertainment spaces caused the recalibration of political actors, coalitions, and styles of municipal leadership. Business elites from finance and insurance, manufacturing and retail once dominated the postwar downtowns. Corporate leaders viewed the positioning of the headquarters of their department stores, banks, and investment firms in these locations as an integral part of their profit strategy. Regional and national outreach efforts could be effectively facilitated from these urban cores. Furthermore, these skyscraper-filled environments projected strength and dominance. Postwar suburbanization and globalization shifted these firms elsewhere and, along with it, their interest in the future of city centers.

A recent analysis of civic leadership in Atlanta, Baltimore, and Philadelphia from 1960 to 1970 and 2007 reveals that the board composition of improvement and management districts changed as the types of industries shifted in their location. Real estate representation, almost absent in the membership of downtown committees of the three cities during 1960 to 1970, emerged as a highly influential and formidable player in 2007. The significant city center residential investments and the increased presence of not-for-profit and educational/cultural institutions are also reflected on these improvement organizations. The comparative study concluded that:

> The dominant business sector on downtown boards today is the real estate industry. On all of today's boards, real estate interests (which include developers and leasing agents) represent approximately a quarter of all representatives. This percentage actually undervalues the importance of real estate to these organizations, however, as many of the law firms and "other professional service" firms (which include a number of architectural firms) are very closely tied to the real estate industry. The combined representation of real estate, nonprofit, and public sectors—

three sectors virtually absent from the earlier boards—now comprises about half of the board in Atlanta (47%) and Baltimore (52%), and over a third in Philadelphia (35%). The constituency working for CBD development, at least as represented on peak business association boards, has clearly changed in ways that reflect the changing value and function of the downtown as productive economic space.[64]

Beyond the changing character of these downtown civic organizations, the formal leadership is also promoting a set of urban policies that are operating within a shifting political and economic framework. Structured around neoliberalism, the outcome of these practices also helps support the creation of the tourist city. Political scientist Larry Bennett in his examination of Chicago's Mayor Richard M. Daley concluded that "by shedding redistributive functions, while emphasizing physical enhancements, stripped down municipal custodianship, and attention-garnering mega-events, Richard M. Daley has turned Chicago's municipal government into a public sector agent in support of corporate investment, upscale residential development, and associated arts, entertainment, and leisure sector functions."[65] The role of neoliberalism in guiding urban promotional activities geared toward cultural consumption and infrastructural growth is found in other cities. Milwaukee managed to transform its downtown by following similar strategies.[66]

These conditions fuel one of the major challenges facing urban tourism and the cities that embrace it as a local economic development strategy. Does it work? If so, who benefits? Sociologist John Hannigan in his examination of the "Fantasy City," a reflection of the postmodern metropolis, concludes that the new entertainment economy has further accelerated fragmentation, supported gated communities, and stripped authenticity. The promotion of the city of play for Hannigan is a corporate tool, only concerned with maximizing profit, resulting in an environment dominated by placelessness and a bland homogeneity. On the issue of economic growth, Hannigan notes, "regarding whether or not wealth is recreated, the answer seems to be a resounding "no." By and large, mega-projects such as downtown shopping malls, festival market places, new sports arenas and

stadiums and urban entertainment centers are loss leaders in which
intangible, image-related 'spillovers' are expected to outweigh the
actual economic benefits for the local community."[67]

In addition to supporting gentrification, the new type of urbanism also affects the nature of public space. Urban tourism transforms
downtowns into theme parks. This in turn pushes out the lower and
middle classes and cultivates gentrification. One interpreter of these
conditions notes that the new downtowns are contributing to "spatial
apartheid":

> The problem with the Dallas system is the spatial injustice it has done
> to the city. While one might try to explain away the social and racial
> segregation of Charlotte or Calgary as the minor inconveniences of
> small and self-correcting cities, to see it on the scale of downtown Dal-
> las brings the metaphor of spatial apartheid home: the nonwhite, the
> socially nonconformist, or the politically dissenting are unlikely ever to
> be allowed to install themselves in the quasiprivate domain of the city's
> elevated and underground shopping concourses.[68]

These debates are intense and the implications go beyond issues
of social justice. For example, urban tourism development causes a
variety of neighborhood impacts. Gentrification and displacement are
just two areas that receive extensive attention and coverage, but even
residents with higher incomes attracted by the cultural and entertainment offerings report difficulties. Further research on the relationship
between locals and the tourist could provide a deeper understanding of
these implications. Tourism cities that successfully embrace the classic tourism model that includes a tourism core, direct support zones,
and indirect support zones cannot avoid these challenges. Charleston,
South Carolina maintains a tourism core district, South of Broad.
Visitors engulf this area which contains housing, stores, entertainment facilities, and parks. Residents find that everyday living is overwhelming given the large number of tourists who dominate the streets
and cause extensive pedestrian and traffic jams. In addition, many
residents feel that that their lives are constantly on display.[69]

While these issues must be taken seriously, it is clear that the emergence of postwar urban tourism breathed new life into many declin-

Figure 7.3   The village of Anafiotika is located directly under the north section of the Acropolis in Athens, Greece. Situated in the popular destination of Plaka, the residents interact daily with tourists, drawn by the traditional setting (Courtesy Ollirg, Shutterstock Images).

ing urban areas, and from that perspective its presence can be assessed as being quite positive. Investments in creating attractions expanded the local economies, improved infrastructure and allowed for property redevelopment and reuse. Furthermore, successful cities came to see increased numbers of new residents, shoppers and tourists walking their once deserted streets. Art districts composed of galleries, restored theaters and mixed-use projects anchoring retail, residential and entertainment helped create an around-the-clock downtown environment. These reformatted settings proved reminiscent of late nineteenth century urban life.

Urban Tourism and the Cities of the Twenty-First Century

As we look into the future, cities will only intensify their pursuit of tourism activities, maintaining a competitive outlook, searching for ways to attract visitors, and capture dollars. In an effort to upgrade their services, cities will also expand their amenities. These amenities will lead to greater residential development, and depending on the nature of local leadership, some cities will emerge more successful than others in achieving their goals. These pacesetters can combat the current unauthentic and mass-produced visitor environments, offering new alternatives to leisure and entertainment. The way manufacturing fueled advancement and positioned cities as centers of building human capital, tourism is currently signaling a new era of urban change. This time it will be within a postindustrial, consumption-driven economy, altering not only the physical environment, but also, once again, keeping cities relevant following the postwar urban decline. Thus, the stage is set for further growth in commerce and culture.

Due to the complementary nature of their goals, partnerships between local governments, convention and tourism bureaus, and business improvement districts will not only persist, but also likely strengthen. These arrangements will become central to the future growth of this industry. At the same time, a greater understanding of these developing and highly influential tourism coalitions is necessary. The maturation of this sector makes these arrangements relevant because of the significant economic ramifications. The future advancement of urban tourism in the United States and many other developed nations will be increasingly tied to lifestyle and quality-of-life arguments and considerations. Investments in new bicycle paths, open spaces, parks, and attractive streetscapes will directly support this goal. On the other hand, developing countries will largely draw from the financial rationales of this strategy. In both cases, it is expected that public expenditures (infrastructure and marketing) will continue because of intercity competition, focusing on attracting businesses, new residents, and visitors.

Increased leisure time and lifestyle changes place tourism in the forefront as a major world industry with a significant impact on many other economic sectors, from transportation to sales. Furthermore, the vast resources developed to serve the consumption desires of visitors necessitate a better understanding of tourist behavior, including the social and economic impacts of these practices. The reliance on cost-benefit analysis has limitations and the politicization of the issues clouds the debates. Regardless of these concerns, a renewed interest in the downtown is evident in both larger and smaller cities. Capital investment is likely to continue as the economic conditions improve. Interestingly, media coverage of the reconstituted CBDs also helped increase federal contributions and leveraged additional types of fundraising. For those that argue that downtowns are dying, urban tourism proves them wrong. Urban sprawl and deconcentrated spatial patterns, visible during the 1970s and 1980s, do not offer the dominant interpretation of urbanization and urbanism anymore. With a new function and a renewed energy, urban centers will continue to be relevant and functional in a highly dynamic, competitive and complex built environment.

However, the tourism industry and cities which view this sector as being central to their economic development strategies must also deal with possible changes. A number of questions emerge as we think about the future of urban tourism. Specifically, what if environmental/energy constraints substantially increase costs and reduce the volume of international tourism? Is there a possibility of building more environmentally sustainable forms of tourism? Can tourism be reshaped to provide more equitable rewards; for example, for service workers in hotels and restaurants? Addressing these issues and the related forces might produce new or even more desirable varieties of urban tourism. This in turn can lead this sector into a new cycle that is not only economically sound but also socially responsive.

Writing, Reflection, and Debate

Discussion Questions

One of the major critiques of urban tourism is that it reduces cultural authenticity. Can you identify ways to reverse that effect? Can sustainability and tourism coexist? What are some ways to achieve that outcome?

Economic impact studies are often employed to rationalize public spending on tourist infrastructure. What are some of the challenges presented by these tools? Are there more measured ways to approach making these large expenditures?

How can the development of urban tourism assist the disadvantaged? How can we ensure that it benefits the community?

NOTES

Chapter 1

1. Furman, Barbara. 1996. *Challenging the Growth Machine: Neighborhood Politics in Chicago and Pittsburgh*. Lawrence, KS: University Press of Kansas.
2. Majors, Dan. 2007. "Pittsburgh Rated 'Most Livable' Once Again: After 22 years, Back Atop." *Pittsburgh Post-Gazette* (April 25).
3. Carpenter, Mackenzie. 2009. "Pittsburgh Ranked Tops in U.S. by *The Economist*." *Pittsburgh Post-Gazette* (June 10).
4. Levy, Francesca. 2010. "America's Most Livable Cities." http://www.forbes.com/2010/04/29/cities-livable-pittsburgh-lifestyle-real-estate-top-ten-jobs-crime-income.html (accessed May 2, 2010).
5. Jacobson, Louis. 2002. "Pittsburgh Rebuilds Its North Shore With Link Across River to Downtown." *Planning* 68(5):34–35.
6. "Pittsburgh: How Now Brown Town? A Former Steel City Is Now Proclaiming its Cleaner Land and Clever Minds." 2006. *The Economist* (September 14).
7. Rotstein, Gary. 2009. "Population of Region Drops, But Rate's Slower" *Pittsburgh Post-Gazette* (March 19).
8. See Mayor's Office, City of Pittsburgh. http://www.city.pittsburgh.pa.us/mayor/ (accessed January 11, 2010).
9. "Pittsburgh: How Now Brown Town?" A Former Steel City is Now Proclaiming its Cleaner Land and Clever Minds." 2006. *The Economist* (14 September).
10. Schooley, Tim. 2005. "South Side Works Adding AmEagle, BCBG." *Pittsburgh Business Times* (January 21).
11. U.S. Census Bureau. *Report on Transportation Business in the United States at the Eleventh Census 1890*, p. 4.
12. Warner, Sam Bass, Jr. 1968. *The Private City*. Philadelphia: University of Pennsylvania Press.
13. Wade, Louise Carol. 2004. "Meatpacking." In *Encyclopedia of Chicago*, J. R. Grossman, A. Durkin Keating, and J. L. Ruff, eds. (pp. 515–517). Chicago: University of Chicago Press.
14. Addams, Jane. 1909. *The Spirit of Youth and the City Streets*. New York: Macmillan.
15. "A Timeline: 1898–1998 (History of Park Organizations Around the US)." 1998. *Parks & Recreation* (July 1).

16.　Ibid.

17.　McLean, Daniel D., Amy R. Hurd, and Nancy Brattain Rogers. 2007. *Recreation and Leisure in Modern Society*. Sudbury, MA: Jones and Bartlett.

18.　Hunnicutt, Benjamin Kline. 1984. "The End of Shorter Hours." *Labor History* 25(3): 373–404.

19.　McLean, Daniel D., Amy R. Hurd, and Nancy Brattain Rogers. 2007. *Recreation and Leisure in Modern Society*. Sudbury, MA.: Jones and Bartlett Publishers.

20.　Currell, Susan. 2005. *The March of Spare Time: The Problem and Promise of Leisure in the Great Depression*. Philadelphia: University of Pennsylvania Press; McLean, Daniel D, Amy R. Hurd, and Nancy Brattain Rogers. 2007. *Recreation and Leisure in Modern Society*. Sudbury, MA: Jones and Bartlett Publishers.

21.　Gems, Gerald R. 2001. "Welfare Capitalism and Blue-Collar Sport: The Legacy of Labour Unrest." *Rethinking History* 1(5): 43–58.

22.　Industrial Recreation Association. 1944. *Annual Conference Proceedings*, April 4–6, Chicago.

23.　Beauregard, Robert A. 1993. *Voices of Decline: The Post-War Fate of US Cities*. Oxford: Blackwell; Judd, Dennis R., and Todd Swanstrom. 1994. *City Politics*. New York: HarperCollins.

24.　Bluestone, Barry, and Bennett Harrison. 1982. *The Deindustrialization of America: Plant Closings, Community Abandonment, and the Dismantling of Basic Industry*. New York: Basic Books.

25.　Levy, Frank. 1998. *The New Dollars and Dreams: American Incomes and Economic Change*. Ithaca, NY: Cornell University Press.

26.　Lundberg, George A., Mirra Komarovsky, and Mary Alice McInerny. 1934. *Leisure: A Suburban Study*. New York: Columbia University Press, p. 78.

27.　Pieper, Josef. 1952. *Leisure: The Basis of Culture*. New York: Pantheon Press, p. 112.

28.　Brooks, John. 1983. "Highbrow, Lowbrow, Middlebrow—Now: An Interview with Russell Lynes." *American Heritage Magazine* 34(4): 25–29.

29.　Judd, Dennis R., and Todd Swanstrom. 1994. *City Politics*. New York: HarperCollins.

30.　Mollenkopf, John. 1975. "The Postwar Politics of Urban Development." *Politics and Society* 5(1): 247–296.

31.　McDonald, John. 2008. *Urban America: Growth, Crisis, and Rebirth*. Armonk, NY: M.E. Sharpe.

32.　Sugrue, Thomas. 1996. *The Origins of the Urban Crisis: Race and Inequality in Postwar Detroit*. Princeton, NJ: Princeton University Press.

33.　Linkon, Sherry Lee, and John Russo. 2002. *Steeltown U.S.A.: Work & Memory in Youngstown*. Lawrence: University Press of Kansas.

34.　Gutman, Marta. 2007. "Equipping the Public Realm: Rethinking Robert Moses and Recreation." In *Robert Moses and the Modern City: The Transformation of New York*, H. Ballon and K. T. Jackson, eds. (pp. 72–85). New York: W.W. Norton.

35.　Caro, Robert. 1974. *The Power Broker: Robert Moses and the Fall of New York*. New York: Knopf.

36.　Levy, Frank. 1998. *The New Dollars and Dreams: American Incomes and Economic Change*. New York: Russell Sage.

37.　Baum, Arthur W. 1953. "The New Leisure: Back-Yard Sports." *Saturday Evening Post* 226(5): 21–58.

38.　Ibid.

39.　Habermas, Jürgen. 1956. "Notizen zum missverhaltnis von kultur und konsum." *Merkur* 10(1): 212–228.

40.　Hemingway, John L. 1996. "Emancipating Leisure: The Recovery of Freedom in Leisure." *Journal of Leisure Research* 28(1): 27–43.

41. Butsch, Richard. 1984. "The Commodification of Leisure: The Case of the Model Airplane Hobby and Industry." *Qualitative Sociology* 7(3):217–235, p. 227.

42. Beauregard, Robert A. 2006. *When America Became Suburban*. Minneapolis: University of Minnesota Press.

43. Beauregard, Robert A. 2001. "Federal Policy and Postwar Urban Decline: A Case of Government Complicity?" *Housing Policy Debate* 12(1):129–151.

44. Garreau, Joel. 1991. *Edge City: Life on the New Frontier*. New York: Doubleday.

45. Lang, Robert, E., and Jennifer LeFurgy. 2003. "Edgeless Cities: Examining the Noncentered Metropolis." *Housing Policy Debate* 14(3):427–460.

46. Stipe, Robert E., and Antoinette J. Lee. 1987. *The American Mosiac: Preserving a Nation's Heritage*. Washington, DC: U.S. Committee, International Council on Monuments and Sites.

47. Satchell, Michael. 1997. "Parks in Peril: The Views Are Still Spectacular, the Wildlife Abundant. Everybody Loves America's National Parks. So Why Are They Under Siege?" *U.S. News and World Report* (July 21).

48. Associated Press. 2009. "Illinois Site Among Nine New Historic Landmarks." (January 17).

49. Schaeffer Munoz, Sara. 2006. "Preserving the Tract Home: Historic Districts on the Rise to Boost Property Values, Owners Seek Designation." *The Wall Street Journal* (March 16).

50. Stanley, Frank. 1953. "They Drive Travel Agents Crazy!" *Saturday Evening Post*, 225(30): 112–118.

51. Beauregard, Robert A. 1998. "Tourism and Economic Development Policy in US Urban Areas." In *The Economic Geography of the Tourist Industry: A Supply-side Analysis*, D. Ioannides and K. G. Debbage, eds. (pp. 220–234). New York: Routledge; Law, Christopher M. 2002. *Urban Tourism: The Visitor Economy and the Growth of Large Cities*. New York: Continuum.

52. Wellner, Alison Stein. 2000. "Where Tourists Spend Big." *American Demographics* 22(12): 22–24.

53. Baedeker, Rob. 2007. "America's 30 Most Visited Cities." *Forbes Traveler* (July 27).

54. Las Vegas Convention and Visitors Authority. 2008. Press Release. "Las Vegas Counts on '21' for New Marketing Campaign." (January 8).

55. Roberts, Dick. 1968. "Postwar Capitalist Development at a Turning Point." *International Socialist Review* 29(2): 35–49.

56. Brozen, Yale. 1954. "Business Leadership and Technological Change." *American Journal of Economics & Sociology* 14(1):13–30.

57. Hunter, Helen. 1978. "Corporate Demand for Cash: The Influence of Corporate Population Growth and Structure." *Review of Economics & Statistics* 60(3):467–471.

58. "The Great American Get-Together." 1969. *Forbes* 103(4): 28–35.

59. Robinson, John, and Geoffrey Godbey. 1999. *Time for Life*. University Park: Pennsylvania State University Press; Juster, Thomas, and Frank Stafford. 1985. *Time Goods and Well-Being*. Ann Arbor: University of Michigan.

60. Aguiar, Mark, and Erik Hurst. 2007. "Measuring Trends in Leisure: The Allocation of Time Over Five Decades." *Quarterly Journal of Economics* 3(8): 969–1006.

61. Robinson, John, Geoffrey Godbey, Jeremy Greenwood, and Guillaume Vandenbroucke. 2005. "Hours Worked: Long-Run Trends" (NBER Working Paper No. 11629). Washington, DC: National Bureau of Economic Research.

62. Statistical Abstract of the United States: 2007, Table 1218; Statistical Abstract of the United States: 1986, Table 385.

63. Coakley, Jay. 2009. *Sports in Society*. New York: McGraw-Hill.

Chapter 2

1. Held, David. 2004. *A Globalizing World? Culture, Economics, Politics*. London: Routledge; Sassen, Saskia. 2006. *Cities in a World Economy*. Thousand Oaks, CA: Pine Forge Press.

2. Plaza, Beatriz. 2000. "Guggenheim Museum's Effectiveness to Attract Tourism." *Annals of Tourism Research* 27(4): 1055–1058.

3. Kong, Lily. 2000. "Cultural Policy in Singapore: Negotiating Economic and Socio-Cultural Agendas." *Geoforum* 31(4): 409–424.

4. Brown, Lester R. and Michael Renner. 1999. *Vital Signs 1999–2000*. London: Earthscan.

5. From http://www.hyatt.com (accessed January 4, 2009).

6. Knowles, Dimitrios Diamantis, and Joudallah Bey El-Mourhabi. 2001. *The Globalization of Tourism and Hospitality: A Strategic Perspective*. London: Continuum.

7. World Travel & Tourism Council. 2008–2009. " Progress and Priorities." London: Author.

8. United Nations World Tourism Organization (UNWTO). 2008. Press Release. "World Tourism Exceeds Expectations in 2007—Arrivals Grow from 800 million to 900 million in Two Years." (January 29).

9. Tourism Market Trends. 2006. "International Tourism Receipts, 1950–2005, Annex 10." Madrid: UNWTO.

10. Hiernaux-Nicolas, Daniel. 1999. "Cancun Bliss in the Tourist City." In *The Tourist City*, D. R. Judd and S. S. Fainstein, eds. (pp. 124–139). New Haven, CT: Yale University Press.

11. "The Globalization of Tourism." 1991. *The Unesco Courier* (July/August).

12. "Hotel Construction Pipeline Growth—Pace Slides in Third Quarter." 2005. *Mortgage Banking* (December 1).

13. "Hotel Construction Pipeline Poised for Record Growth." 2006. *Mortgage Banking* (April 1).

14. McCord, Michael. 2005. "Construction of Downtown Hotel Signals New Era in City." *Portsmouth Herald* (May 1); Forster, Dave. 2008. "Suffolk Centerpiece Hilton Garden Inn to be Sold." *The Virginian-Pilot* (May 21); Long, Tom. 2008. "All Ahead Slow: Fiscal Crunch Delays Portsmouth Development." *Boston Globe* (October 26).

15. HOTELS Giants Survey 2008.

16. Derek Gale. 2008. "Hotels' 325." *Hotels* (July 1).

17. "Household Data Annual Averages: Employed persons by Detailed Industry, Sex, Race, And Hispanic Or Latino Ethnicity, 2003, 2007." Labor Force Statistics (Current Population Survey).

18. Suro, Robert. 2005. *Attitudes about Immigration and Major Demographic Characteristics*. Washington, DC: Pew Hispanic Center (March 2).

19. Gladstone David L., and Susan S. Fainstein. 2003. "Regulating Hospitality: Tourism Workers in New York and Los Angeles." In *Cities and Visitors: Regulating People, Markets, and City Space*, L. M. Hoffman, S. S. Fainstein, and D. R. Judd, eds. (pp. 145–166). Oxford, UK: Blackwell.

20. Altshuler, Alan, and David Luberoff. 2003. *Mega-Projects: The Changing Politics of Urban Public Investment*. Washington, DC: The Brookings Institution.

21. Fainstein, Susan S. 2004. "Tourism and Globalization." Lecture presented at the University of Tenerife, Canary Islands.

22. Kotler, Philip, Donald H. Haider, and Irving Rein. 1993. *Marketing Places: Attracting Investment, Industry, and Tourism to Cities, States and Nations*. New York: Free Press.

23. Lane, Amy. 2005. "Getting the Word Out." *Crain's Detroit Business* (July 4).

24. Oregon Tourism Commission. 2009. *Travel Oregon: Strategic Marketing Plan and Budget, 2007–2009*. Salem, OR: Author.

25. Powell, Ronald W. 2007. "Tourism District OK'd by Council." *The San Diego Union Tribune* (October 17).

26. Duxbury, Sarah. 2008. "SF Hotels to Boost City's Tourism Funds." *San Francisco Business Times* (October 22).

27. Iuspa, Paola. 2001. "Half-Billion Targeted for City of Miami Capital Projects." *Miami Today* (October 18).

28. Fenton, Susan. 2007. "China Says Tourism Surge Challenges Infrastructure." *Reuters News Service* (June 18).

29. Herd, John, and George Griffiths. 1980. *Discovering Dunedin*. Dunedin, New Zealand: McIndoe.

30. Malcolm Farry. 2007. "The Dunedin Stadium Project." Presentation at the City and Sport Symposium, University of Otago (November 4).

31. Williams, John. 2009. "Dunedin Residents' Support for Public Funding of the Proposed Otago Stadium." Department of Marketing, University of Otago (January 19).

32. Gustafson, Sven. 2007. "Detroit Gambles to Increase Tourism. *USA Today* (September 4).

33. Laseca, Erick. 2006. "Private Investment in Mexico's Tourism Sector Booming." Press Release. Mexico Tourism Board Chicago (July 31).

34. Government of Western Australia. 2000. "$1.1 Billion Earmarked for Private Tourism Development in WA." Media Release (February 29).

35. David C. Perry. 2003. "Urban Tourism and the Privatizing Discourses of Public Infrastructure." In *The Infrastructure of Play: Building the Tourist City,* D. R. Judd, ed. (pp. 19–49). Armonk, NY: M.E. Sharpe.

36. Meyer, Gregory. 2007. "Movement on McCormick Hotel Expansion to Wait." *Crain's Chicago Business* (February 6).

37. Noludwe, Ncokazi. 2007. "US City Links/SACN Led Knowledge Exchange Programme." Buffalo City and Virginia Beach Case Report, Buffalo City, South Africa.

38. Hackett, Kim. 2008. "Stadium Strike-Out: After a Last Inning Defeat, Is the Game Really Over for the Reds and their Supporters?" *Sarasota Magazine* (February 1).

39. Balko, Radley. 2008. "So Long, Seattle: Stadium Welfare Schemes." *Reason* (May 1).

40. Strasburg, Jenny. 2004. "Will They Visit S.F.? Budget Battle Pits Funding for Tourism Bureau vs. Social Services." *San Francisco Chronicle* (December 11).

41. Norris, Donald F. 2003. "If We Built, They Will Come! Tourism-Based Economic Development in Baltimore." In *The Infrastructure of Play: Building the Tourist City* D. R. Judd, ed. (pp. 125–167). Armonk, NY: M. E. Sharpe.

42. Walker, Andrea K. 2008. "Harborplace Up For Sale." *Baltimore Sun* (December 19).

43. "Baltimore Remains a Top Destination For Tourists." 1999. Press Release. Baltimore Area Convention and Visitors Association (August 23); "Baltimore Fast Facts for Meeting Planners." 2006. Press Release. Baltimore Area Convention and Visitors Association (September 12).

44. TSA Tourism Satellite Accounting. 2008. *The Travel and Tourism Economic Research: United States*. London, UK: World Travel & Tourism Council.

45. Jasen Lee, and Roche, Lisa Riley. 2008. "State's Tourism Ad Budget May be cut." *Desert News* (December 23).

46. Sealover, Ed. 2009. "State Spending on Tourism a Hot Potato for Lawmakers: Debate Centers on Lean Times vs. Promoting Visits." *Rocky Mountain News*

(January 12); Moore, Paula. 2003. "Tourism Boosters Lag Competition." *Denver Business Journal* (November 28).

47. Lerner, Jill. 2003. "Officials Try to Save Fund From Budget Tax." *Boston Business Journal* (May 16).

48. Ryan Kate. 2006. "Chicago's Tourism Budget a Straggler." *Crain's Chicago Business* (June 5).

49. Kotler, Philip, Donald H. Haider and Irving Rein. 1993. *Marketing Places: Attracting Investment, Industry, and Tourism to Cities, States, and Nations.* New York: Free Press.

50. Aguilar, Louis. 2007. "Tourism Office Puts Spin on Detroit: Visitors Bureau Unveils Glitzy New Push to Sell City's Assets—Music, Cars, Gaming—to Tourists." *Detroit News* (February 1).

51. Bradley, Andrew, Tim Hall, and Margaret Harrison. 2002. "Promoting New Images for Meetings Tourism." *Cities* 19(1): 61.

52. "Decision 1419/1999 of the European Parliament and of the Council." 1999. European Parliament (May).

53. Laider, Dorota. 2003. "Interview with Director of European Integration, Department of Cooperation and Promotion." Krakow City Hall (November 26).

54. Zyrkowski, Artur. 2003."Interview with Director of Promotion of Tourism, Department of Cooperation and Promotion." Krakow City Hall (November 27).

55. "Krakow in Numbers, 2007." 2008. Municipality of Krakow, City Strategy and Development Department Report (February 5).

56. Lee, Denny. 2007. "Poland's Second City is First Choice for the Young. *The New York Time*s (May 27).

57. Giuliani, Rudolph, W. 1997. "The Entrepreneurial City." Speech at The Manhattan Institute, New York City (December 3).

58. Goldsmith, Stephen. 1999. *The Entrepreneurial City: A How-To Handbook for Urban Innovators.* New York: Manhattan Institute.

59. Porter, Michael, E. 2005. "More Tales of the Inner City." *Inc. Magazine* (June).

60. Andranovich, Greg, Matthew J. Burbank, and Charles H. Heying. 2001. "Olympic Cities: Lessons Learned from Mega-Event Politics." *Journal of Urban Affairs* 23(2): 113–131.

61. Preuss, Holger, and Marcia Semitiel Garcia. 2004. *The Economics of Staging the Olympics: A Comparison of the Games, 1972–2008.* Northampton, MA: Edward Elgar.

62. Collison, Kevin. 2007. "Add Students to Urban Revival: Downtown Backers Plan Charter Middle School as Part of Downtown's Renaissance." *The Kansas City Star* (March 9).

63. Pinsky, Mark. 2007. "As Do*wntown* is Reborn, So Are Its Churches: Orlando's Rapid Residential R*evival* Creates the Possibility of a Religious Resurrection." *The Orlando Sentinel* (March 18).

64. Crowe, Robert. 2005. "Popular Houston Cultural Festival to Return to Downtown." *Houston Chronicle* (January 13).

65. City of Toronto, Canada. http://www.toronto.ca/index.htm (accessed January 15, 2009).

Chapter 3

1. Judd, Dennis R., and Susan S. Fainstein, 1999. *The Tourist City.* New Haven, CT: Yale University Press; Gottdiener, Mark, Claudia C. Collins, and David R. Dickens. 1999. *Las Vegas: The Social Production of an All-American City.* Malden, MA:

Blackwell; Gotham, Kevin Fox. 2007. *Authentic New Orleans: Tourism, Culture, and Race in the Big Easy*. New York: New York University Press.

2. Zukin, Sharon. 1991. *Landscapes of Power: From Detroit to Disney World*. Berkeley: University of California Press; Zukin, Sharon. 1995. *The Culture of Cities*. Oxford: Blackwell.

3. Wan, Yee Lai. 2006. "Overall Performance and Issues and Challenges of the Penang Tourism Industry." Paper presented at the Penang Tourism Seminar, Socio-Economic & Environmental Research Institute (SERI), Penang, Malaysia (November 7).

4. Peggy Teo. 2003. "Limits of Imagineering: A Case Study of Penang." *International Journal of Urban and Regional Research* 27(3): 545–63.

5. Biles, Anthony. 2001. "A Day Trip to the Urban Jungle." *Regeneration and Renewal* (August 17); Shaw, Stephen J. 2007. "Ethnoscapes as Cultural Attractions in Canadian 'World Cities.'" In *Tourism, Culture and Regeneration*, M. K. Smith, ed. (pp. 49–58). Wallingford, UK: CABI.

6. Lemcke, Warren. 2007. "Granville Entertainment District: Administrative Report." Vancouver City Council (October 30).

7. Cohen, Eric. 2004. *Contemporary: Tourism, Diversity and Change*. London: Elsevier.

8. Shaw, Stephen J. 2007. "Ethnoscapes as Cultural Attractions in Canadian 'World Cities.'" In *Tourism, Culture and Regeneration*, M. K.Smith, ed. (pp. 49–58). Wallingford, UK: CABI.

9. National Register of Historic Places. 2004. "National Register Federal Program Regulations" (July 1).

10. Robinson, Katharine S. 2005. *Save the Heritage of New Orleans*. Charleston, SC: Historic Charleston Foundation (October 1).

11. "Estimation of Tourism Economic Impacts in the Charleston Area, 2008." 2009. Office of Tourism Analysis, College of Charleston.

12. Ashworth, Gregory J. 2008. "Grote Markt Groningen: The Re-Heritagization of the Public Realm." In *City Spaces, Tourist Places: Urban Tourism Precincts*, B. Hayllar, T. Griffin, and D. Edwards, eds. (pp. 261–274). Oxford, UK: Butterworth-Heinemann.

13. Spirou, Costas. 2007. "Cultural Policy and Urban Restructuring in Chicago." In *Tourism, Culture and Regeneration*, M. K. Smith, ed. (pp. 123–131). Wallingford, UK: CABI.

14. "Crain's List Largest Tourist Attractions (Sightseeing): Ranked by 2007 Attendance." 2008. *Crain's Chicago Business* (June 23).

15. Edwards, Deborah, Tony Griffin, and Bruce Hayllar. 2008. "Darling Harbour: Looking Back and Moving Forward." In *City Spaces, Tourist Places: Urban Tourism Precincts*, B. Hayllar, T. Griffin, and D. Edwards, eds. (pp. 274–294). Oxford, UK: Butterworth-Heinemann.

16. Bailey, Christopher. 1993. "The Politics of Work in an Enterprise Culture: Technology Networks and the Revival of the Inner Cities." *Journal of Design History* 6(3): 185–197.

17. Loney, Nick, Jaime Carpenter, and Clive Dutton. 2004. "Risks in Regeneration." *Regeneration & Renewal* (July 30).

18. Liverpool City. 2004. *Council Regeneration and Development in Liverpool City Centre, 1995–2004* (July).

19. Hodgson, Neil. 2007. "People Power to Decide Fate of New Waterfront." *Liverpool Daily Echo* (March 7).

20. Coligan, Nick. 2007. "Waterfront Mile Gets Facelift: 20 Projects Change the Shape of City." *Liverpool Daily Echo* (August 7).

21. Gunby, Emma. 2007. "Liverpool Waterside Will Rival that of Manhattan." *Liverpool Daily Post* (March 7); Neild, Larry. 2007. "Visionary Design for City's Front Porch; Is Liverpool the New Shanghai?" *Liverpool Daily Post* (March 7).

22. Sasaki Associates, ERA. 2005 "Kansas City Downtown Corridor Strategy." Prepared for The Civic Council of Greater Kansas City (June).

23. Kind, Mark. 2005. "Analyst Proposes $357M Downtown Stadium." *Kansas City Business Journal* (October 12).

24. Kyriazi, Gary. 1997. *Amusement Parks: A Pictorial History.* Secaucus, NJ: Castle Books; Braun, Michael. 2001. "The Economic Impact of Theme Parks on Regions." Paper prepared for NEURUS—Network of European and US Regional and Urban Studies (November 21).

25. Jeffers, Gene, and Judith Rubin. 2008. "Theme Park Attendance Report for 2007." Report by the Themed Entertainment Association (TEA) and Economics Research Associates (REA).

26. Associated Press. 2006. "Disney Future: More Ships, Urban Hotels?" (February 12).

27. Foglesong, Richard. 1999. "Walt Disney World and Orlando: Deregulation as a Strategy for Tourism." In *The Tourist City*, D. Judd and S. S. Fainstein, eds. (pp. 89–106). New Haven, CT: Yale University Press.

28. "The International Drive Master Transit & Improvement District." 2007, Presentation on International Drive Resort Area Development Update and Profiles (June).

29. Loukaki, Argyro. 1997. "Whose Genius Loci? Contrasting Interpretations of the Sacred Rock of the Athenian Acropolis." *Annals of the Association of American Geographers* 87(2): 306–329.

30. Deffner, Alex. M. 2005. "The Combination of Cultural and Time Planning: A New Direction for the Future of European Cities." *City* 9(1): 125–141.

31. Spirou, Costas. 2008. "The Evolution of the Tourism Precinct." In *City Spaces, Tourist Places: Urban Tourism Precincts*, B. Hayllar, T. Griffin, and D. Edwards, eds. (pp. 19–38). Oxford, UK: Butterworth-Heinemann.

32. Coates, Dennis, and Victor A. Matheson. 2009. "Mega-Events and Housing Costs: Raising the Rent while Raising the Roof?"International Association of Sports Economists, Working Paper Series, No. 09-02) (February).

33. Hersh, Philip. 2008. "Athens Post-Olympics Legacy: Empty Spaces, Unsightly Venues, Uncertain Tomorrow." *Chicago Tribune* (August 4).

34. Andranovich, Greg, Matthew J. Burbank and Charles H. Heying. 2001."Olympic Cities: Lessons Learned from Mega-Event Politics." *Journal of Urban Affairs* 23(2): 113–131.

35. Ryan Ong. 2004. "New Beijing, Great Olympics: Beijing and its Unfolding Olympic Legacy." *Stanford Journal of East Asian Affairs* 4(2): 35–49.

36. Hofstede Geert. 2001. *Culture's Consequences.* Thousand Oaks: Sage.

37. Ng, Siew Imm, Julie Anne Lee, and Geoffrey N. Soutar. 2007. "Tourists' Intention to Visit a Country: The Impact of Cultural Distance." *Tourism Management* 28(6): 1497–1506.

38. Weed, Mike. 2008. *Olympic Tourism.* Oxford, UK: Butterworth-Heinemann.

39. Chi-Chu, Tschang. 2008. *"Olympic* Vacancies Haunt *Beijing* Hotels.*" Business Week* (October 20).

40. Liu, Melinda. 2009. "The Empty-Nest Syndrome." *Newsweek* (March 30).

41. Ibid.

Chapter 4

1. Spirou, Costas. 2007. "Cultural Policy and Urban Restructuring in Chicago." In *Culture, Tourism and Regeneration*, M. Smith ed. (pp. 123–131). Wallingford, UK: CABI.

2. Spirou, Costas. 2006. "Urban Beautification: The Construction of a New Identity in Chicago." In *The New Chicago: A Social and Cultural Analysis*, J. Koval, L. Bennett, M. Bennett, F. Demissie, R. Garner, and K. Kim, eds. (pp. 294–302). Philadelphia: Temple University Press.

3. Spirou, Costas. 2006. "Infrastructure Development and the Tourism Industry in Chicago." In *Chicago's Geographies: A 21st Century Metropolis,* R. Greene, M. Bouman, and D. Grammenos, eds. (pp. 113–128). Washington, DC: Association of American Geographers Press.

4. Judd, Dennis R. 1999. "Constructing the Tourist Bubble." In *The Tourist City*, D. Judd and S. S. Fainstein eds. (pp. 35–53). New Haven, CT: Yale University Press; Judd, Dennis. 2003. *The Infrastructure of Play: Building the Tourist City*. Armonk, NY: M. E. Sharpe.

5. Regional Results: Americas. 2007. "Tourism Highlights, 2007." Madrid, Spain: World Tourism Organization.

6. Wilkinson, Tracy. 2007. "A Long View of History—In Greece, an Art Deco Landmark May Fall to Clear an Acropolis Vista." *Los Angeles Times* (October 15).

7. Ehrlich, Bruce and Peter Dreier. 1999. "The New Boston Discovers the Old Tourism and the Struggle for a Livable City." In *The Tourist City*, D. Judd and S. S. Fainstein eds. (pp. 155–178). New Haven, CT: Yale University Press.

8. Law, Christopher. 2002. *Urban Tourism: The Visitor Economy and the Growth of Large Cities*. London: Continuum.

9. Aviva, Aron-Dine, Chad Stone, and Richard Kogan. 2008. *How Robust Was the 2001–2007 Economic Expansion?* Washington, DC: Center on Budget and Policy Priorities. (April 22)

10. Glaeser, Edward, and Jesse Shapiro. 2001. "Is There a New Urbanism? The Growth of U.S. Cities in the 1990s." Harvard Institute of Economic Research. (Discussion Paper #1925) (June 12).

11. Judd, Dennis, R., William Winter, William R. Barnes, and Emily Stern. 2003. "Tourism and Entertainment as Local Economic Development: A National Survey." In *The Infrastructure of Play: Building the Tourist City,* D. R. Judd, ed. (pp. 50–74). Armonk, NY: M. E. Sharpe.

12. Ibid.

13. "Hilton Austin in Top 25 in Chain." 2005. *Austin Business Journal* (April 6); "Refinancing of Hilton Debt Saves Taxpayers Millions." 2007. *Austin Business Journal* (March 20).

14. Sunnucks, Mike. 2005. "Skeptics Concerned About Viability of City-Funded Hotel." *Phoenix Business Journal* (March 18).

15. Quirk, James, and Rodney Fort. 1992. *Pay Dirt: The Business of Professional Team Sports*. Princeton, NJ: Princeton University Press.

16. Solomon, John. 2004. "Public Wises Up, Baulks at Paying for New Stadiums." *USA Today* (April 1).

17. Johnson, Arthur, T. 1993. *Minor League Baseball and Local Economic Development*. Champaign, IL: University of Illinois Press.

18. Spirou, Costas. forthcoming 2011. "Cultural Policy and the Dynamics of Stadium Development." In *Sport in the City: Cultural Connections*, M. Sam and J. E. Hughson, eds. London: Routledge.

19.   Norton, Robert D. 1979. *City Life-Cycles and American Urban Policy*. New York: Academic Press; Smith, Fred. 2003. "Decaying at the Core: Urban Decline in Cleveland, Ohio." *Research in Economic History* 21(1): 135–184.

20.   Strauss, Robert. 1999. "Hoping Ball Parks Succeed In Speeding Urban *Revival*." *The New York Times* (September 26).

21.   Chapin, Timothy S. 2004. "Sports Facilities as Urban Redevelopment Catalysts." *Journal of the American Planning Association* 70(2): 193–209.

22.   "Back From the Dead." 2007. *Economist* (October 27).

23.   Zerlin, Kerri. 2008. "15 Convention Center Openings Slated." *Tradeshow Week* (September 15).

24.   "2007 TSW 200." 2008. *Tradeshow Week Magazine* (May 14).

25.   Spirou, Costas. 2006. "Expansion Projects Like McCormick Place Can be Risky." *Crain's Chicago Business* (April 24).

26.   Finnegan, Amanda. 2009. "Reports: Gaming Revenue Down, Casino Debt Climbing." *Las Vegas Sun* (January 30).

27.   Parker, Robert, E. 1999. "Las Vegas: Casino Gambling and Local Culture." In *The Tourist City*, D. Judd and S. S. Fainstein, eds. (pp. 107–123). New Haven, CT: Yale University Press.

28.   Gottdiener, Mark, Claudia Collins, and David Dickens. 1999. *Las Vegas: The Social Production of an All-American City*. Oxford, UK: Blackwell.

29.   Rivlin, Gary. 2007. "In Las Vegas, Too Many Hotels Are Never Enough." *The New York Times* (April 24).

30.   2010 *State of the States: The AGA Survey of Casino Entertainment*. 2010. Washington, DC: American Gaming Association.

31.   Rephann, Terance J., Margaret Dalton, Anthony Stair, and Andrew Isserman. 1997. "Casino Gambling As An Economic Development Strategy." *Tourism Economics* 3(2): 161–83.

32.   "Copenhagen's Waterfront Development." 2009. *Travel + Leisure* (March).

33.   Marshall, Richard. 2001. *Waterfronts in Post-Industrial Cities*. New York: Spoon Press; Craig-Smit, Stephen J., and Michael Fagence. 1995. *Recreation and Tourism as a Catalyst for Urban Waterfront Redevelopment: An International Survey*. Westport, CT: Praeger.

34.   Cornell, Susan E. 2003. "Less than the Sum of Its Parts." *Business New Haven* (May 12).

35.   CIC Research. 2008. "2007 Market Profile and Economic Impact of Seattle-King County Visitors." Seattle Convention and Visitors Bureau (July 2).

36.   Webster, Richard A. 2008. "Summer Tourists Hit New Orleans in Droves." *New Orleans City Business* (August 19).

37.   Crompton, John L. 2005. *City Park Forum Briefing Papers #9: Promote Tourism*. Chicago: American Planning Association.

38.   Spirou, Costas. 2006. "Urban Beautification: The Construction of a New Identity in Chicago." In *The New Chicago: A Social and Cultural Analysis*, J. Koval, L. Bennett, M. Bennett, F. Demissie, R. Garner, and K. Kim, eds. (pp. 294–302). Philadelphia: Temple University Press.

39.   Herrick, Thaddeus. 2004. "Houston Knows We Have a Problem—They're Working on It." *The Wall Street Journal* (January 22).

40.   Rodriguez, Lori. 2007. "Arbor Day 2007: Beautification Fund will Bring 20,000 Trees to Houston." *The Houston Chronicle* (January 26).

41.   Van Dongen, Rachel. 2003. "Despite Kidnappings, Columbia Urges Travel." *The Christian Science Monitor* (October 20).

42. "International Tourism Arrivals by Country of Destination." 2005. *Tourism Market Trends, 2005 edition*. Geneva, Switzerland: World Trade Organization; Brodzinsky, Sibylla. 2006. "Hot Destination: Colombia." *The Christian Science Monitor* (May 9).

43. Montezuma, Ricardo. 2005. "The Transformation of Bogota, Colombia, 1995–2000: Investing in Citizenship and Urban Mobility." *Global Urban Development* 1(1): 1–10.

Chapter 5

1.   Glaeser, Edward. 1998. "Are Cities Dying?" *Journal of Economic Perspectives* 12(2):139–160; Mathur, Vijay, K. 1999. "Human Capital-Based Strategy for Regional Economic Development." *Economic Development Quarterly* 13(3): 203–216; Simon, Curtis. 1998. "Human Capital and Metropolitan Employment Growth." *Journal of Urban Economics* 43(2): 223–243.

2.   Clark, Terry Nichols, ed. 2004. *The City as an Entertainment Machine*. Boston, MA: JAI/Elsevier; Clark, Terry Nichols, Richard Lloyd, Kenneth Wong, and Pushpam Jain. 2002. "Amenities Drive Urban Growth" *Journal of Urban Affairs* 24(5): 493–515.

3.   Clark, Terry Nichols, and L. C. Ferguson. 1983. *City Money: Political Process, Fiscal Strain and Retrenchment*. New York: Columbia University Press.

4.   Florida, Richard. 2002. *The Rise of the Creative Class*. New York: Basic Books.

5.   Taylor, Paul. 2009. "Denver Tops List of Favorite Cities: For Nearly Half of America, Grass is Greener Somewhere Else." Pew Research Center: Social & Demographic Trends (January 29)

6.   Weiler, Stephan. 2000. "Pioneers and Settlers in Lo-Do Denver: Private Risk and Public Benefits in Urban Development." *Urban Studies* 37(1): 167–179.

7.   Marsh, Steve. 1993. "The Renaissance of Denver's LoDo." *Colorado Business Magazine* 20(11):35.

8.   Murray, Michael. 2002. "Denver." *Cities* 19(4): 283–295.

9.   Glaeser, Edward, Jose Scheinkman, and Andrei Shleifer. 1995. "Economic Growth in a Cross-Section of Cities." *Journal of Monetary Economics* 36(1): 117–143; Barro, Robert. 1991. "Economic Growth in a Cross Section of Countries." *Quarterly Journal of Economics* 106(2): 407–443; Barro, Robert, and X. Salai-Martin. 1995. *Economic Growth*. New York: McGraw-Hill.

10. Lochner, Lance, and Enrico Moretti. 2004 "The Effect of Education on Crime: Evidence from Prison Inmates, Arrests, and Self Reports." *American Economic Review* 94(1): 155–189; Dee, Thomas. 2004. "Are There Civic Returns to Education?" *Journal of Public Economics* 88(9–10): 1697–1720; Glaeser, Edward, and Raven Saks. 2004. "Corruption in America." Harvard Institute of Economic Research (Discussion Paper no. 2043).

11. Wheeler, Christopher. 2005. "Human Capital Growth in a Cross Section of U.S. Metropolitan Areas." Federal Reserve Bank of St. Louis, Working Papers Series (September).

12. Ibid.

13. Glaeser, Edward, L. 1999. "Learning in Cities." *Journal of Urban Economics* 46(2): 254–277.

14. Peri, Giovanni. 2002. "Young Workers, Learning, and Agglomerations." *Journal of Urban Economics* 52(3): 582–607.

15. Harden, Blaine. 2002. "The Year in Ideas: Intellectual Magnet *Cities*." *New York Times Magazine* (December 15).

16.   Costa, Dora, and Matthew Kahn. 2000. "Power Couples: Changes in the Loca-
      tional Choice of the College Educated, 1940–1990." *Quarterly Journal of Economics*
      115(4): 1287–1315.

17.   Glaeser, Edward, and Jesse Shapiro. 2003. "*Urban Growth* in the 1990s: Is City Liv-
      ing Back?" *Journal of Regional Science* 43(1): 139–165.

18.   Simon, Curtis, J., and Clark Nardinelli. 2002. "Human Capital and the Rise of
      American Cities, 1900–1990." *Regional Science and Urban Economics* 32(1): 59–96.

19.   Florida, Richard. 2002. *The Rise of the Creative Class*. New York: Basic Books.

20.   Bell, Daniel. 1979. *The Cultural Contradictions of Capitalism*. London: Heinemann,
      p. 71.

21.   Brooks, David. 2001. *Bobos in Paradise: The New Upper Class and How They Got There*.
      New York: Simon & Schuster.

22.   Brooks, David. 2000. "A conversation with…." NewsHour with Jim Lehrer (Gwen
      Ifill), PBS (May 9 transcript).

23.   Florida, Richard. 2003. *The Rise of the Creative Class*. New York: Basic Books.

24.   Hoyman, Michele, and Christopher Faricy. 2009. "It Takes a Village: A Test of the
      Creative Class, Social Capital, and Human Capital Theories." *Urban Affairs Review*
      44(3): 311–333.

25.   Donegan, Mary, Joshua Drucker, Harvey Goldstein, Nichola Lowe, and Emil Mal-
      izia. 2008. "Which Indicators Explain Metropolitan Economic Performance Best?
      Traditional or Creative Class." *Journal of the American Planning Association* 74(2):
      180–195.

26.   Wilson, David, and Roger Keil. 2008. "The Real Creative Class." *Social & Cultural
      Geography* 9(8): 841–847.

27.   Florida, Richard. 2003. "Cities and the Creative Class." *City & Community* 2(1):
      3–19.

28.   Taylor, Paul. 2009. "Denver Tops List of Favorite Cities: For Nearly Half of Amer-
      ica, Grass is Greener Somewhere Else." Pew ResearchCenter: Social & Demo-
      graphic Trends (January 29).

29.   Storper, Michael, and Michael Manville. 2006 "Behaviour, Preferences and Cities:
      Urban Theory and Urban Resurgence." *Urban Studies* 43(8): 1247–1274.

30.   Gyourko, Joseph, and Tracy, Joseph. 1991. "The Structure of Local Political Finance
      and the Quality of Life." *Journal of Political Economy* 99(4): 774–806.

31.   Swope, Christopher. 2003. "Chasing the Rainbow: Is a Gay Population an Engine
      of Urban Revival?" *Governing* 17(1): 18–24.

32.   Terry Nichols Clark, Richard Lloyd, Kenneth Wong and Pushpam Jain. 2002.
      "Amenities Drive Urban Growth." *Journal of Urban Affairs* 24(5): 493–515.

33.   Ibid.

34.   Clark, Terry Nichols, ed. 2004. *The City as an Entertainment Machine*. Boston, MA:
      JAI/Elsevier.

35.   Kirchberg, Volker. 2006. [Book Review] *The City as an Entertainment Machine* Terry
      Nichols Clark, ed. (Research in Urban Policy, Vol. 9). Boston, MA: Elsevier. *City &
      Community* 5(2): 199–202.

36.   Storper, Michael and Michael Manville. 2006. "Behaviour, Preferences and Cities:
      Urban Theory and Urban Resurgence." *Urban Studies* 43(8): 1247–74.

37.   Shapiro, Jesse M. 2006. "Smart Cities: Quality of Life, Productivity, and the Growth
      Effects of Human Capital." *Review of Economics and Statistics* 88(2): 324–335.

38.   Garcia, Beatriz. 2005. "From Glasgow to Liverpool. Understanding the Long Term
      Legacies of Becoming European City of Culture." Guest seminar presented at Uni-
      versity of Glasgow, *Urban Studies Department* (October 8, 2004); University of *Glas-
      gow, Geography Department* (January 14, 2005); and *Glasgow Caledonian University,
      Division of Media, Culture and Leisure Management* (April 14, 2005).

39. "The Price of Civic Pride." 2001. *The Economist* 358(8212): 56.
40. Tretter, Eliot. 2009. "The Cultures of Capitalism: Glasgow and the Monopoly of Culture." *Antipode* 41(1): 111–132.
41. García, Beatriz. 2005. "Deconstructing the City of Culture: The Long-Term Cultural Legacies of Glasgow 1990." *Urban Studies* 42(5/6): 841–868.
42. Hanley, Lynsey. 2005. "Roll over London—Here's Glasgow." *The Daily Telegraph* (June 17).
43. Malanga. Steven 2004. "The Curse of the Creative Class: A New Age Theory of Urban Development Amounts to Economic Snake Oil." *Wall Street Journal* (January 19).
44. Rexhausen, Jeff, and George Vredeveld. 2003. "Riverfront Investment." *Economic Development Journal* 2(1): 8–15.
45. Shilling, Dan. 2007. *Civic Tourism: the Poetry and Politics of Place.* Prescott, AZ: Sharlot Hall Museum Press.
46. Coletta, Carol. 2008. "Fostering the Creative City. Report for the Wallace Foundation." *CEOs for Cities* (August).
47. Atkinson, Rowland, and Hazel Easthope. 2009. "The Consequences of the Creative Class: The Pursuit of Creativity Strategies in Australia's Cities." *International Journal of Urban and Regional Research* 33(1): 64–79.
48. Brisbane City Council. 2003. Creative City: Brisbane City Council's Cultural Strategy 2003–2008. Brisbane: Cultural Policy Unity, Community & Economic Development, Brisbane City Council.
49. Atkinson, Rowland, and Hazel Easthope. 2009. "The Consequences of the Creative Class: The Pursuit of Creativity Strategies in Australia's Cities." *International Journal of Urban and Regional Research* 33(1): 64–79.

Chapter 6

1. Hof, Reiner M. 1990. "San Diegans, Inc.: The Formative Years, 1958–63, The Redevelopment of Downtown San Diego." *The Journal of San Diego History* 36(1): 48-64.
2. Brown, Peter Hendee. 2009. *America's Waterfront Revival: Port Authorities and Urban Redevelopment.* Philadelphia: University of Pennsylvania Press.
3. Chapin, Tim. 2002. "Beyond the Entrepreneurial City: Municipal Capitalism in San Diego." *Journal of Urban Affairs* 24(5): 565-581.
4. Population and Housing Estimates: Subregional Area 1-Central San Diego. 2008. SANDAG, Current Estimates (October).
5. Birch, Eugenie L. 2005. *Who Lives Downtown.* Washington, DC: The Brookings Institution, Living Cities Census Series.
6. Spirou, Costas. Forthcoming 2011. "Back to the Center: Metropolitan Expansion and the New Downtowns of Culture and Urban Tourism." In *The City Revisited: Perspectives from New York, Chicago, and Los Angeles*, D. Judd and D. Simpson, eds. Minneapolis: University of Minnesota Press.
7. As quoted in Lees, Loretta, Tom Slater, and Elvin Wyly. 2008. *Gentrification.* New York: Routledge, p. 4.
8. Lees, Slater, and Wyly. 2008. *Gentrification.* New York: Routledge.
9. Butler, Tim and Garry Robson. 2003. *London Calling: The Middle Classes and the Remaking of Inner London.* London: Berg.
10. Lees, Loretta. 2003. "Super-Gentrification: The Case of Brooklyn Heights, New York City." *Urban Studies* 40(12): 2487–2509.

11. Spirou, Costas. 2006. "Infrastructure Development and the Tourism Industry in Chicago." In *Chicago's Geographies: A 21st Century Metropolis* R. Greene, M. J. Bouman, and D. Grammenos, eds. (pp. 113–128). Washington, DC: Association of American Geographers Press.

12. Sarzynski, Brian. 2004. "Up and Coming. What Price Downtown Asheville?" *Mountain Xpress* (April 14).

13. DiMassa, Cara Mia. 2007. "It's Looking Up Downtown." *Los Angeles Times* (March 30).

14. *As We Build Our City, Let Us Think That Are Building Forever.* 2004. Report by Houston Downtown Development Framework (October) http://www.centralhouston.org/Home/DowntownHouston/FrameworkfortheFuture/Cover/Cover.PDF (accessed August 10, 2009)

15. Central Houston, Inc. 2004. *Downtown and Inner City Residential Overview.* http://www.centralhouston.org/Home/Programs/PlanningandDevelopment/DowntownResidentalOver/Downtown%20Residental%20Overview.PDF (accessed August 16, 2009).

16. Cole, Heather. 2006. "Go West: Developers Plan $150 Million in Projects for Western Regions of Downtown." *St. Louis Business Journal* (February 17).

17. Smith, Ray. 2003. "Lofts Lift Smaller Cities—Developers around U.S. Take Cue From Megalopolises, Turn Old Factories Into Apartments." *Wall Street Journal* (May 28).

18. Templin, Neal. 1997. "Downtown Lofts Beckon Sunbelt-Moving Where Earlier Generations Feared to Tread." *Wall Street Journal* (November 26).

19. North Central Texas. 2003. *Demographic Forecast: Dallas CBD.* North Central Texas Council of Governments http://www.nctcog.org/ris/demographics/forecast/query.asp?thefield=citycode&thevalue=DAL1 (accessed March 15, 2009)

20. *Annual Report 2008.* 2009. Nashville Downtown Partnership, Nashville, Tennessee. http://www.nashvilledowntown.com/pdf/2008_Annual_Report.pdf (accessed October 18, 2009).

21. Ibid.

22. Ibid.

23. Hunter Interests Inc. 2005. *Final Report: Tampa Downtown Vision and Action Program.* (March). http://www.tampasdowntown.com/userfiles/files/Reports/Vision%20Plan%20Part%201.pdf (accessed September 2009).

24. Zink, Janet. 2006. "City Puts Pricetag on Riverwalk." *St. Petersburg Times* (February 15); Allman, John W. 2007. "Central Park Village Demolished." *The Tampa Tribune* (July 31); Welch, Amy. 2002. "Makeover: Tampa is Hoping that Residential Development Will Give Downtown Life After Dark." *Florida Trend* (December 1).

25. Bigda, Carolyn, Erin Chambers, Lawrence Lanahan, Joe Light, Sarah Max, and Jennifer Merritt. 2007. "Best Places to Retire." *Money Magazine.* http://money.cnn.com/magazines/moneymag/bpretire/2007/index.html (accessed October 20, 2009).

26. Walker, Sam. 1995. "Detroit Battles Decay, Joblessness in Ultimate US Test of Renewal." *Christian Science Monitor* (February 9); Bachelor, Lynn W. 1998. "Stadiums As Solution Sets: Revival of Downtown Detroit." *Policy Studies Review* 15(1): 89–101.

27. Beebe, Katherine, and Associates. 2006. "Downtown Detroit Residential Market Study." Produced for the Lower Woodward Housing Fund. (September 23) http://www.detinvfund.com/ReportFinal_0601005.pdf (accessed July 23, 2009).

28. Ibid, p. 30.

29. *Stroller, Gary. 2004. "Conventions* Come to Risky Areas? *USA Today* (July 27).

30. Booza, Jason C. 2008. "Reality v. Perceptions: Analysis of 2007 Cime and Safety in Downtown Detroit." Report prepared by Wayne State University (July 26) http://www.tedconline.com/uploads/Downtown_Detroit_Crime_Study_2006.pdf (accessed June 12, 2009).

31. Grossman, Andrew. 2009. "Retailers Head for Exits in Detroit." *The Wall Street Journal* (June 16).

32. Eisinger, Peter. 2003. "Reimagining Detroit." *City & Community* 2(2): 85–99.

33. Judd, Dennis. 2006. "Commentary: Tracing the Commodity Chain of Global Tourism." *Tourism Geographies: An International Journal of Tourism Space, Place and Environment* 8(4): 323–336; Lorentzen, Anne. 2009. "Cities in the Experience Economy." *European Planning Studies* 17(6): 829–845.

34. Spirou, Costas. Forthcoming 2011. "Back to the Center: Metropolitan Expansion and the New Downtowns of Culture and Urban Tourism." In *The City Revisited: Perspectives from New York, Chicago, and Los Angeles*, D. Judd and D. Simpson, eds. Minneapolis: University of Minnesota Press.

35. U.S. Census. Population, 1960, 1970, 1980, 1990, 2000.

36. "Syracuse Convention & Visitors Bureau Releases 2008 Destination Image Marketing Campaign ROI Results." 2009. Press Release. Syracuse Convention & Visitors Bureau (February 6).

37. *Inside Downtown Newsletter*. 2008. Downtown Committee of Syracuse, Inc. (October); *Inside Downtown Newsletter*. 2009. Downtown Committee of Syracuse, Inc. (February); *Inside Downtown Newsletter*. 2009. Downtown Committee of Syracuse, Inc. (March).

38. Tveidt, Tom. 2008. *2008 Asheville Metro Economic Outlook*. Asheville, NC: Asheville Metro Business Research Center, Asheville Area Chamber of Commerce (July 23).

39. Ibid.

40. Asheville Chamber of Commerce. 2008. "2008 Legislative Agenda State Priorities" (March) http://www.ashevillechamber.org/economicdevelopment/documents/2008StateAgenda.pdf (accessed, August 14, 2009).

41. Ibid.

42. Hatcher, Chris, and Dedra Ragland. 2002. "White Paper: Downtown Master Plan." City of Denton Planning and Development Department, City Hall, Denton, TX.; Fleischauser, Eric. 2007. "Public-Private Partnerships Spur Downtown Growth in Greenville, SC." *The Decatur Daily* (November 25).

43. Ibid., p. 62.

44. Ibid, p. 18.

45. Whitworth, Nancy P., and Mary Douglas Neal. 2008. "How Greenville, South Carolina, Brought Downtown Back: A Case Study in 30 Years of Successful Public/Private Collaboration." *Real Estate Review* 37(1) 9–23.

Chapter 7

1. United Nations World Tourism Organization. 2009. *UNWTO World Tourism Barometer* 7(2): 15.

2. Ibid.

3. World Travel and Tourism Council. *The Economic Impact of Travel & Tourism. 2010*. London: Author.

4. *Tourism Highlights*. 2008. Madrid, Spain: World Tourism Organization.

5. Personal communication, October 20, 2007.

6. Hannigan, John. 1998. *Fantasy City*. London: Routledge; Davis, Mike. 1990. *City of Quartz*. New York: Verso; Rothman, Hal, and Mike Davis. 2002. *The Grit Beneath the Glitter*. Berkeley: University of California Press.

7. Richards, Greg, and Julie Wilson. 2006. "Developing Creativity in Tourist Experiences: A Solution to the Serial Reproduction of Culture?" *Tourism Management* 27(6): 1209–1223.

8. Harvey, David. 1989. *The Condition of Postmodernity*. Oxford, UK: Blackwell.

9. Judd, Dennis R. 1999. "Constructing the Tourist Bubble." In *The Tourist City*, D. R. Judd and S. S. Fainstein, eds. (pp. 35–53). New Haven, CT: Yale University Press.

10. Ritzer, George, and Allan Liska. 1997. "'McDisneyization' and 'Post-Tourism': Complementary Perspectives on Contemporary Tourism." In *Touring Cultures: Transformations in Travel and Theory*, C. Rojek and J. Urry, eds. (pp. 96–109). London: Routledge.

11. Ritzer, George. 1993. *The McDonaldization of Society: An Investigation into the Changing Character of Contemporary Social Life*. London: Sage.

12. Ritzer, George. 2004. *The Globalization of Nothing*. Thousand Oaks, CA: Pine Fore Press, p. 6.

13. Judd, Dennis. 2006. "Commentary: Tracing the Commodity Chain of Global Tourism." *Tourism Geographies: An International Journal of Tourism Space, Place and Environment* 8(4): 323–336.

14. McClinchey, Kelly. 2008. "Urban Ethnic Festivals, Neighborhoods, and the Multiple Realities of Marketing Place." *Journal of Travel & Tourism* 25(3/4): 251–264.

15. Hall, Michael. 2008. "Servicescapes, Designscapes, Branding, and the Creation of Place-Identity: South of Litchfield, Christchurch." *Journal of Travel & Tourism Marketing* 25(3/4): 233–250.

16. Green, Garth. 2007. "Come to Life: Authenticity, Value, and the Carnival as Cultural Commodity in Trinidad and Tobago." *Identities* 14 (1/2): 203–224.

17. Schoorl, Fred. 2005. "On *Authenticity* and Artificiality in Heritage Policies in the Netherlands." *Museum International* 57(3): 79–85.

18. Sharma, Bishnu, and Pam Dyer. 2009. "An Investigation of Differences in Residents' Perceptions on the Sunshine Coast: *Tourism* Impacts and Demographic Variables." *Tourism Geographies* 11(2): 187–213.

19. Bai, Zhihong. 2007. "Ethnic Identities under the Tourist Gaze." *Asian Ethnicity* 8(3): 245–259.

20. Barthel-Bouchier, Diane. 2001. "Authenticity and Identity." *International Sociology* 16(2): 221–239.

21. McIntosh, Alison, and Anne Zahra. 2007. "A Cultural Encounter through Volunteer Tourism: Towards the Ideals of Sustainable Tourism?" *Journal of Sustainable Tourism* 15(5): 541–556.

22. Richards, Greg, and Julie Wilson. 2006. "Developing Creativity in Tourist Experiences: A Solution to the Serial Reproduction of Culture?" *Tourism Management* 27(6), 1209–1223.

23. Department of Housing and Urban Development 2004. "HUD Publishes 'Preserving America'—A How-to Guide to Promote Historic Preservation and Tourism." HUD No. 04-150 (News Release. December 16). Washington, DC: Department of Housing and Urban Development.

24. VISA Corporation. 2009. *Tourism Outlook: USA* (June 2) http://corporate.visa.com/_media/tourism-outlook-usa-2009.pdf (accessed September 13, 2009).

25. Brewer, Pauleen. 2005. "Letter to the Editor: Stadium Poor Use of Funds." *The Washington Post* (April 10).

26. Davis, Kate, and Chauna Brocht. 2002. *Subsidizing the Low Road: Economic Development in Baltimore*. Washington, DC: Good Jobs First (September).

27. Ibid.
28. Maharaj, Brij and Kem Ramballi. 1998. "Local Economic Development Strategies in an Emerging Democracy: The Case of Durban in South Africa." *Urban Studies* 35(1): 131–148.
29. Maharaj, Brij, Reshma Sucheran, and Pillay Vino. 2006. *"Durban—A Tourism Mecca?* Challenges of the Post-Apartheid Era." *Urban Forum* 17(3): 262–281.
30. Loftman, Patrick, and Brendan Nevin. 1996. "Going for Growth: Prestige Projects in Three British Cities." *Urban Studies* 33(6): 991–1019.
31. Ibid, p. 1001.
32. Ibid, p. 1006.
33. Ibid. p. 1012.
34. Mollenkopf, John Hull, and Manuel Castells. 1991. *The Dual City: Restructuring New York.* New York: Russell Sage.
35. Squires, Gregory, D., and Charis E. Kubrin. 2005. "Privileged Places: Race, Uneven Development and the Geography of Opportunity in Urban America." *Urban Studies* 42(1): 47–68.
36. Mills, Karen, G., Elisabeth B. Reynolds, and Andrew Reamer. 2008. *Clusters and Competitiveness: A New Federal Role for Stimulating Regional Economies.* Washington, DC: Brookings Institution (April).
37. Rothman, Hal, and Mike Davis. 2002. *The Grit Beneath the Glitter.* Berkeley: University of California Press.
38. Carlino, Gerald A., and Albert Saiz. 2008. *Beautiful City: Leisure Amenities and Urban Growth.* FRB of Philadelphia (Working Paper No. 08-22). (December 6).
39. Ibid. p. 27.
40. Ibid. pp. 33–34.
41. Spivak, Jeffrey. 2006. "Neighborhood Leaders Want City Investment." *The Kansas City Star* (December 9).
42. Stolte, John. 2005. "Help Neighborhoods." *The Kansas City Star* (December 1).
43. Meyers, Jessica. 2007. "Hession Announces Urban Design Competition: City Hopes to Promote Livable *Neighborhoods." The Spokesman-Review* (June 4).
44. Cambell, Matt. 2007. "Attention to Basic Services Is a Priority: She Wants to Extend the Downtown Renaissance into Kansas City's Neighborhoods by Combating Blight." *The Kansas City Star* (February 8).
45. Gotham, Kevin Fox. 2005. "Tourism Gentrification: The Case of New Orleans' Vieux Carre (French Quarter)." *Urban Studies* 42(7): 1099–1121.
46. Brown-Saracino, Japonica. 2010. *The Gentrification Debates.* New York: Routledge; Brown-Saracino, Japonica. 2010. *A Neighborhood that Never Changes: Gentrification, Social Preservation, and the Search for Authenticity.* Chicago: University of Chicago Press.
47. Betancur, John. 2005. "Gentrification *before* Gentrification? The Plight of Pilsen in Chicago." A Nathalie P. Voorhees Center for Neighborhood and Community Improvement White paper (Summer) http://www.uic.edu/cuppa/voorheesctr/Publications/Gentrification%20before%20Gentrification.pdf (accessed October 29, 2009).
48. Boyd, Michelle. 2000. "Reconstructing Bronzeville: Racial Nostalgia and Neighborhood Redevelopment." *Journal of Urban Affairs* 22(2): 107–122.
49. Bromley, Rosemary D. F., and Peter Mackie. 2009. *"Displacement* and the New Spaces for Informal Trade in the Latin American City Centre." *Urban Studies* 46(7): 1485–1506.
50. Edwards, Johnny. 2009. "Harrisburg Protest March Set for Fourth." *The Augusta Chronicle* (July 1).

51. Judd, Dennis R., and Todd Swanstrom. 2008. *City Politics: The Political Economy of Urban America*. New York: Pearson/Longman.
52. Ibid, p, 200.
53. Panella, Adolph, Jr. 2007. "Paying for More Sports." *The Tampa Tribune* (June 22).
54. Nothdurft, John. 2009. "Oversight Warranted on Stadium Project." *Miami Herald* (July 16).
55. Brown, Clyde, and David M. Paul. 2002. "The Political Scorecard of Professional Sports Facility Referendums in the United States, 1984–2000." *Journal of Sport & Social Issues* 26(3): 248–267.
56. Coates, Dennis, and Brad R. Humphreys. 2003. *Professional Sports Facilities, Franchises and Urban Economic Development* (Working Paper 03-103). Baltimore, MD: University of Maryland, Baltimore County (UMBC) Economics Department.
57. Mondello, Michael, and Paul Anderson. 2004. "Stadiums, Arenas, and Sports Referendums: A Comparative Analysis of Cities Involved in the Stadium Game." *International Journal of Sport Management* 5(1): 43–71.
58. Naccarato, Rose. 2007. *Staff Research Brief: Tax Increment Financing Opportunities and Concerns*. Nashville, TN: The Tennessee Advisory Committee on Intergovernmental Affairs.
59. National Education Association. 2003. "Protecting Public Education Property Tax Abatements, Tax Increment Financing, and Funding for Schools" (NEA Research Working Paper). Washington, DC: Author (January).
60. "Regenerating Cities: TIFs and Urban Development Britain Looks Westward for Tips on Tarting Up Its Towns." 2009. *The Economist* (June 27).
61. Haywood, Michael. K. 1998. "Economic Business Cycles and the Tourism Life-Cycle Concept." In *The Economic Geography of the Tourism Industry*, D. Ioannides and K. G. Debbage, eds. (pp. 273–284). New York: Routledge.
62. Butler, Richard.W. 1980. "The Concept of Tourism Area Cycle of Evolution: Implications for Management of Resources." *Canadian Geographer* 24(1):5–12.
63. Jafari, Jafar. 1989. "Sociocultural Dimensions of Tourism: An English Language Literature Review." In *Tourism as a Factor of Changes: A Sociocultural Study*, J. Bystrzanowski, ed. (pp. 17–60). Vienna, Austria: Centre for Research and Documentation in Social Sciences.
64. Strom, Elizabeth. 2008. "Rethinking the Politics of Downtown Development." *Journal of Urban Affairs* 30(1): 37–61.
65. Bennett, Larry. Forthcoming 2011. "The Mayor Among His Peers: Interpreting Richard M. Daley." In *The City Revisited: Perspectives from Chicago, Los Angeles and New York*, D. R. Judd and D. Simpson, eds. Minneapolis: University of Minnesota Press.
66. Zimmerman, Jeffrey. 2008. "From Brew Town to Cool Town: Neoliberalism and the Creative City Development Strategy in Milwaukee." *Cities* 25(4): 230–242.
67. Hannigan, John. 1998. *Fantasy City: Pleasure and Profit in the Postmodern Metropolis*. New York: Routledge.
68. Boddy, Trevor. 1992. "Underground and Overhead: Building the Analogous City." In *Variations on a Theme Park: The New American City and the End of Public Space*, M. Sorkin, ed. (pp. 123–153). New York: Hill and Wang.
69. Harrill, Rich, and Thomas D. Potts. 2003. "Tourism Planning in Historic Districts." *Journal of the American Planning Association* 69(3): 233–244.

INDEX

Page numbers in italics refer to figures or tables.

Made in the USA
Lexington, KY
18 August 2016